Natural Language Processing with Spark NLP
Learning to Understand Text at Scale

Alex Thomas

Beijing · Boston · Farnham · Sebastopol · Tokyo

Natural Language Processing with Spark NLP

by Alex Thomas

Published by O'Reilly Media, Inc., 1005 Gravenstein Highway North, Sebastopol, CA 95472.

O'Reilly books may be purchased for educational, business, or sales promotional use. Online editions are also available for most titles (*http://oreilly.com*). For more information, contact our corporate/institutional sales department: 800-998-9938 or *corporate@oreilly.com*.

Acquisitions Editor: Mike Loukides
Developmental Editors: Nicole Taché, Gary O'Brien
Production Editor: Beth Kelly
Copyeditor: Piper Editorial
Proofreader: Athena Lakri

Indexer: WordCo, Inc.
Interior Designer: David Futato
Cover Designer: Karen Montgomery
Illustrator: Rebecca Demarest

July 2020:   First Edition

Revision History for the First Edition

2020-06-24:   First Release

See *http://oreilly.com/catalog/errata.csp?isbn=9781492047766* for release details.

978-1-492-04776-6

[LSI]

Table of Contents

Part I.   Basics

Part II.   Building Blocks

Part IV.   Building NLP Systems

Preface

Why Natural Language Processing Is Important and Difficult

Natural language processing (NLP) is a field of study concerned with processing language data. We will be focusing on text, but natural language audio data is also a part of NLP. Dealing with natural language text data is difficult. The reason it is difficult is that it relies on three fields of study: linguistics, software engineering, and machine learning. It is hard to find the expertise in all three for most NLP-based projects. Fortunately, you don't need to be a world-class expert in all three fields to make informed decisions about your application. As long as you know some basics, you can use libraries built by experts to accomplish your goals. Consider the advances made in creating efficient algorithms for vector and matrix operations. If the common linear algebra libraries that deep learning libraries use were not available, imagine how much harder it would have been for the deep learning revolution to begin. Even though these libraries mean that we don't need to implement cache aware matrix multiplication for every new project, we still need to understand the basics of linear algebra and the basics of how the operations are implemented to make the best use of these libraries. I believe the situation is becoming the same for NLP and NLP libraries.

Applications that use natural language (text, spoken, and gestural) will always be different than other applications due to the data they use. The benefit and draw to these applications is how much data is out there. Humans are producing and churning natural language data all the time. The difficult aspects are that people are literally evolved to detect mistakes in natural language use, and the data (text, images, audio, and video) is not made with computers in mind. These difficulties can be overcome through a combination of linguistics, software engineering, and machine learning.

This book deals with text data. This is the easiest of the data types that natural language comes in, because our computers were designed with text in mind. That being said, we still want to consider a lot of small and large details that are not obvious.

Background

A few years ago, I was working on a tutorial for O'Reilly. This tutorial was about building NLP pipelines on Apache Spark. At the time, Apache Spark 2.0 was still relatively new, but I was mainly using version 1.6. I thought it would be cool to build an annotation library using the new DataFrames and pipelines; alas, I was not able to implement this for the tutorial. However, I talked about this with my friend (and tutorial copresenter) David Talby, and we created a design doc. I didn't have enough time to work on building the library, so I consulted Saif Addin, whom David had hired to work on the project. As the project grew and developed, David, Claudiu Branzan (another friend and colleague), and I began presenting tutorials at conferences and meetups. It seemed like there was an interest in learning more about the library and an interest in learning more about NLP in general.

People who know me know I am rant-prone, and few topics are as likely to get me started as NLP and how it is used and misused in the technology industry. I think this is because of my background. Growing up, I studied linguistics as a hobby—an all-consuming hobby. When I went to university, even though I focused on mathematics, I also took linguistics courses. Shortly before graduating, I decided that I also wanted to learn computer science, so I could take the theoretical concepts I had learned and create something. Once I began in the industry, I learned that I could combine these three interests into one: NLP. This gives me a rare view of NLP because I studied its components first individually and then combined.

I am really excited to be working on this book, and I hope this book helps you in building your next NLP application!

Philosophy

An important part of the library is the idea that people should build their own models. There is no one-size-fits-all method in NLP. If you want to build a successful NLP application, you need to understand your data as well as your product. Prebuilt models are useful for initial versions, demos, and tutorials. This means that if you want to use Spark NLP successfully, you will need to understand how NLP works. So in this book we will cover more than just Spark NLP API. We will talk about how to use Spark NLP, but we will also talk about how NLP and deep learning work. When you combine an understanding of NLP with a library that is built with the intent of customization, you will be able to build NLP applications that achieve your goals.

Conventions Used in This Book

The following typographical conventions are used in this book:

Italic
> Indicates new terms, URLs, email addresses, filenames, and file extensions.

`Constant width`
> Used for program listings, as well as within paragraphs to refer to program elements such as variable or function names, databases, data types, environment variables, statements, and keywords.

`Constant width bold`
> Shows commands or other text that should be typed literally by the user.

`Constant width italic`
> Shows text that should be replaced with user-supplied values or by values determined by context.

 This element signifies a general note.

Using Code Examples

Supplemental material (code examples, exercises, etc.) is available for download at *https://oreil.ly/SparkNLP*.

If you have a technical question or a problem using the code examples, please send an email to *bookquestions@oreilly.com*.

This book is here to help you get your job done. In general, if example code is offered with this book, you may use it in your programs and documentation. You do not need to contact us for permission unless you're reproducing a significant portion of the code. For example, writing a program that uses several chunks of code from this book does not require permission. Selling or distributing examples from O'Reilly books does require permission. Answering a question by citing this book and quoting example code does not require permission. Incorporating a significant amount of example code from this book into your product's documentation does require permission.

We appreciate, but generally do not require, attribution. An attribution usually includes the title, author, publisher, and ISBN. For example: *Natural Language*

Processing with Spark NLP by Alex Thomas (O'Reilly). Copyright 2020 Alex Thomas, 978-1-492-04776-6."

If you feel your use of code examples falls outside fair use or the permission given above, feel free to contact us at *permissions@oreilly.com*.

O'Reilly Online Learning

 For more than 40 years, *O'Reilly Media* has provided technology and business training, knowledge, and insight to help companies succeed.

Our unique network of experts and innovators share their knowledge and expertise through books, articles, and our online learning platform. O'Reilly's online learning platform gives you on-demand access to live training courses, in-depth learning paths, interactive coding environments, and a vast collection of text and video from O'Reilly and 200+ other publishers. For more information, visit *http://oreilly.com*.

How to Contact Us

Please address comments and questions concerning this book to the publisher:

> O'Reilly Media, Inc.
> 1005 Gravenstein Highway North
> Sebastopol, CA 95472
> 800-998-9938 (in the United States or Canada)
> 707-829-0515 (international or local)
> 707-829-0104 (fax)

We have a web page for this book, where we list errata, examples, and any additional information. You can access this page at *https://oreil.ly/NLPSpark*.

Email *bookquestions@oreilly.com* to comment or ask technical questions about this book.

For news and information about our books and courses, visit *http://oreilly.com*.

Find us on Facebook: *http://facebook.com/oreilly*

Follow us on Twitter: *http://twitter.com/oreillymedia*

Watch us on YouTube: *http://youtube.com/oreillymedia*

Acknowledgments

I want to thank my editors at O'Reilly Nicole Taché and Gary O'Brien for their help and support. I want to thank the tech reviewers who were of great help in restructuring the book. I also want to thank Mike Loukides for his guidance in starting this project.

I want to thank David Talby for all his mentorship. I want to thank Saif Addin, Maziyar Panahi and the rest of the John Snow Labs team for taking the initial design David and I had, and making it into a successful and widely used library. I also want to thank Vishnu Vettrivel for his support and counsel during this project.

Finally, I want to thank my family and friends for their patience and encouragement.

PART I

Basics

## CHAPTER 1

Getting Started

Introduction

This book is about using Spark NLP to build *natural language processing (NLP)* applications. Spark NLP is an NLP library built on top of Apache Spark. In this book I'll cover how to use Spark NLP, as well as fundamental natural language processing topics. Hopefully, at the end of this book you'll have a new software tool for working with natural language and Spark NLP, as well as a suite of techniques and some understanding of why these techniques work.

Let's begin by talking about the structure of this book. In the first part, we'll go over the technologies and techniques we'll be using with Spark NLP throughout this book. After that we'll talk about the building blocks of NLP. Finally, we'll talk about NLP applications and systems.

When working on an application that requires NLP, there are three perspectives you should keep in mind: the software developer's perspective, the linguist's perspective, and the data scientist's perspective. The software developer's perspective focuses on what your application needs to do; this grounds the work in terms of the product you want to create. The linguist's perspective focuses on what it is in the data that you want to extract. The data scientist's perspective focuses on how you can extract the information you need from your data.

Following is a more detailed overview of the book.

Part I, *Basics*

- Chapter 1 covers setting up your environment so you can follow along with the examples and exercises in the book.

- Chapter 2, *Natural Language Basics* is a survey of some of the linguistic concepts that help in understanding why NLP techniques work, and how to use NLP techniques to get the information you need from language.

- Chapter 3, *NLP on Apache Spark* is an introduction to Apache Spark and, most germane, the Spark NLP library.

- Chapter 4, *Deep Learning Basics* is a survey of some of the deep learning concepts that we'll be using in this book. This book is *not* a tutorial on deep learning, but we'll try and explain these techniques when necessary.

Part II, *Building Blocks*

- Chapter 5, *Processing Words* covers the classic text-processing techniques. Since NLP applications generally require a pipeline of transformations, understanding the early steps well is a necessity.

- Chapter 6, *Information Retrieval* covers the basic concepts of search engines. Not only is this a classic example of an application that uses text, but many NLP techniques used in other kinds of applications ultimately come from information retrieval.

- Chapter 7, *Classification and Regression* covers some well-established techniques of using text features for classification and regression tasks.

- Chapter 8, *Sequence Modeling with Keras* introduces techniques used in modeling natural language text data as sequences. Since natural language is a sequence, these techniques are fundamental.

- Chapter 9, *Information Extraction* shows how we can extract facts and relationships from text.

- Chapter 10, *Topic Modeling* demonstrates techniques for finding topics in documents. Topic modeling is a great way to explore text.

- Chapter 11, *Word Embeddings* discusses one of the most popular modern techniques for creating features from text.

Part III, *Applications*

- Chapter 12, *Sentiment Analysis and Emotion Detection* covers some basic applications that require identifying the sentiment of a text's author—for example, whether a movie review is positive or negative.

- Chapter 13, *Building Knowledge Bases* explores creating an ontology, a collection of facts and relationships organized in a graph-like manner, from a corpus.

- Chapter 14, *Search Engine* goes deeper into what can be done to improve a search engine. Improving is not just about improving the ranker; it's also about facilitating the user with features like facets.

- Chapter 15, *Chatbot* demonstrates how to create a chatbot—this is a fun and interesting application. This kind of application is becoming more and more popular.
- Chapter 16, *Object Character Recognition* introduces converting text stored as images to text data. Not all texts are stored as text data. Handwriting and old texts are examples of texts we may receive as images. Sometimes, we also have to deal with nonhandwritten text stored in images like PDF images and scans of printed documents.

Part IV, *Building NLP Systems*
- Chapter 17, *Supporting Multiple Languages* explores topics that an application creator should consider when preparing to work with multiple languages.
- Chapter 18, *Human Labeling* covers ways to use humans to gather data about texts. Being able to efficiently use humans to augment data can make an otherwise impossible project feasible.
- Chapter 19, *Productionizing NLP Applications* covers creating models, Spark NLP pipelines, and TensorFlow graphs, and publishing them for use in production; some of the performance concerns that developers should keep in mind when designing a system that uses text; and the quality and monitoring concerns that are unique to NLP applications.

Other Tools

In addition to Spark NLP, Apache Spark, and TensorFlow, we'll make use of a number of other tools:

- Python (*https://www.python.org*) is one of the most popular programming languages used in data science. Although Spark NLP is implemented in Scala, we will be demonstrating its use through Python.
- Anaconda (*https://www.anaconda.com*) is an open source distribution of Python (and R, which we are not using). It is maintained by Anaconda, Inc., who also offer an enterprise platform and training courses. We'll use the Anaconda package manager, conda, to create our environment.
- Jupyter Notebook (*https://jupyter.org*) is a tool for executing code in the browser. Jupyter Notebook also allows you to write markdown and display visualizations all in the browser. In fact, this book was written as a Jupyter notebook before being converted to a publishable format. Jupyter Notebook is maintained by Project Jupyter, which is a nonprofit dedicated to supporting interactive data-science tools.

- Docker (*https://www.docker.com*) is a tool for easily creating virtual machines, often referred to as *containers*. We'll use Docker as an alternative installation tool to setting up Anaconda. It is maintained by Docker, Inc.

Setting Up Your Environment

In this book, almost every chapter has exercises, so it is useful to make sure that the environment is working at the beginning. We'll use Jupyter notebooks in this book, and the kernel we'll use is the baseline Python 3.6 kernel. The instructions here use Continuum's Anaconda to set up a Python virtual environment.

You can also use the docker image (*https://oreil.ly/iFqgI*) for the necessary environment.

These instructions were created from the set-up process for Ubuntu. There are additional set-up instructions online at the project's GitHub page.

Prerequisites

1. Anaconda
   - To set up Anaconda, follow the instructions (*https://oreil.ly/8rbHS*).
2. Apache Spark
   - To set up Apache Spark, follow the instructions (*https://oreil.ly/egGoQ*).
   - Make sure that SPARK_HOME is set to the location of your Apache Spark installation.
     — If you are on Linux or macOS, you can put export SPARK_HOME="/path/to/spark"
     — If you are on Windows, you can use System Properties to set an environment variable named SPARK_HOME to "/path/to/spark"
   - This was written on Apache Spark 2.4

Optional: Set up a password (*https://oreil.ly/yymsW*) for your Jupyter notebook server.

Starting Apache Spark

```
$ echo $SPARK_HOME

/path/to/your/spark/installation

$ spark-shell

Using Spark's default log4j profile: org/apache/spark/log4j-defaults.prope
rties
Setting default log level to "WARN".
To adjust logging level use sc.setLogLevel(newLevel). For SparkR, use
```

```
setL ogLevel(newLevel).
...
Spark context Web UI available at localhost:4040
Spark context available as 'sc' (master = local[*], app id = ...).
Spark session available as 'spark'.
Welcome to
      ____              __
     / __/__  ___ _____/ /__
    _\ \/ _ \/ _ `/ __/  '_/
   /___/ .__/\_,_/_/ /_/\_\   version 2.3.2
      /_/

Using Scala version 2.11.8 (Java HotSpot(TM) 64-Bit Server VM, Java 1.8.0
_102)
Type in expressions to have them evaluated.
Type :help for more information.

scala>
```

Checking Out the Code

1. Go to the GitHub repo (*https://oreil.ly/DrWtE*) for this project

2. Check out the code, and run the following code examples in a terminal:

   a. Clone the repo
   ```
   git clone https://github.com/alexander-n-thomas/spark-nlp-book.git
   ```

   b. Create the Anaconda environment—this will take a while
   ```
   conda env create -f environment.yml
   ```

   c. Activate the new environment
   ```
   source activate spark-nlp-book
   ```

   d. Create the kernel for this environment
   ```
   ipython kernel install --user --name=sparknlpbook
   ```

   e. Launch the notebook server
   ```
   jupyter notebook
   ```

   f. Go to your notebook page at localhost:8888

Getting Familiar with Apache Spark

Now that we're all set up, let's start using Spark NLP! We will be using the *20 News-groups* Data Set (*https://oreil.ly/gXmnY*) from the University of California–Irvine Machine Learning Repository. For this first example we use the mini_newsgroups data set (*https://oreil.ly/W1iwn*). Download the TAR file and extract it into the data folder for this project.

```
! ls ./data/mini_newsgroups
```

```
alt.atheism                rec.autos            sci.space
comp.graphics              rec.motorcycles      soc.religion.christian
comp.os.ms-windows.misc    rec.sport.baseball   talk.politics.guns
comp.sys.ibm.pc.hardware   rec.sport.hockey     talk.politics.mideast
comp.sys.mac.hardware      sci.crypt            talk.politics.misc
comp.windows.x             sci.electronics      talk.religion.misc
misc.forsale               sci.me
```

Starting Apache Spark with Spark NLP

There are many ways we can use Apache Spark from Jupyter notebooks. We could use a specialized kernel, but I generally prefer using a simple kernel. Fortunately, Spark NLP gives us an easy way to start up.

```
import sparknlp

import pyspark
from pyspark import SparkConf
from pyspark.sql import SparkSession
from pyspark.sql import functions as fun
from pyspark.sql.types import *

%matplotlib inline
import matplotlib.pyplot as plt

packages = ','.join([
    "JohnSnowLabs:spark-nlp:1.6.3",
])

spark_conf = SparkConf()
spark_conf = spark_conf.setAppName('spark-nlp-book-p1c1')
spark_conf = spark_conf.setAppName('master[*]')
spark_conf = spark_conf.set("spark.jars.packages", packages)
spark = SparkSession.builder.config(conf=spark_conf).getOrCreate()

%matplotlib inline
import matplotlib.pyplot as plt
```

Loading and Viewing Data in Apache Spark

Let's look at how we can load data with Apache Spark and then at some ways we can view the data.

```
import os

mini_newsgroups_path = os.path.join('data', 'mini_newsgroups', '*')

texts = spark.sparkContext.wholeTextFiles(mini_newsgroups_path)

schema = StructType([
    StructField('filename', StringType()),
    StructField('text', StringType()),
```

```
])
texts_df = spark.createDataFrame(texts, schema)

texts_df.show()

+--------------------+--------------------+
|            filename|                text|
+--------------------+--------------------+
|file:/home/alext/...|Path: cantaloupe....|
|file:/home/alext/...|Newsgroups: sci.e...|
|file:/home/alext/...|Newsgroups: sci.e...|
|file:/home/alext/...|Newsgroups: sci.e...|
|file:/home/alext/...|Xref: cantaloupe....|
|file:/home/alext/...|Path: cantaloupe....|
|file:/home/alext/...|Xref: cantaloupe....|
|file:/home/alext/...|Newsgroups: sci.e...|
|file:/home/alext/...|Newsgroups: sci.e...|
|file:/home/alext/...|Xref: cantaloupe....|
|file:/home/alext/...|Path: cantaloupe....|
|file:/home/alext/...|Newsgroups: sci.e...|
|file:/home/alext/...|Path: cantaloupe....|
|file:/home/alext/...|Path: cantaloupe....|
|file:/home/alext/...|Path: cantaloupe....|
|file:/home/alext/...|Xref: cantaloupe....|
|file:/home/alext/...|Path: cantaloupe....|
|file:/home/alext/...|Newsgroups: sci.e...|
|file:/home/alext/...|Newsgroups: sci.e...|
+--------------------+--------------------+
only showing top 20 rows
```

Looking at the data is important in any data-science project. When working with structured data, especially numerical data, it is common to explore data with aggregates. This is necessary because data sets are large, and looking at a small number of examples can easily lead to misrepresentation of the data. Natural language data complicates this. On one hand, humans are really good at interpreting language; on the other, humans are also really good at jumping to conclusions and making hasty generalizations. So we still have the problem of creating a representative summary for large data sets. We'll talk about some techniques to do this in Chapters 10 and 11.

For now, let's talk about ways we can look at a small amount of data in DataFrames. As you can see in the preceding code example, we can show the output of a DataFrame using .show().

Let's look at the arguments:

1. n: number of rows to show.

2. truncate: if set to True, truncates strings longer than 20 characters by default. If set to a number greater than one, truncates long strings to length truncate and aligns cells right.

3. `vertical`: if set to True, prints output rows vertically (one line per column value).

Let's try using some of these arguments:

```
texts_df.show(n=5, truncate=100, vertical=True)

-RECORD
0------------------------------------------------------------------------------
------------------------
 filename | file:/home/alext/projects/spark-nlp-book/data/mini_newsgroups/
sci.electronics/54165
 text     | Path: cantaloupe.srv.cs.cmu.edu!magnesium.club.cc.cmu.edu!
news.sei.cmu.edu!cis.ohio-state.edu!zap...
-RECORD
1------------------------------------------------------------------------------
------------------------
 filename | file:/home/alext/projects/spark-nlp-book/data/mini_newsgroups/
sci.electronics/54057
 text     | Newsgroups: sci.electronics
Path: cantaloupe.srv.cs.cmu.edu!magnesium.club.cc.cmu.edu!news.sei.cm...
-RECORD
2------------------------------------------------------------------------------
------------------------
 filename | file:/home/alext/projects/spark-nlp-book/data/mini_newsgroups/
sci.electronics/53712
 text     | Newsgroups: sci.electronics
Path: cantaloupe.srv.cs.cmu.edu!das-news.harvard.edu!noc.near.net!how...
-RECORD
3------------------------------------------------------------------------------
------------------------
 filename | file:/home/alext/projects/spark-nlp-book/data/mini_newsgroups/
sci.electronics/53529
 text     | Newsgroups: sci.electronics
Path: cantaloupe.srv.cs.cmu.edu!crabapple.srv.cs.cmu.edu!bb3.andrew.c...
-RECORD
4------------------------------------------------------------------------------
------------------------
 filename | file:/home/alext/projects/spark-nlp-book/data/mini_newsgroups/
sci.electronics/54042
 text     | Xref: cantaloupe.srv.cs.cmu.edu comp.os.msdos.programmer:23292
alt.msdos.programmer:6797 sci.elec...
only showing top 5 rows
```

The `.show()` method is good for a quick view of data, but if the data is complicated, it doesn't work as well. In the Jupyter environment, there are some special integrations with pandas, and pandas `DataFrames` are displayed a little more nicely. Table 1-1 is an example.

```
texts_df.limit(5).toPandas()
```

Table 1-1. pandas DataFrame output in Jupyter notebook

	filename	text
0	file:/home/alext/projects/spark-nlp-book/data...	Path: cantaloupe.srv.cs.cmu.edu!magne...
1	file:/home/alext/projects/spark-nlp-book/data...	Newsgroups: sci.electronics\nPath: cant...
2	file:/home/alext/projects/spark-nlp-book/data...	Newsgroups: sci.electronics\nPath: cant...
3	file:/home/alext/projects/spark-nlp-book/data...	Newsgroups: sci.electronics\nPath: cant...
4	file:/home/alext/projects/spark-nlp-book/data...	Xref: cantaloupe.srv.cs.cmu.edu comp.o...

Notice the use of `.limit()`. The `.toPandas()` method pulls the Spark `DataFrame` into memory to create a pandas `DataFrame`. Converting to pandas can also be useful for using tools available in Python, since pandas `DataFrame` is widely supported in the Python ecosystem.

For other types of visualizations, we'll primarily use the Python libraries matplotlib and seaborn. In order to use these libraries we will need to create pandas `DataFrames`, so we will either aggregate or sample Spark `DataFrames` into a manageable size.

Hello World with Spark NLP

We have some data, so let's use Spark NLP to process it. First, let's extract the newsgroup name from the filename. We can see the newsgroup as the last folder in the filename. Table 1-2 shows the result.

```
texts_df = texts_df.withColumn(
    'newsgroup',
    fun.split('filename', '/').getItem(7)
)

texts_df.limit(5).toPandas()
```

Table 1-2. Table with newsgroup column

	filename	text	newsgroup
0	file:/home/alext/projects/spark...	Path: cantaloupe.srv.cs.cmu.edu!mag...	sci.electronics
1	file:/home/alext/projects/spark...	Newsgroups: sci.electronics\nPath: ca...	sci.electronics
2	file:/home/alext/projects/spark...	Newsgroups: sci.electronics\nPath: ca...	sci.electronics
3	file:/home/alext/projects/spark...	Newsgroups: sci.electronics\nPath: ca...	sci.electronics
4	file:/home/alext/projects/spark...	Xref: cantaloupe.srv.cs.cmu.edu comp...	sci.electronics

Let's look at how many documents are in each newsgroup. Figure 1-1 shows the bar chart.

```
newsgroup_counts = texts_df.groupBy('newsgroup').count().toPandas()

newsgroup_counts.plot(kind='bar', figsize=(10, 5))
plt.xticks(
```

```
    ticks=range(len(newsgroup_counts)),
    labels=newsgroup_counts['newsgroup']
)
plt.show()
```

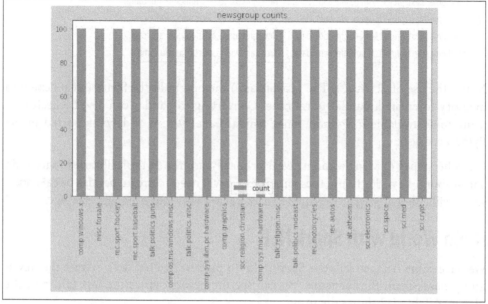

Figure 1-1. Mini-newsgroups counts

Because the mini_newsgroups data set is a subset of the Twenty Newsgroups Data Set, we have the same number of documents in each newsgroup. Now, let's use the Explain Document ML (*https://oreil.ly/8wH1V*):

```
from sparknlp.pretrained import PretrainedPipeline
```

The explain_document_ml is a pretrained pipeline that we can use to process text with a simple pipeline that performs basic processing steps. In order to understand what the explain_document_ml is doing, it is necessary to give a brief description of what the annotators are. An *annotator* is a representation of a specific NLP technique. We will go more in depth when we get to Chapter 3.

The annotators work on a document, which is the text, associated metadata, and any previously discovered annotations. This design helps annotators reuse work of previous annotators. The downside is that it is more complex than libraries like NLTK, which are uncoupled collections of NLP functions.

The explain_document_ml has one Transformer and six annotators:

DocumentAssembler
> A Transformer that creates a column that contains documents.

Sentence Segmenter
> An annotator that produces the sentences of the document.

Tokenizer
> An annotator that produces the tokens of the sentences.

SpellChecker
> An annotator that produces the spelling-corrected tokens.

Stemmer
> An annotator that produces the stems of the tokens.

Lemmatizer
> An annotator that produces the lemmas of the tokens.

POS Tagger
> An annotator that produces the parts of speech of the associated tokens.

There are some new terms introduced here that we'll discuss more in upcoming chapters:

```
pipeline = PretrainedPipeline('explain_document_ml', lang='en')
```

The .annotate() method of the BasicPipeline can be used to annotate singular strings, as well as DataFrames. Let's look at what it produces.

```
pipeline.annotate('Hellu wrold!')

{'document': ['Hellu wrold!'],
 'spell': ['Hello', 'world', '!'],
 'pos': ['UH', 'NN', '.'],
 'lemmas': ['Hello', 'world', '!'],
 'token': ['Hellu', 'wrold', '!'],
 'stems': ['hello', 'world', '!'],
 'sentence': ['Hellu wrold!']}
```

This a good amount of additional information, which brings up something that you will want to keep in mind—annotations can produce a lot of extra data.

Let's look at the schema of the raw data.

```
texts_df.printSchema()

root
 |-- filename: string (nullable = true)
 |-- text: string (nullable = true)
 |-- newsgroup: string (nullable = true)
```

Now, let's annotate our `DataFrame` and look at the new schema.

```
procd_texts_df = basic_pipeline.annotate(texts_df, 'text')

procd_texts_df.printSchema()

root
 |-- filename: string (nullable = true)
 |-- text: string (nullable = true)
 |-- newsgroup: string (nullable = true)
 |-- document: array (nullable = true)
 |    |-- element: struct (containsNull = true)
 |    |    |-- annotatorType: string (nullable = true)
 |    |    |-- begin: integer (nullable = false)
 |    |    |-- end: integer (nullable = false)
 |    |    |-- result: string (nullable = true)
 |    |    |-- metadata: map (nullable = true)
 |    |    |    |-- key: string
 |    |    |    |-- value: string (valueContainsNull = true)
 |    |    |-- embeddings: array (nullable = true)
 |    |    |    |-- element: float (containsNull = false)
 |    |    |-- sentence_embeddings: array (nullable = true)
 |    |    |    |-- element: float (containsNull = false)
 |-- sentence: array (nullable = true)
 |    |-- element: struct (containsNull = true)
 |    |    |-- annotatorType: string (nullable = true)
...
```

That schema is quite complex! To break it down, let's look at the token column. It has an `Array` type column, and each element is a `Struct`. Each element has the following:

annotatorType
:   The type of annotation.

begin
:   The starting character position of the annotation.

end
:   The character position after the end of the annotation.

result
:   The output of the annotator.

metadata
:   A `Map` from `String` to `String` containing additional, potentially helpful, information about the annotation.

Let's look at some of the data using `.show()`.

```
procd_texts_df.show(n=2)

+-------------------+-------------------+---------------+---------
----------+-------------------+-------------------+-------------
```

```
------+-------------------+-------------------+------------------
-+
|          filename|            text|      newsgroup|
   document|          sentence|              token|
  spell|          lemmas|              stems|              po
s|
+-------------------+-------------------+---------------+---------
-----------+-------------------+-------------------+-------------
------+-------------------+-------------------+------------------
-+
|file:/home/alext/...|Path: cantaloupe....|sci.electronics|[[documen
t, 0, 90...|[[document, 0, 46...|[[token, 0, 3, Pa...|[[token, 0, 3,
 Pa...|[[token, 0, 3, Pa...|[[token, 0, 3, pa...|[[pos, 0, 3, NNP,..
.|
|file:/home/alext/...|Newsgroups: sci.e...|sci.electronics|[[documen
t, 0, 19...|[[document, 0, 40...|[[token, 0, 9, Ne...|[[token, 0, 9,
 Ne...|[[token, 0, 9, Ne...|[[token, 0, 9, ne...|[[pos, 0, 9, NNP,..
.|
+-------------------+-------------------+---------------+---------
-----------+-------------------+-------------------+-------------
------+-------------------+-------------------+------------------
-+
only showing top 2 rows
```

This is not very readable. Not only is the automatic formatting doing poorly with this data, but we can hardly see our annotations. Let's try using some other arguments.

```
procd_texts_df.show(n=2, truncate=100, vertical=True)

-RECORD 0----------------------------------------------------------
---------------------------------------------
 filename  | file:/home/alext/projects/spark-nlp-book/data/mini_news
groups/sci.electronics/54165
 text      | Path: cantaloupe.srv.cs.cmu.edu!magnesium.club.cc.cmu.e
du!news.sei.cmu.edu!cis.ohio-state.edu!zap...
 newsgroup | sci.electronics

 document  | [[document, 0, 903, Path: cantaloupe.srv.cs.cmu.edu!mag
nesium.club.cc.cmu.edu!news.sei.cmu.edu!ci...
 sentence  | [[document, 0, 468, Path: cantaloupe.srv.cs.cmu.edu!mag
nesium.club.cc.cmu.edu!news.sei.cmu.edu!ci...
 token     | [[token, 0, 3, Path, [sentence -> 0], [], []], [token,
4, 4, :, [sentence -> 0], [], []], [token,...
 spell     | [[token, 0, 3, Path, [sentence -> 0], [], []], [token,
4, 4, :, [sentence -> 0], [], []], [token,...
 lemmas    | [[token, 0, 3, Path, [sentence -> 0], [], []], [token,
4, 4, :, [sentence -> 0], [], []], [token,...
 stems     | [[token, 0, 3, path, [sentence -> 0], [], []], [token,
4, 4, :, [sentence -> 0], [], []], [token,...
 pos       | [[pos, 0, 3, NNP, [word -> Path], [], []], [pos, 4, 4,
:, [word -> :], [], []], [pos, 6, 157, JJ,...
-RECORD 1----------------------------------------------------------
---------------------------------------------
```

```
 filename     | file:/home/alext/projects/spark-nlp-book/data/mini_news
groups/sci.electronics/54057
 text         | Newsgroups: sci.electronics
Path: cantaloupe.srv.cs.cmu.edu!magnesium.club.cc.cmu.edu!news.sei.c
m...
 newsgroup    | sci.electronics

 document     | [[document, 0, 1944, Newsgroups: sci.electronics Path:
cantaloupe.srv.cs.cmu.edu!magnesium.club.c...
 sentence     | [[document, 0, 408, Newsgroups: sci.electronics Path: c
antaloupe.srv.cs.cmu.edu!magnesium.club.cc...
 token        | [[token, 0, 9, Newsgroups, [sentence -> 0], [], []], [t
oken, 10, 10, :, [sentence -> 0], [], []],...
 spell        | [[token, 0, 9, Newsgroups, [sentence -> 0], [], []], [t
oken, 10, 10, :, [sentence -> 0], [], []],...
 lemmas       | [[token, 0, 9, Newsgroups, [sentence -> 0], [], []], [t
oken, 10, 10, :, [sentence -> 0], [], []],...
 stems        | [[token, 0, 9, newsgroup, [sentence -> 0], [], []], [to
ken, 10, 10, :, [sentence -> 0], [], []], ...
 pos          | [[pos, 0, 9, NNP, [word -> Newsgroups], [], []], [pos,
10, 10, :, [word -> :], [], []], [pos, 12,...
only showing top 2 rows
```

Better, but this is still not useful for getting a general understanding of our corpus. We at least have a glimpse of what our pipeline is doing.

Now, we need to pull out the information we might want to use in other processes—that is why there is the `Finisher Transformer`. The `Finisher` takes annotations and pulls out the pieces of data that we will be using in downstream processes. This allows us to use the results of our NLP pipeline in generic Spark. For now, let's pull out all the lemmas and put them into a `String`, separated by spaces.

```
from sparknlp import Finisher

finisher = Finisher()
finisher = finisher
# taking the lemma column
finisher = finisher.setInputCols(['lemmas'])
# separating lemmas by a single space
finisher = finisher.setAnnotationSplitSymbol(' ')

finished_texts_df = finisher.transform(procd_texts_df)

finished_texts_df.show(n=1, truncate=100, vertical=True)

-RECORD 0--------------------------------------------------------
----------------------------------------------------
filename          | file:/home/alext/projects/spark-nlp-book/data/mini
_newsgroups/sci.electronics/54165
text              | Path: cantaloupe.srv.cs.cmu.edu!magnesium.club.cc.
cmu.edu!news.sei.cmu.edu!cis.ohio-state.edu!zap...
newsgroup         | sci.electronics
```

```
finished_lemmas | [Path, :, cantaloupe.srv.cs.cmu.edu!magnesium.club
.cc.cmu.edu!news.sei.cmu.edu!cis.ohio-state.edu...
only showing top 1 row
```

Normally, we'll be using the `.setOutputAsArray(True)` option so that the output is an `Array` instead of a `String`.

Let's look at the final result on the first document.

```
finished_texts_df.select('finished_lemmas').take(1)
```

```
[Row(finished_lemmas=['Path', ':', 'cantaloupe.srv.cs.cmu.edu!magnes
ium.club.cc.cmu.edu!news.sei.cmu.edu!cis.ohio-state.edu!zaphod.mps.o
hio-state.edu!news.acns.nwu.edu!uicvm.uic.edu!u19250', 'Organization
', ':', 'University', 'of', 'Illinois', 'at', 'Chicago', ',', 'acade
mic', 'Computer', 'Center', 'Date', ':', 'Sat', ',', '24', 'Apr', '1
993', '14:28:35', 'CDT', 'From', ':', '<U19250@uicvm.uic.edu>', 'Mes
sage-ID', ':', '<93114.142835U19250@uicvm.uic.edu>', 'Newsgroups', '
:', 'sci.electronics', 'Subject', ':', 'multiple', 'input', 'for', '
PC', 'Lines', ':', '0', 'Can', 'anyone', 'offer', 'a', 'suggestion',
 'on', 'a', 'problem', 'I', 'be', 'have', '?', 'I', 'have', 'several
', 'board', 'whose', 'sole', 'purpose', 'be', 'to', 'decode', 'DTMF'
, 'tone', 'and', 'send', 'the', 'resultant', 'in', 'ASCII', 'to', 'a
', 'PC', '.', 'These', 'board', 'run', 'on', 'the', 'serial', 'inter
face', '.', 'I', 'need', 'to', 'run', 'A', 'of', 'the', 'board', 'so
mewhat', 'simultaneously', '.', 'I', 'need', 'to', 'be', 'able', 'to
', 'ho', 'ok', 'they', 'up', 'to', 'a', 'PC', '>', 'The', 'problem',
 'be', ',', 'how', 'do', 'I', 'hook', 'up', '8', '+', 'serial', 'dev
ice', 'to', 'one', 'PC', 'inexpensively', ',', 'so', 'that', 'all',
'can', 'send', 'data', 'simultaneously', '(', 'or', 'close', 'to', '
it', ')', '?', 'Any', 'help', 'would', 'be', 'greatly', 'appreciate'
, '!', 'Achin', 'Single'])]
```

It doesn't look like much has been done here, but there is still a lot to unpack. In the next chapter, we will explain some basics of linguistics that will help us understand what these annotators are doing.

## CHAPTER 2

Natural Language Basics

What Is Natural Language?

One of the most important faculties humanity has is language. Language is an essential part of how our society operates. Although it is such an integral function of humanity, it's still a phenomenon that is not fully understood. It is primarily studied by observing usage and by observing pathologies. There has also been much philosophical work done exploring meaning and language's relationship to cognition, truth, and reality. What makes language so difficult to understand is that it is ubiquitous in our experiences. The very act of producing and consuming statements about language contains the biases and ambiguity that permeate language itself. Fortunately, we do not need to go into such high philosophies! However, I like to keep in mind the grandeur and mystery of language as an anchor as we dive into the material in this book.

Many animals have complex communication systems, and some even have complex societies, but no animal has shown the ability to communicate such complex abstractions as humans do. This complexity is great if you are looking to survive the Neolithic period or to order a pizza, but if you are building an application that processes language, you have your work cut out for you. Human language appears to be much more complex than any other communication system. Not only do the rules of our language allow infinite unique sentences (e.g., "The first horse came before the second horse, which came before the third, which came before the fourth. . ."), they also allow us to create incredible abstractions. Both of these aspects relate to other human cognitive abilities.

Let's take a brief foray into the origins of language and writing in order to appreciate this phenomenon that we will be working with.

Origins of Language

There is a lot of debate about the origins of human language. We're not even entirely sure when or where modern human language first developed or if there is a single place and time where language originated. The gestural theory suggests that sign language originated first, followed later by verbal language, which developed alongside the physiological traits necessary for making more and more complex sounds. Another interesting debate is whether language developed in stages or all at once.

Even the mechanisms children use to acquire language are not fully understood. In the Middle Ages, it was thought that if a child was not taught language they would speak the "original" or "natural" language. There are stories of such intentional and unintentional experiments being performed, and various results have been claimed. In modern times, there have been some tragedies that have let us observe what happens when a human is not exposed to language in early childhood. When children are not exposed to language until after a *critical* period, they have a severe difficulty in learning and understanding complex grammar. There appears to be something special about young children's language acquisition that allows them to learn our complex communication system.

In these tragic situations, in which a child doesn't acquire a language in the critical period, the victims are still able to learn words, but they have difficulty learning complex syntax. Another tragedy that has taught us about language is the FOXP2 gene and its effect on those who have mutations in it. It appears that some mutations of this gene lead to *verbal dyspraxia*, a difficulty or inability to speak. One difficulty experienced by those with verbal dyspraxia is the inability to form long or complex sequences of sounds or words. The existence of this gene, which appears to allow us to create complex sequences, raises questions about the origins of language. If we did not have complex language before evolving the FOXP2 gene, what advantage could this gene have imparted that led to it being selected?

In the 1980s, a number of schools for deaf children were built in Nicaragua. Initially, these children communicated using "home signs," or rudimentary and highly motivated signs. A *motivated sign* is one whose form is determined, or at least influenced, by that which it represents—for example, pantomiming the act of putting something in one's mouth to represent food. Over time, the younger children combined these different sign systems into a more and more complex, and abstract, sign language. Eventually, a completely new language was born, with fully complex grammar and abstract *unmotivated signs*.

Regardless of how, when, and where language originated, we know that the written form came much later.

Spoken Language Versus Written Language

Written language was developed only a few thousand years ago. Written language does not, and cannot, represent all the nuances possible in spoken or gestured language. Language is more than a sequence of sounds or gestures. It is combined with facial gestures and changes in the manner of the production of sounds or gestures. These are called *paralinguistic features*.

There are a few ways in which paralinguistic features can be written. When they are present, they can be used to access complex intents.

Click sounds are often seen as an exotic feature of some languages in southern Africa, but they are also used as a paralinguistic feature in some European languages. In English, the "tsk tsk" or "tut tut" sound indicates disappointment, annoyance, or even disgust. Although there are agreed-upon written representations, these aren't true words. Outside of depictions of spoken language, you will rarely find these represented in text.

Tone is another sound used as a linguistic feature in some languages, and as a paralinguistic feature in others. Mandarin uses four tones, but English uses tone as a paralinguistic feature. Chinese logograms represent entire words and so don't need to represent tone separately, but the Latin-based Pinyin writing system used to phonetically represent Mandarin represents tone by marks over the vowels. English has some ways to represent these sort of paralinguistic features. Consider the difference between the following:

> You know the king.
> You know the king?

The difference between these two sentences is purely tone and pitch. The question mark indicates that the sentence should be interpreted as a question, and so it also indicates the general tone and pitch of the sentence.

Facial gesturing is an example of a paralinguistic feature that is not possible to represent in traditional text. In modern writing, facial gestures are arguably represented by emojis or emoticons. There is still much nuance that is difficult to interpret.

Let's consider the scenario in which you ask to reschedule a lunch with a friend. Say they respond with the following:

> OK :)

In that response, you can't tell what the smile indicates. They could be using it because you are known for rescheduling, so this is humorously expected. They could be using it out of habit. On the other hand, say they respond with the following:

OK...

In this response, the ellipsis is much harder to interpret. It could represent annoyance, or it could simply be an indicator that there is another message forthcoming. If this exchange had been communicated in person, there would be less ambiguity, because these things can be perceived in facial gestures and other paralinguistic features.

Let's look now at the field of linguistics, as this will give us a structured way of exploring these considerations when looking at language data.

Linguistics

Linguistics is the study of human language. There are many subfields of linguistics, but there are generally two types: one focused around elements of language and one focused around how language is used. There are also a number of interdisciplinary fields that connect linguistics and another field. Let's look at a few subfields.

Phonetics and Phonology

Phonetics is the study of the sounds used in verbal languages. Because we will be focusing on text data, we will not be using this subfield much. The fundamental unit is the phone or phoneme (these are different things but are used in different kinds of analysis). These units are represented using the *International Phonetic Alphabet (IPA)*. The IPA uses symbols to represent a great variety of sounds. I will use it in this section without much explanation, but if you are interested in learning more about IPA and its symbols, there are plenty of great resources online.

Languages have *phonologies*, which are collections of *phonemes* and rules about how to use and realize the phonemes. When a phoneme is realized it is a *phone*. In English, /t/ is a phoneme (/*/ is the convention for writing phonemes, and [*] is the convention for phones), and /t/ has multiple possible realizations:

[tʰ]

At the beginning of a stressed syllable: "team," "return"

[t]

After an /s/ like "stop," at the end of a word like "pot," and even between vowels in some dialects (UK, India), or at the beginning of an unstressed syllable like "matter" or "technique"

[ɾ]

A flap sound in some dialects (North America, Australia, New Zealand) between vowels

[2]
    A glottal stop in some dialects (UK) between vowels

Generally when working with text data, we are not concerned with phonetics, but it can be useful if we want to search using sound similarity. For example, we may want to search a list of names for someone named Katherine, but *Katherine* can be spelled in many different ways (Katheryn, Catharine, Katharine, etc.). Using an algorithm called Soundex we can search for similar sounding names by representing the query phonetically.

Morphology

Morphology is the study of morphemes. *Morphemes* are the smallest element that can carry meaning. There are four kinds of morphemes, defined by *unbound* versus *bound* and *content* versus *functional*:

Unbound content morphemes, content morphemes, or lexical morphemes
    Words that represent things or concepts themselves

    Examples: "cat," "remember," "red," "quickly"

Unbound functional morphemes or functional morphemes
    Words that perform a function in a sentence

    Examples: "they," "from," "will" (when used to make the future tense)

Bound content morphemes or derivational affixes
    Affixes that turn one word into another

    Examples: "-ty" ("royal" + "-ty" = "royalty"), "-er" ("call" + "-er" = "caller")

Bound functional morphemes or inflectional affixes
    Affixes that indicate the function of a word in a sentence

    Examples: "-(e)s" (plural, "cat" + "-(e)s" = "cats," "pass" + "-(e)s" = "passes"), "-ed" (past tense, "melt" + "-ed" = "melted")

There are some text processing algorithms that can be easily explained as removing or simplifying some kind of morpheme. Understanding these differences is a good start to understanding where you want to look for information in your text data. This information is language specific. What are *functional morphemes* in some languages are *inflectional affixes* in other languages, so understanding these distinctions can help inform your decisions in the basic processing for different languages.

One important distinction in morphology is whether the language is *synthetic* or *analytic*. This can be considered as a ratio of *inflectional affixes* to *functional morphemes*. The more *inflectional affixes* are used, the more synthetic the language is. English is considered a mostly analytic language, as is Mandarin, and can be referred to as *isolating.* Russian and Greek are more middle-of-the-road and can sometimes be called *fusional.* Turkish and Finnish are quite synthetic and are referred to as *agglutinative.* The typology of a language is vital to determining how to do the basic text processing. We will cover this in more depth when we discuss building applications for multiple languages.

Morphology is very closely related to syntax; in fact, both are often considered under an umbrella concept of *morpho-syntax.*

Syntax

Syntax is the study of how words are combined into phrases and sentences. There are multiple competing models for syntax. The models that are popular in the field of linguistics are not necessarily the popular models in computational linguistics and NLP.

The most common way that syntax is introduced is with *phrase structure trees (PSTs).* Let's look at the PST in Figure 2-1 for the following sentence:

I saw the man with the hat.

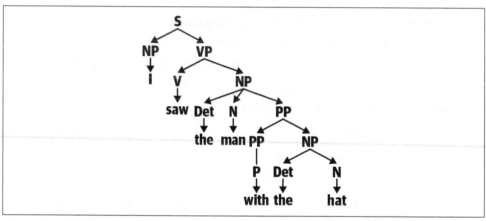

Figure 2-1. Phrase structure tree

PSTs are not really used outside of introducing syntax. Minimalist program grammars, tree-adjoint grammars, and head-driven phrase structure grammar are the popular models in linguistics, NLP, and computational linguistics, respectively. There are many different kinds of grammars, and we will go into them more when we cover syntactic parsers.

The difficult part of researching syntax is that models either are not sufficiently constrained—that is, they allow structures that are not observed in nature—or are excessively constrained, meaning they cannot express structures that are observed in nature. All the well-known grammars handle simple sentences, so theoretically for most NLP uses any model would work.

Syntax is a central aspect of human language, and extracting the information encoded with syntax can be computationally intensive. There are many ways to approximate the extraction. We will generally see that when we want to extract information, we will try and do so without actually creating a parsed structure. The reason for this is, as we said before, there are infinite potential phrases and sentences in the syntax of human languages. The algorithms that parse sentences are often quite expensive because of this.

Semantics

Semantics is the study of the meaning of linguistic elements. This field has close ties to various fields in philosophy, especially logic. One aspect of the field of semantics is modeling how meaning is composed from the structures of language, so semantics is most closely related to syntax. There are aspects of language meaning that can be seen as compositional; others are more complicated. Phrases and sentences can generally be decomposed, but dialogues, poems, and books are not so easily analyzed.

It would seem that we are always interested in extracting the semantics in text, and this is true after a fashion. What we should always keep in mind is that a text, a sentence, or even a word can have many different meanings. We'll need to know what we are interested in before we build our NLP pipeline.

Most projects that use NLP are looking for the meaning in the text being analyzed, so we will be revisiting this field multiple times.

There are a couple of other subfields we should keep in mind—sociolinguistics and pragmatics.

Sociolinguistics: Dialects, Registers, and Other Varieties

Sociolinguistics is the study of language in society. It is an interdisciplinary field between sociology and linguistics. Understanding the social context of text is important in understanding how to interpret the text. This field also gives us a framework to understand how different data sets might be related to each other. This will be useful when we look at transfer learning.

A useful concept from sociolinguistics is the idea of language varieties, which covers the subjects of dialects and slang. The idea is that a language is a collection of varieties, and people have their own individual collection of varieties. The collection of varieties that an individual speaks can be considered an *idiolect*. The different varieties that an individual uses are called *registers*. Registers covers the concept of formality as well as other manners of speech, gesture, and writing.

Formality

Because language is a fundamental tool of human social interaction, many aspects of social behavior have representations in language. One aspect is the idea of formality. Formality is often talked about as a single spectrum from casual to formal, but it is more complex than this. The level of formality that a person working in retail is required to use with a customer is different from the levels of formality required when someone is applying for graduate school or talking to a grandparent. Very formal and very informal registers can lead to complications.

Highly formal registers often include content that doesn't convey much meaning but is there to indicate formality. Consider the following hypothetical dialogue between a retail worker and a customer:

> *Customer*: Hello. Do you have any mangoes?
> *Retail worker*: Hmmm. . .I don't think so, sir.

The customer's question is relatively straightforward. Most people interpret the retail worker's response as effectively equivalent in meaning to "No." The initial "Hmm. . ." is either because the retail worker does not know and needs to consider whether the store carries mangoes, or because they are pretending to consider the request. An abrupt answer of "I don't think so, sir" could be considered rude or dismissive. Similarly, the retail worker can't just say "Hmm. . .no, sir" because that could be considered curt. The "sir" is purely a formal marker called an honorific.

Informal registers can be difficult to parse because shorthand and slang are commonly used within them. Additionally, we often use informal contexts with people we are closest to. This means that much of our communication in informal registers is in a deeply shared context. This can make using the most informal communication difficult.

Context

Registers are based not only on formality but also on context. Registers affect the pronunciation, morphosyntax, and even word meanings. When working with text data sets with language from different varieties, we must always keep in mind how the different varieties in our data set may be expressed.

Consider the meaning of the word "quiet" in two different kinds of reviews:

> The hotel room was quiet.
> The headphones are quiet.

In the first, "quiet" is a positive attribute, whereas it is likely negative in the second. This is a relatively straightforward example; the differences can be much more subtle, and they need to be taken into consideration when attempting to combine data sets or do transfer learning.

There is an entire subfield dedicated to understanding the use of language in context: pragmatics.

Pragmatics

Pragmatics is a subfield that looks at the use and meaning of language in context. Understanding pragmatics will help us understand the intent behind the text data we have. Pragmatics is a subfield that I think any NLP practitioner will come back to again and again.

Roman Jakobson

Although it is now somewhat old, I like the Roman Jakobson model of pragmatics (see Figure 2-2). The model is built around a simple abstract model of communication. The idea is that there are six different parts or factors to communications.

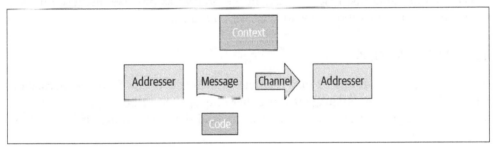

Figure 2-2. Roman Jakobson's functions of language

In this model, there are six factors in communication, along with six functions. Each function focuses on its associated factor. Following are the six functions (with the associated factor):

Emotive (the addresser)
> Messages that communicate the state of the addresser ("uh-oh!")

Conative (the addressee)
> Messages that have an intended effect on the addressee ("Open the window.")

Poetic (the message)
> Messages that are for the message's own sake (poetry, scatting)

Metalingual (the code)
> Messages about the code in which the message is encoded ("What do you call this?")

Phatic (the channel)
Messages that establish or relate to the communication channel ("Hello!", small talk)

Referential (the context)
Messages that convey information from the context ("It's raining.")

This model of pragmatics considers messages as focusing on some combination of these factors. It is often explained with examples of messages that focus mostly on one factor, but it should be kept in mind that most speech acts are a combination of focusing on several factors.

How To Use Pragmatics

When working with text data sets, it is worthwhile to consider why the messages were written. Understanding this requires a mix of pragmatics, sociolinguistics, and domain expertise. We might not always have access to a domain expert, but we can make educated interpretations of the pragmatics and social context of the data. These considerations should be made as early in the process as possible, because this will inform many decisions about how to work with our data.

Writing Systems

In this chapter we've discussed many aspects of language, but so far we've focused on aspects that are part of language that is either only spoken or both spoken and written. There is a great variety of writing systems, and they can strongly influence how we process our data.

Origins

Although writing is a recent development in human history, there still appears to be a physical adaptation. When a person becomes literate, part of the brain that specializes in character recognition, the letterbox, is activated. The letterbox is located in a similar place for all people regardless of which language they learn. There are different theories of its origin, but the existence of the letterbox is yet another example of how specialized humans and our language faculties are.

Writing appears to have been invented multiple times throughout history. There does appear to be a pattern of first creating highly motivated symbols that may not even correspond to words, also known as pictographs, which then get transformed and specialized.

The origin of the Latin alphabet has many interesting twists and turns. The generally accepted chain of cultures through which it evolved is as follows: The Latins borrowed from a Greek alphabet, but keep in mind that there were multiple Greek alphabets in the classical era. The Greeks in turn borrowed their characters from the Phoenicians, with the addition of some innovated letters. The Phoenicians were a tribe of Canaanites who lived on the coast of the Levant. The Canaanites all shared the same or similar characters in their writing system. This writing system appears to be based on simplified versions of Egyptian characters. Egyptian writing was a mix of logograms and phonetic symbols (similar to modern Japanese). The Canaanites took some of the phonetic symbols of Egyptian writing and adapted them to their own language, and then they simplified the appearance of these symbols until the pictographic elements were no longer noticeable. The Egyptians appear to have innovated their own writing system from a system of pictographs. At the same time, writing systems were being innovated in Sumer (modern-day Iraq), and China.

Figure 2-3 displays some letters and their origins in ancient pictograms.

Latin	Cyrillic	Greek	Hebrew	Phoenician	Name	Name (tr.)
A/a	A/a	A/α	א	ﬡ	Alep	Ox
B/b	Б/б, В/в	B/β	ב	ﬤ	Bet	House
C/c	Г/г	Γ/γ	ג	ﬧ	Giml	Camel
F/f			ו	﬩	Waw	Hook
K/k	К/к	K/κ	ך/כ	ﬦ	Kap	Palm (hand)
O/o	О/о	O/ο	ע	O	Ayin	Eye
P/p	П/п	Π/π	ף/פ	ﬨ	Pe	Mouth
Q/q			ק	ﬦ	Qop	Needle eye
R/r	Р/р	P/ρ	ר	ﬧ	Resh	Head
S/s	С/с	Σ/σ/ς	ש	W	Shin	Tooth or Bow
T/t	T/т	T/τ	ת	X	Taw	Tally mark
U/u	У/у	Y/υ	ו	Y	Waw	Hook

Figure 2-3. Origins of some letters of the alphabet

Alphabets

An *alphabet* is a phonetic-based writing system that represents consonants and vowels. Here are some examples of alphabets:

Latin

Latin is used throughout the world. Its use was spread during the colonial age. In order to be adapted to many different languages, many new characters were invented. The English alphabet is relatively simple (and arguably ill-fitted to

English). Its modern form was defined in the early days of printing when special characters were more difficult or even impossible to represent.

English: "Hello!" pronounced /hɛˈloʊ/

Cyrillic

Cyrillic is used in many countries in Eastern Europe, Central Asia, and North Asia. Its name comes from Saint Cyril, a ninth-century Byzantine monk who invented (or at least formalized) Glagolitic, the precursor alphabet to Cyrillic.

Russian: "Привет!" pronounced /prʲɪˈvʲet/

Greek

Greek is used by modern Greek and its dialects, as well as by some minority languages in Greek-speaking majority areas. The Greek alphabet today is from the Attic (Athenian) Greek alphabet of the classical era.

Greek: "Γειά σου!" pronounced /ja su/

Hangul

Hangul is used to write Korean and was invented in the 15th century under King Sejong. Korean is different from other alphabets in that the symbols are combined into syllable blocks. Consider the following example:

Korean: "ㅇ+ㅏ+ㄴ ㄴ+ㅕ+ㅇ" <- + a + n n + yeo + ng> becomes "안녕" pronounced /anɲjʌŋ/

Alphabetic scripts are generally straightforward, but be mindful of languages that use *diacritics*, marks on characters. Sometimes we may want to remove these as part of normalizing our data, and this can be complicated. However, this generally can be solved in a rule-based manner.

Abjads

An *abjad* is a phonetic-based writing system that primarily represents consonants and only optionally vowels. These writing systems are almost entirely written right-to-left, which is something to keep in mind when creating UIs for languages that use these scripts. Here are some examples of abjads:

Arabic

Arabic (writing system) is used in writing Arabic (language), Farsi, Punjabi, and Urdu. Its use was spread with the rise of Islam. Arabic (writing system) is descended from the Aramaic abjad, which spread into the Arabian peninsula and developed a cursive form that we see today.

Arabic: "مرحبا" <m + r + h + b + a> pronounced [mær.ħɑ.bæː]

Hebrew

> Hebrew (writing system) is used in writing Hebrew (language), Aramaic, Yiddish, Ladino, and other languages of the Jewish diaspora. It developed from the ancient Canaanite abjads.

> Hebrew: "שלום" <sh + l + o + m> pronounced /ʃaˈlom/

It may seem that not writing vowels would make it difficult to read. However, it is difficult only for those learning the language. This is why most abjads have optional marks for indicating vowels to help children and second-language learners. When we talk about different morphosyntactic systems we will see why writing vowels is less of a hindrance for Semitic languages.

Abugidas

An *abugida* is a phonetic-based writing system in which each character represents a syllable. Instead of having a separate character for each possible syllable (which is what a syllabary is), an abugida has one character per starting consonant with a default vowel and marks that change the vowel. Consider the most widely used abugida today, Devanagari. There is a character, क, that represents /ka/. If we want to change the vowel to /u/, we add the necessary mark, कु, and that represents /ku/. It is also common for there to be a special mark that indicates no vowel, which is generally used to represent consonants that occur at the end of a syllable. Historically, some languages did not have such a mark and relied on various conventions to indicate syllable-final consonants. The following are some examples of abugidas:

Devanagari

> Devanagari originated some time before the 10th century AD, developed from the earlier Brahmi script. We are not sure where the Brahmi script comes from, though it is thought to be derived from the Aramaic abjad.

> Hindi: "नमस्ते" <na + ma + s - + te> pronounced /nəˈmə.ste/

Thai

> Thai (writing system) also derives from the Brahmi script. One interesting thing about the Thai writing system is that it also represents tone. There are special characters to mark tone, as well as intrinsic tones that are associated with certain characters.

> Thai: "สวัสดี" <s + wa + s + di> pronounced /sa˩˩.wat˩˩.di˩/

Geʾez

> Geʾez (writing system) is used in East Africa to write various languages of Ethiopia. It is developed from a South Arabian script, likely unrelated to modern Arabic (writing system), which itself is a descendant from the earliest Canaanite scripts. Originally, Geʾez was an abjad, but over time a default vowel developed,

and the vowel marks became mandatory. Because the marks that change the default vowel sometimes change the shape of the character, it can be argued that Ge'ez might be a syllabary.

Amharic: "ሰላም" <sə + la + mə> ppronounced /səlam/

Syllabaries

A *syllabary* is a phonetic-based system of writing in which there is a different symbol for each possible syllable in a language. Unlike the other phonetic-based systems, syllabaries are often invented, instead of being derived. There are not many still in use today. Syllabaries, like alphabets, are generally pretty simple and straightforward, which makes working with them as data easier. The following are some examples of syllabaries:

Hiragana
> Hiragana is one of the syllabaries used to write Japanese. The other is Katakana, which is also used to write Ainu, an interesting language spoken in northern Japan and unrelated to Japanese. Hiragana and Katakana were developed from simplified representations of Chinese logographs, similar to how the Canaanite writing system developed from Egyptian. Japanese uses Hanji, Chinese logographs, combined with Hiragana. This is necessary because Japanese and Chinese are such different languages, with Japanese being an agglutinative language and Chinese being highly analytic. Katakana is used to write borrowed words and onomatopoeia (like English "woof," and "bang").
>
> Japanese: "今日は" <kon + nichi + ha> pronounced "konît͡ɕiwa

Tsalagi
> Tsalagi is the syllabary invented by Sequoyah for writing his native Cherokee language. If you speak English you will recognize some of the characters, but that will not help in pronouncing them. The characters' pronunciation has no connection to their pronunciation in English.
>
> Tsalagi: "ᏏᏲ" <si + yo> pronounced /sijo/

Logographs

A *logographic* (also *logosyllabic*) system is a system based on a combination of semantics and phonetics. This is a somewhat miscellaneous category, since these systems often work very differently from one another. There is only one such system widely used today—Han Chinese characters. It is used to write most of the languages of China, as well as Japanese (Hanji, mentioned previously). These writing systems can make processing easier, because there is generally less decomposition possible, so basic text processing can be simplified. They can also complicate matters because they are often written without word separators (e.g., the space character), and they require more in-depth knowledge of the language to deal with nuanced processing.

Han Chinese

Han Chinese characters use a logographic writing system in which each character generally represents a syllable in Chinese languages, though this is not necessarily the case in Japanese.

Chinese: "你好" <"you" + "good"> pronounced "ni˧˩ hau˧˩" in Mandarin Chinese, "nei˩˧ hou˧˥" in Cantonese

Encodings

When we work with text data, we are working with written data that has been encoded into some binary format. This may seem like a small matter, but it is a frequent source of difficulties, especially when working with non-English languages. Because the English-speaking world played such a large part in the development of modern computers, many defaults make sense only for English.

Let's go over some details about encoding to keep in mind when (not if) we run into encoding issues.

ASCII

American Standard Code for Information Interchange (ASCII) is a mapping of control characters, Latin punctuation, Arabic numerals (as used in Europe), and English characters. It was originally designed for representing characters in teleprinters, aka teletypewriters, which is the origin of the abbreviation TTY.

Although this is an old standard, some legacy systems still support only ASCII.

Unicode

Since text is ultimately represented using bytes, there must be some mapping between numbers and characters. Your computer has no notion of "a," it knows only numbers. Unicode is the standardized set of character-number mappings maintained by the Unicode Consortium. For example, "a" is mapped to 97. Characters are generally represented with a specific formatted hexadecimal number—for example "a" is U+0061. U+#### is the standard format for representing Unicode values. The characters are grouped by language generally. Here are some examples of *blocks*:

- Basic Latin (U+0000–U+007F): ASCII characters
- Latin-1 Supplement (U+0080–U+00FF): additional control codes, additional European punctuation, and common Latin characters used in Europe

- Cyrillic (U+0400–U+04FF): the characters for most languages that use a Cyrillic writing system

Unicode is implemented in different encodings. The most common of these encodings are maintained by the Unicode Consortium itself, and some by ISO and IEC.

UTF-8

8-bit Unicode Transformation Format (UTF-8) is *variable width* implementation of Unicode. It is variable width because characters in different ranges require a different number of bytes. It uses one byte to represent the ASCII characters. It uses two bytes to represent U+0080 to U+07FF, which covers the most commonly used alphabets and abjads (except Hangul). Three bytes covers CJK (Chinese-Japanese-Korean) characters, South Asian scripts, and most other currently used languages. Four bytes covers the rest of Unicode. It supports this by using a prefix of bits on a byte to indicate that it is part of a multibyte pattern.

UTF-8 has taken over as the most common encoding from ASCII and ISO-8859-1 (aka Latin-1). Unlike ASCII and ISO-8859-1, it supports languages outside of Western Europe. Data that is ASCII encoded is not a problem, since that represents the one-byte UTF-8 characters. However, ISO-8859-1 represents the Latin-1 Supplement with one byte as well. This leads to a common problem of data being encoded one way and decoded another. Let's look at how "ñ" is represented and potentially mangled.

char	latin1 enc	utf-8 enc	latin1 enc to utf-8 dec	utf-8 enc to latin1 dec
a	61	61	a	a
ñ	F1	C3 B1	INVALID	Ã±

We'll cover this topic more when we talk about productionization and multilanguage systems.

Exercises: Tokenizing

One of the most fundamental text processing techniques is *tokenization*. This is the process of taking a string of characters and breaking it into pieces, often words. This seems like a simple task, but since it is such an early stage in any NLP pipeline, getting it correct is vital. It is also going to be affected by the writing system of the language you are working with.

Let's look at what might be some challenges for tokenizing a language. Let's start with some basic tokenizers.

Whitespace tokenizer

Tokens are defined as the non-whitespace character sequences on either side of a whitespace character sequence.

ASCII tokenizer

Tokens are defined as a sequence of ASCII letters or digits.

The `gaps` parameter tells us how the tokenizer is defining a token. If it is set to `True`, then the `pattern` argument is defining what separates tokens. If `False`, it represents the tokens themselves.

```
from nltk import nltk.tokenize.RegexpTokenizer

whitespace_tokenizer = RegexpTokenizer(r'\s+', gaps=True)
ascii_tokenizer = RegexpTokenizer(r'[a-zA-Z0-9_]+', gaps=False)
```

Tokenize English

Tokenizing English is relatively straightforward. We can split on whitespaces:

```
whitespace_tokenizer.tokenize('Hello world!')
```

```
['Hello', 'world!']
```

Or we can use the ASCII tokenizer:

```
ascii_tokenizer.tokenize('Hello world!')
```

```
['Hello', 'world']
```

Tokenize Greek

Greek uses the same space character as English to separate words, so the whitespace tokenizer will work here:

```
whitespace_tokenizer.tokenize('Γειά σου Κόσμε!')
```

```
['Γειά', 'σου', 'Κόσμε!']
```

The ASCII tokenizer won't work here, since Greek is not supported by ASCII:

```
ascii_tokenizer.tokenize('Γειά σου Κόσμε!')
```

```
[]
# Define a regex with gaps=False that will tokenize Greek
pattern = r''
greek_tokenizer = RegexpTokenizer(pattern, gaps=False)

#assert greek_tokenizer.tokenize('Γειά σου Κόσμε!') == ['Γειά', 'σου', 'Κόσμε']
```

Tokenize Ge'ez (Amharic)

Amharic does not use the same character to separate tokens as English does, so the whitespace tokenizer won't work:

```
whitespace_tokenizer.tokenize('በላም፡አቡል!')

['በላም፡አቡል!']

# Define a regex with gaps=True that will tokenize Amharic
pattern = r''
amharic_sep_tokenizer = RegexpTokenizer(pattern, gaps=True)

#assert amharic_sep_tokenizer.tokenize('በላም፡አቡል!') in (['በላም', 'አቡል!'],
['በላም', 'አቡል'])
```

Similarly, the ASCII tokenizer doesn't work here either:

```
ascii_tokenizer.tokenize('በላም፡አቡል!')

[]

# Define a regex with gaps=False that will tokenize Amharic
pattern = r''
amharic_tokenizer = RegexpTokenizer(pattern, gaps=False)

#assert amharic_tokenizer.tokenize('በላም፡አቡል!') == ['በላም', 'አቡል']
```

Resources

- International Phonetic Association (*https://oreil.ly/yg0Ca*): the home page of the organization that maintains the international phonetic alphabet
- Omniglot (*https://www.omniglot.com*): an online encyclopedia of writing systems
- Unicode Consortium (*https://home.unicode.org*): the home page of the organization that maintains Unicode
- YouTube channels:
  — Langfocus: this channel does explorations of different languages
  — NativLang: this channel covers interesting aspects and histories of languages
  — Wikitongues: this is the channel of a nonprofit that gathers videos of people speaking different languages from around the world
- *The Cambridge Encyclopedia of Language* by David Crystal (Cambridge University Press)
  — This is a great resource for many aspects of language and linguistics. If you are trying to deal with an aspect of language that you are unfamiliar with, you can probably get a start on what to research here.
- *Course in General Linguistics* by Ferdinand de Saussure (Open Court)

— Saussure is the father of modern linguistics. Although many of the hypotheses are outdated, the approach he takes is very informative. The way in which he breaks phonemes into features is still useful today.

- *Fundamentals of Psycholinguistics* by Eva M. Fernández and Helen Smith Cairns (Wiley-Blackwell)

  — This is a great textbook for approaching psycholinguistics from a linguistics perspective. It includes a great deal of information that will help an NLP data scientist better understand the natural phenomenon they wish to model.

- *Handbook of the IPA* (Cambridge University Press)

  — If you are looking to go deeper into linguistics, you will need to have an understanding of IPA. This book can also be helpful if you want to focus on speech instead of text.

- *Language Files* by the Department of Linguistics (Ohio State University Press)

  — This is the first textbook I used when studying linguistics. Textbooks for Intro to Linguistics courses can be useful to those working with NLP. If you run into a problem and need a better understanding of the underlying linguistics, such a textbook can point you in the right direction.

## CHAPTER 3

NLP on Apache Spark

It's no longer news that there is a data deluge. Every day, people and devices are creating huge amounts of data. Text data is definitely one of the main kinds of data that humans produce. People write millions of comments, product reviews, Reddit messages, and tweets per day. This data is incredibly valuable—for both research and commerce. Because of the scale at which this data is created, our approach to working with it has changed.

Most of the original research in NLP was done on small data sets with hundreds or thousands of documents. You may think that it would be easier to build NLP applications now that we have so much more text data with which to build better models. However, these pieces of text have different pragmatics and are of different varieties, so leveraging them is more complicated from a data-science perspective. From the software engineering perspective, big data introduces many challenges. Structured data has predictable size and organization, which makes it easier to store and distribute efficiently. Text data is much less consistent. This makes parallelizing and distributing work more important and potentially more complex. Distributed computing frameworks like Spark help us manage these challenges and complexities.

In this chapter, we will discuss the Apache Spark and Spark NLP. First, we will cover some basic concepts that will help us understand distributed computing. Then, we will talk briefly about the history of distributed computing. We will talk about some important modules in Spark—*Spark SQL* and *MLlib*. This will give us the background and context needed to talk about Spark NLP in technical detail.

Now, we'll cover some technical concepts that will be helpful in understanding how Spark works. The explanations will be high level. If you are interested in maximizing performance, I suggest looking more into these topics. For the general audience, I hope this material will give you the intuition necessary to help make decisions when designing and building Spark-based applications.

Parallelism, Concurrency, Distributing Computation

Let's start by defining some terms. A *process* can be thought of as a running program. A *process* executes its code using an allotted portion of memory also known as a *memory space*. A *thread* is a sequence of execution steps within a process that the operating system can schedule. Sharing data between processes generally requires copying data between the different memory spaces. When a Java or Scala program is run, the *Java Virtual Machine (JVM)* is the process. The threads of a process share access to the same memory space, which they access *concurrently*.

Concurrent access of data can be tricky. For example, let's say we want to generate word counts. If two threads are working on this process, it's possible for us to get the wrong count. Consider the following program (written in pseudo-Python). In this program, we will use a thread pool. A *thread pool* is a way to separate partitioning work from scheduling. We allocate a certain number of threads, and then we go through our data asking for threads for the pool. The operating system can then schedule the work.

```
0:  def word_count(tokenized_documents): # list of lists of tokens
1:      word_counts = {}
2:      thread_pool = ThreadPool()
3:      i = 0
4:      for thread in thread_pool
5:          run thread:
6:              while i < len(tokenized_documents):
7:                  doc = tokenized_documents[i]
8:                  i += 1
9:                  for token in doc:
10:                     old_count = word_counts.get(token, 0)
11:                     word_counts[token] = old_count + 1
12:     return word_counts
```

This looks reasonable, but we see that the code under `run thread` references data in the shared memory space like `i` and `word_counts`. Table 3-1 shows the execution of this program with two `threads` in the `ThreadPool` starting at line 6.

Table 3-1. Two threads in the `ThreadPool`

time	thread1	thread2	i	valid_state
0	while i < len(tokenized_documents)		0	yes
1		while i < len(tokenized_documents)	0	yes
2	doc = tokenized_documents[i]		0	yes
3		doc = tokenized_documents[i]	0	**NO**

At time 3, thread2 will be retrieving tokenized_documents[0], while thread1 is already set to work on the first document. This program has a *race condition*, in which we can get incorrect results depending on the sequence of operations done in the different threads. Avoiding these problems generally involves writing code that is safe for concurrent access. For example, we can pause thread2 until thread1 is finished updating by *locking* on tokenized_documents. If you look at the code, there is another race condition, on i. If thread1 takes the last document, tokenized_documents[N-1], thread2 starts its while-loop check, thread1 updates i, then thread2 uses i. We will be accessing tokenized_documents[N], which doesn't exist. So let's lock on i.

```
0:  def word_count(tokenized_documents): # list of lists of tokens
1:      word_counts = {}
2:      thread_pool = ThreadPool()
3:      i = 0
4:      for thread in thread_pool
5:          run thread:
6:              while True:
7:                  lock i:
8:                      if i < len(tokenized_documents)
9:                          doc = tokenized_documents[i]
10:                         i += 1
11:                     else:
12:                         break
13:                 for token in doc:
14:                     lock word_counts:
15:                         old_count = word_counts.get(token, 0)
16:                         word_counts[token] = old_count + 1
17:     return word_counts
```

Now, we are locking on i and checking i in the loop. We also lock on word_counts so that if two threads want to update the counts of the same word, they won't accidentally pull a stale value for old_count. Table 3-2 shows the execution of this program now from line 7.

Table 3-2. Locking on i and word_counts

time	thread1	thread2	i	valid state
0	lock i		0	yes
1	if i < len(tokenized_documents)	blocked	0	yes
2	doc = tokenized_documents[i]	blocked	0	yes
3	i += 1	blocked	0	yes
4		lock i	1	yes
5	lock word_counts		1	yes

time	thread1	thread2	i	valid state
6		if i < len(tokenized_documents)	1	yes
7	old_count = word_counts.get(token, 0)		1	yes
8		doc = tokenized_documents[i]	1	yes
9	word_counts[token] = old_count + 1		1	yes
10		i += 1	1	yes
11	lock word_counts		2	yes
12	old_count = word_counts.get(token, 0)	blocked	2	yes
13	word_counts[token] = old_count + 1	blocked	2	yes
14		lock word_counts	2	yes
15	blocked	old_count = word_counts.get(token, 0)	2	yes
16	blocked	word_counts[token] = old_count + 1	2	yes

We fixed the problem, but at the cost of frequently blocking one of the threads. This means that we are getting less advantage of the parallelism. It would be better to design our algorithm so that the threads don't share state. We will see an example of this when we talk about MapReduce.

Sometimes, parallelizing on one machine is not sufficient, so we *distribute* the work across many machines grouped together in a *cluster*. When all the work is done on a machine, we are bringing the data (in memory or on disk) to the code, but when distributing work we are bringing the code to the data. Distributing the work of a program across a cluster means we have new concerns. We don't have access to a shared memory space, so we need to be more thoughtful in how we design our algorithms. Although processes on different machines don't share a common memory space, we still need to consider concurrency because the threads of the process on a given machine of the cluster still share common (local) memory space. Fortunately, modern frameworks like Spark mostly take care of these concerns, but it's still good to keep this in mind when designing your programs.

Programs that work on text data often find some form of parallelization helpful because processing the text into structured data is often the most time-consuming stage of a program. Most NLP pipelines ultimately output structured numeric data, which means that the data that's loaded, the text, can often be much larger than the data that is output. Unfortunately, because of the complexity of NLP algorithms, text processing in distributed frameworks is generally limited to basic techniques. Fortunately, we have Spark NLP, which we will discuss shortly.

Parallelization Before Apache Hadoop

HTCondor (*https://oreil.ly/_asEi*) is a framework developed at the University of Wisconsin–Madison starting in 1988. It boasts an impressive catalog of uses. It was used by NASA, the Human Genome Project, and the Large Hadron Collider. Technically, it's not just a framework for distributing computation—it also can manage resources. In fact, it can be used with other frameworks for distributing computation. It was built with the idea that machines in the cluster may be owned by different users, so work can be scheduled based on available resources. This is from a time when clusters of computers were not as available.

GNU parallel (*https://oreil.ly/6eFIg*) and pexec (*https://oreil.ly/mHLdC*) are UNIX tools that can be used to parallelize work on a single machine, as well as across machines. This requires that the distributable portions of work be run from the command line. These tools allow us to utilize resources across machines, but it doesn't help with parallelizing our algorithms.

MapReduce and Apache Hadoop

We can represent distributed computation with two operations: map and reduce. The map operation can be used to transform, filter, or sort data. The reduce operation can be used to group or summarize data. Let's return to our word count example to see how we can use these two operations for a basic NLP task.

```python
def map(docs):
    for doc in docs:
        for token in doc:
            yield (token, 1)

def reduce(records):
    word_counts = {}
    for token, count in records:
        word_counts[token] = word_counts.get(token, 0) + count
    for word, count in word_counts.items():
        yield (word, count)
```

The data is loaded in partitions, with some documents going to each mapper process on the cluster. There can be multiple mappers per machine. Each mapper runs the map function on their documents and saves the results to the disk. After all of the mappers have completed, the data from the mapper stage is *shuffled* so that, all the records with the same key (word in this case), are in the same partition. This data is now sorted so that within a partition, all the records are ordered by key. Finally, the sorted data is loaded and the reduce step is called for each partition reducer process combining all of the counts. In between stages, the data is saved to the disk.

MapReduce can express most distributed algorithms, but some are difficult or downright awkward in this framework. This is why abstractions to MapReduce were developed rather quickly.

Apache Hadoop (*https://hadoop.apache.org*) is the popular open source implementation of MapReduce along with a distributed file system, *Hadoop Distributed File System (HDFS)*. To write a Hadoop program, you need to select or define an input format, mapper, reducer, and output format. There have been many libraries and frameworks to allow higher levels of implementing a program.

Apache Pig (*https://pig.apache.org*) is a framework for expressing MapReduce programs in procedural code. Its procedural nature makes implementing *extract, transform, load (ETL)* programs very convenient and straightforward. However, other types of programs, model training programs for example, are much more difficult. The language that Apache Pig uses is called *Pig Latin*. There is some overlap with SQL, so if someone knows SQL well, learning Pig Latin is easy.

Apache Hive (*https://hive.apache.org*) is a data warehousing framework originally built on Hadoop. Hive allows users to write SQL that is executed with MapReduce. Now, Hive can run using other distributed frameworks in addition to Hadoop, including Spark.

Apache Spark

Spark (*https://spark.apache.org*) is a project started by Matei Zaharia. Spark is a distributed computing framework. There are important differences in how Spark and Hadoop process data. Spark allows users to write arbitrary code against distributed data. Currently, there are official APIs for Spark in Scala, Java, Python, and R. Spark does not save intermediate data to disk. Usually, Spark-based programs will keep data in memory, though this can be changed by configuration to also utilize the disk. This allows for quicker processing but can require more *scale out* (more machines), or more *scale up* (machines with more memory).

Let's look at word_count in Spark.

Architecture of Apache Spark

Spark is organized around a driver that is running the program, a master that manages resources and distributes work, and workers that execute computation. There are a number of possible masters. Spark ships with its own master, which is what is used in standalone and local modes. You can also use Apache YARN or Apache Mesos. In my experience, Apache YARN is the most common choice for enterprise systems.

Let's take a more detailed look at Spark's architecture.

Physical Architecture

We start our program on the *submitting machine* which submits an *application*. This *driver* runs the application on the *client machine* and sends jobs to the *spark master* to be distributed to the *workers*. The spark master may not be a completely separate machine. That machine may also be doing work on the cluster and so would be a worker as well. Also, you may be running your program on the spark master, and so it could also be the client machine.

There are two modes that you can use to start a Spark application: *cluster mode* and *client mode*. If the machine submitting the application is the same machine that runs the application, you are in client mode, because you are submitting from the client machine. Otherwise, you are in cluster mode. Generally, you use client mode if your machine is inside the cluster and cluster mode if it is not (see Figures 3-1 and 3-2).

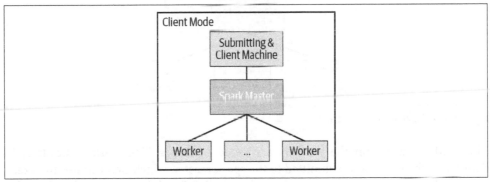

Figure 3-1. Physical architecture (client mode)

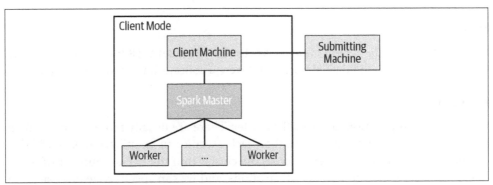

Figure 3-2. Physical architecture (cluster mode)

You can also run Spark in local mode in which, as the name implies, client machine, spark master, and worker are all the same machine. This is very useful for developing and testing Spark applications. It is also useful if you want to parallelize work on one machine.

Now that we have an idea of the physical architecture, let's look at the logical architecture.

Logical Architecture

In looking at the logical architecture of Spark, we will treat the client machine, spark master, and worker as if they are different (see Figure 3-3). The driver is a JVM process that will submit work to the spark master. If the program is a Java or Scala program, then it is also the process running the program. If the program is in Python or R, then the driver process is a separate process from that running the program.

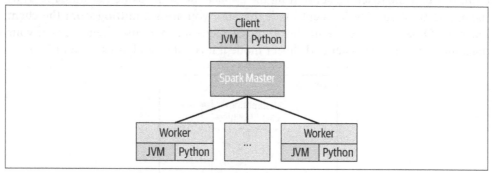

Figure 3-3. Logical architecture

The JVM processes on the workers are called *executors*. The work to be done is defined on the driver and submitted to the spark master, which orchestrates the executors to do the work. The next step in understanding Spark is understanding how the data is distributed.

RDDs

Spark distributes data in `resilient distributed datasets` (RDDs). RDDs allow users to work with distributed data almost as if it were a collection located in the driver.

Partitioning

In Spark, data is partitioned across the cluster. There are usually more partitions than executors. This allows for each thread on each executor to be utilized. Spark will distribute the data in the RDD evenly across the cluster into the default number of partitions. We can specify the number of partitions, and we can specify a field to partition by. This can be very useful when your algorithm requires some degree of locality—for example, having all the tweets from a single user.

Serialization

Any code that is shipped to the data should refer only to serializable objects. `NotSer ializableException` errors are common and can be nearly inscrutable to those new to Spark. When we map over an RDD, we are creating a `Function` and sending it to the machines with the data. A function is the code that defines it, and the data needed in the definition. This second part is called the *closure* of the function. Identifying what objects are needed for a function is a complicated task, and sometimes extraneous objects can be captured. If you are having problems with serializability, there are a couple of possible solutions. The following are questions that can help you find the right solution:

- Are you using your own custom classes? Make sure that they are serializable.
- Are you loading a resource? Perhaps your distributed code should load it lazily so that it is loaded on each executor, instead of being loaded on the driver and shipped to the executors.
- Are Spark objects (`SparkSession`, RDDs) being captured in a closure? This can happen when you are defining your function anonymously. If your function is defined anonymously, perhaps you can define it elsewhere.

These tips can help find common errors, but the solution to this problem is something that can be determined only on a case-by-case basis.

Ordering

When working with distributed data, there is not necessarily a guaranteed order to the items in your data. When writing your code, keep in mind that the data exists in partitions across the cluster.

This is not to say that we cannot define an order. We can define an order on the partitions by an index. In this situation, the "first" element of the RDD will be the first element of the first partition. Furthermore, let's say we want to order an `RDD[Int]` ascending by value. Using our ordering on partitions, we can shuffle the data such that all elements in partition i are less than all elements in partition i+1. From here, we can sort each partition. Now we have a sorted RDD. This is an expensive operation, however.

Output and logging

When writing functions that are used to transform data, it is often useful to print statements or, preferably, to log statements to look at the state of variables in the function. In a distributed context, this is more complicated because the function is not running on the same machine as the program. Accessing the logs and the `stdout` generally depends on the configuration of the cluster and which master you are using. In some situations, it may suffice to run your program on a small set of data in local mode.

Spark jobs

A Spark-based program will have a `SparkSession`, which is how the driver talks to the master. Before Spark version 2.x, the `SparkContext` was used for this. There is still a `SparkContext`, but it is part of the `SparkSession` now. This `SparkSession` represents the `App`. The `App` submits `jobs` to the master. The `jobs` are broken into `stages`, which are logical groupings of work in the `job`. The `stages` are broken into `tasks`, which represent the work to be done on each partition (see Figure 3-4).

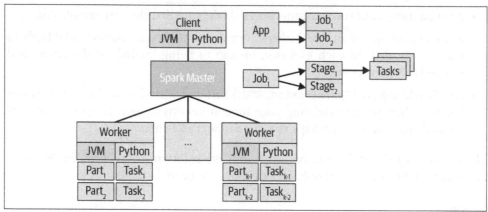

Figure 3-4. Spark jobs

Not every operation on data will start a job. Spark is lazy—in a good way. Execution is done only when a result is needed. This allows the work done to be organized into an execution plan to improve efficiency. There are certain operations, sometimes referred to as actions, that will cause execution immediately. These are operations that return specific values, e.g. `aggregate`. There are also operations where further execution planning becomes impossible until computed, e.g. `zipWithIndex`.

This execution plan is often referred to as the *Directed Acyclic Graph (DAG)*. Data in Spark is defined by its DAG, which includes its sources and whatever operations were run to generate it. This allows Spark to remove data from memory as necessary without losing reference to the data. If data that was generated and removed is referred to later, it will be regenerated. This can be time-consuming. Fortunately, we can instruct Spark to keep data if we need to.

Persisting

The basic way of persisting data in Spark is with the persist method. This creates a checkpoint. You can also use the cache method and provide options for configuring how the data will be persisted. The data will still be generated lazily, but once it is generated, it will be kept.

Let's look at an example:

```
from operator import concat, itemgetter, methodcaller
import os
from time import sleep

import pyspark
from pyspark import SparkConf
from pyspark.sql import SparkSession
from pyspark.sql import functions as fun
from pyspark.sql.types import *

packages = ','.join([
    "com.johnsnowlabs.nlp:spark-nlp_2.11:2.4.5",
])

def has_moon(text):
    if 'moon' in text:
        sleep(1)
        return True
    else:
        return False

# RDD containing filepath-text pairs
path = os.path.join('data', 'mini_newsgroups', 'sci.space')
text_pairs = spark.sparkContext\
    .wholeTextFiles(path)
texts = text_pairs.map(itemgetter(1))
lower_cased = texts.map(methodcaller('lower'))
moon_texts = texts.filter(has_moon).persist()
print('This appears quickly because the previous operations are '
      'all lazy')
print(moon_texts.count())
print('This appears slowly since the count method will call '
      'has_moon which sleeps')
print(moon_texts.reduce(concat)[:100])
print('This appears quickly because has_moon will not be '
      'called due to the data being persisted')

This appears quickly because the previous operations are all lazy
11
This appears slowly since the count method will call has_moon which
sleeps
Newsgroups: sci.space
Path: cantaloupe.srv.cs.cmu.edu!das-news.harvard.edu!noc.near.net!
uunet!zaphod
```

> This appears quickly because has_moon will not be called due to the
> data being persisted

Now that we have an idea of how Spark works, let's go back to our word-count problem.

```python
from collections import Counter
from operator import add

from nltk.tokenize import RegexpTokenizer

# RDD containing filepath-text pairs
texts = spark.sparkContext.wholeTextFiles(path)
print('\n\nfilepath-text pair of first document')
print(texts.first())

tokenizer = RegexpTokenizer(r'\w+', gaps=False)
tokenized_texts = texts.map(
    lambda path_text: tokenizer.tokenize(path_text[1]))
print('\n\ntokenized text of first document')
print(tokenized_texts.first())

# This is the equivalent place that the previous implementations
# started
document_token_counts = tokenized_texts.map(Counter)
print('\n\ndocument-level counts of first document')
print(document_token_counts.first().most_common(10))

word_counts = token_counts = document_token_counts.reduce(add)
print('\n\nword counts')
print(word_counts.most_common(10))
```

```
filepath-text pair of first document
('file:/.../spark-nlp-book/data/mini_news...')


tokenized text of first document
['Xref', 'cantaloupe', 'srv', 'cs', 'cmu', ..., 'cantaloupe', 'srv']


document-level counts of first document
[('the', 13), ('of', 7), ('temperature', 6), ..., ('nasa', 4)]


word counts
[('the', 1648), ('of', 804), ..., ('for', 305), ('cmu', 288)]
```

As you see, we use the map and reduce methods here. Spark allows you to implement MapReduce-style programs, but you can also implement in many other ways.

Python and R

Spark is primarily implemented in Scala. The Java API is there to allow more idiomatic Java use of Spark. There is also a Python API (PySpark) and an R API (SparkR). Spark-based programs implemented in Scala or Java run on the same JVM that serves as the driver. Programs implemented in PySpark or SparkR run in Python and R processes, respectively, with the `SparkSession` ultimately in a different process. This generally does not affect the performance, unless we use functions defined in Python or R.

As can be seen in the previous example, when we are tokenizing, counting, and combining counts we are calling Python code to process our data. This is accomplished by the JVM process serializing and shipping the data to the Python process, which is then deserialized, processed, serialized, and shipped back to the JVM to be deserialized. This adds a lot of extra work to our job. When using PySpark or SparkR it will be faster to use internal Spark functions whenever possible.

Not using custom functions in Python or R seems restrictive when using RDDs, but most likely, your work will be using the `DataFrames` and `DataSets` that we discuss in the next section.

Spark SQL and Spark MLlib

Since the release of Spark 2, the primary intended way to work with data within Spark is through the `Dataset`. The `Dataset[T]` is an object that allows us to treat our distributed data as tables. The type parameter `T` is the type used to represent the rows of the table. There is a special kind of `Dataset` in which the type of the rows is `Row`, which allows us to have tabular data without defining new classes—this does come at the cost of losing some type safety. The examples we'll be using will generally be with `DataFrames`, since they are the best way to work with data in PySpark.

The `Dataset` and `DataFrame` are defined in the Spark SQL module, since one of the greatest benefits is the ability to express many operations with SQL. The prebuilt *user-defined functions (UDFs)* are available in all the APIs. This allows us to do most kinds of processing in the non-JVM languages with the same efficiency as if we were using Scala or Java.

Another module we need to introduce before we begin talking about Spark NLP is MLlib. *MLlib* is a module for doing machine learning on Spark. Before Spark 2, all the MLlib algorithms were implemented on RDDs. Since then, a new version of MLlib was defined using `Datasets` and `DataFrames`. MLlib is similar in design, at a high level, to other machine learning libraries, with a notion of transformers, models, and pipelines.

Before we talk about MLlib, let's load some data into a `DataFrame`, since MLlib is built using `DataFrames`. We will be using the Iris data set (*https://oreil.ly/my69i*), which is often used as an example in data science. It's small, easy to understand, and can work for clustering and classification examples. It is structured data, so it doesn't give us any text data to work with. Table-like structure is generally designed around structured data, so this data will help us explore the API before getting into using Spark for text.

The `iris.data` file does not have a header, so we have to tell Spark what the columns are when they are loaded. Let's construct a schema. The *schema* is the definition of the columns and their types in the `DataFrame`. The most common task is to build a model to predict what class an iris flower is (I. virginica, I. setosa, or I. versicolor) based on its sepals and petals.

```
from pyspark.sql.types import *

schema = StructType([
    StructField('sepal_length', DoubleType(), nullable=False),
    StructField('sepal_width', DoubleType(), nullable=False),
    StructField('petal_length', DoubleType(), nullable=False),
    StructField('petal_width', DoubleType(), nullable=False),
    StructField('class', StringType(), nullable=False)
])
```

Now that we have created the schema, we can load our CSV. Table 3-3 shows the summary of the data.

```
iris = spark.read.csv('./data/iris/iris.data', schema=schema)

iris.describe().toPandas()
```

Table 3-3. Summary of the Iris data

	summary	sepal_length	sepal_width	petal_length	petal_width	class
0	count	150	150	150	150	150
1	mean	5.843	3.054	3.759	1.199	None
2	stddev	0.828	0.434	1.764	0.763	None
3	min	4.3	2.0	1.0	0.1	Iris-setosa
4	max	7.9	4.4	6.9	2.5	Iris-virginica

Let's start by looking at the classes (species of Iris) in our data (see Table 3-4).

```
iris.select('class').distinct().toPandas()
```

Table 3-4. Classes in the Iris data

	class
0	Iris-virginica
1	Iris-setosa
2	Iris-versicolor

Let's start by looking at some of the summary stats for the *Iris setosa* class, shown in Table 3-5.

```
iris.where('class = "Iris-setosa"').drop('class').describe().toPandas()
```

Table 3-5. Summary of tthe setosa examples

	summary	sepal_length	sepal_width	petal_length	petal_width
0	count	50	50	50	50
1	mean	5.006	3.418	1.464	0.244
2	stddev	0.352	0.381	0.174	0.107
3	min	4.3	2.3	1.0	0.1
4	max	5.8	4.4	1.9	0.6

We can *register* a DataFrame, which will allow us to interact with it purely through SQL. We will be registering our DataFrame as a temporary table. This means that the table will exist only for the lifetime of our App, and it will be available only through our App's SparkSession (see Table 3-6).

```
iris.registerTempTable('iris')

spark.sql('''
SELECT *
FROM iris
LIMIT 5
''').toPandas()
```

Table 3-6. Five records from the Iris dataset

	sepal_length	sepal_width	petal_length	petal_width	class
0	5.1	3.5	1.4	0.2	Iris-setosa
1	4.9	3.0	1.4	0.2	Iris-setosa
2	4.7	3.2	1.3	0.2	Iris-setosa
3	4.6	3.1	1.5	0.2	Iris-setosa
4	5.0	3.6	1.4	0.2	Iris-setosa

Let's look at some of the fields grouped by their class in Table 3-7.

```
spark.sql('''
SELECT
    class,
    min(sepal_length), avg(sepal_length), max(sepal_length),
    min(sepal_width), avg(sepal_width), max(sepal_width),
    min(petal_length), avg(petal_length), max(petal_length),
    min(petal_width), avg(petal_width), max(petal_width)
FROM iris
GROUP BY class
''').toPandas()
```

Table 3-7. The min/average/max for attributes by class

class	Iris-virginica	Iris-setosa	Iris-versicolor
min(sepal_length)	4.900	4.300	4.900
avg(sepal_length)	6.588	5.006	5.936
max(sepal_length)	7.900	5.800	7.000
min(sepal_width)	2.200	2.300	2.000
avg(sepal_width)	2.974	3.418	2.770
max(sepal_width)	3.800	4.400	3.400
min(petal_length)	4.500	1.000	3.000
avg(petal_length)	5.552	1.464	4.260
max(petal_length)	6.900	1.900	5.100
min(petal_length)	1.400	0.100	1.000
avg(petal_length)	2.026	0.244	1.326
max(petal_length)	2.500	0.600	1.800

Transformers

A Transformer is a piece of logic that transforms the data without needing to learn or fit anything from the data. A good way to understand transformers is that they represent functions that we wish to map over our data. All stages of a pipeline have parameters so that we can make sure that the transformation is being applied to the right fields and with the desired configuration. Let's look at a few examples.

SQLTransformer

The SQLTransformer has only one parameter—statement—which is the SQL statement that will be executed against our DataFrame. Let's use an SQLTransformer to do the group-by we performed previously. Table 3-8 shows the result.

```
from pyspark.ml.feature import SQLTransformer

statement = '''
SELECT
```

```
        class,
        min(sepal_length), avg(sepal_length), max(sepal_length),
        min(sepal_width), avg(sepal_width), max(sepal_width),
        min(petal_length), avg(petal_length), max(petal_length),
        min(petal_width), avg(petal_width), max(petal_width)
    FROM iris
    GROUP BY class
    '''

    sql_transformer = SQLTransformer(statement=statement)

    sql_transformer.transform(iris).toPandas()
```

Table 3-8. Output from the SQLTransformer

class	Iris-virginica	Iris-setosa	Iris-versicolor
min(sepal_length)	4.900	4.300	4.900
avg(sepal_length)	6.588	5.006	5.936
max(sepal_length)	7.900	5.800	7.000
...			

We get the same output as when we ran the SQL command.

SQLTransformer is useful when you have preprocessing or restructuring that you need to perform on your data before other steps in the pipeline. Now let's look at a transformer that works on one field and returns the original data with a new field.

Binarizer

The Binarizer is a Transformer that applies a threshold to a numeric field, turning it into 0s (when below the threshold) and 1s (when above the threshold). It takes three parameters:

inputCol
    The column to be binarized

outputCol
    The column containing the binarized values

threshold
    The threshold we will apply

Table 3-9 shows the results.

```
    from pyspark.ml.feature import Binarizer

    binarizer = Binarizer(
        inputCol='sepal_length',
        outputCol='sepal_length_above_5',
```

```
    threshold=5.0
)

binarizer.transform(iris).limit(5).toPandas()
```

Table 3-9. Output from Binarizer

	sepal_length	...	class	sepal_length_above_5
0	5.1	...	Iris-setosa	1.0
1	4.9	...	Iris-setosa	0.0
2	4.7	...	Iris-setosa	0.0
3	4.6	...	Iris-setosa	0.0
4	5.0	...	Iris-setosa	0.0

Unlike the `SQLTransformer`, the `Binarizer` returns a modified version of the input `DataFrame`. Almost all `Transformers` behave this way.

The `Binarizer` is used when you want to convert a real valued property into a class. For example, if we want to mark social media posts as "viral" and "not-viral" we could use a `Binarizer` on the views property.

VectorAssembler

Another import `Transformer` is the `VectorAssembler`. It takes a list of numeric and vector-valued columns and constructs a single vector. This is useful because all MLlib's machine learning algorithms expect a single vector-valued input column for features. The `VectorAssembler` takes two parameters:

`inputCols`
   The list of columns to be assembled

`outputCol`
   The column containing the new vectors

```
from pyspark.ml.feature import VectorAssembler

assembler = VectorAssembler(
    inputCols=[
        'sepal_length', 'sepal_width',
        'petal_length', 'petal_width'
    ],
    outputCol='features'
)
```

Let's persist this data (see Table 3-10).

```
iris_w_vecs = assembler.transform(iris).persist()

iris_w_vecs.limit(5).toPandas()
```

Table 3-10. Output from VectorAssembler

	sepal_length	sepal_width	petal_length	petal_width	class	features
0	5.1	3.5	1.4	0.2	Iris-setosa	[5.1, 3.5, 1.4, 0.2]
1	4.9	3.0	1.4	0.2	Iris-setosa	[4.9, 3.0, 1.4, 0.2]
2	4.7	3.2	1.3	0.2	Iris-setosa	[4.7, 3.2, 1.3, 0.2]
3	4.6	3.1	1.5	0.2	Iris-setosa	[4.6, 3.1, 1.5, 0.2]
4	5.0	3.6	1.4	0.2	Iris-setosa	[5.0, 3.6, 1.4, 0.2]

Now we have our features as vectors. This is what the machine learning Estimators in MLlib need to work with.

Estimators and Models

Estimators allow us to create transformations that are informed by our data. Classification models (e.g., decision trees) and regression models (e.g., linear regressions) are prominent examples, but some preprocessing algorithms are like this as well. For example, preprocessing that needs to know the whole vocabulary first will be Estimators. The Estimator is fit with a DataFrame and returns a Model, which is a kind of Transformer. The Models created from classifier and regression Estimators are PredictionModels.

This is a similar design to *scikit-learn*, with the exception that in scikit-learn when we call fit we mutate the estimator instead of creating a new object. There are pros and cons to this, as there always are when debating mutability. Idiomatic Scala strongly prefers immutability.

Let's look at some examples of Estimators and Models.

MinMaxScaler

The MinMaxScaler allows us to scale our data to be between 0 and 1. It takes four parameters:

inputCol
> The column to be scaled

outputCol
> The column containing the scaled values

max
> The new maximum value (optional, default = 1)

min
> The new minimum value (optional, default = 0)

The results are shown in Table 3-11.

```
from pyspark.ml.feature import MinMaxScaler

scaler = MinMaxScaler(
    inputCol='features',
    outputCol='petal_length_scaled'
)

scaler_model = scaler.fit(iris_w_vecs)

scaler_model.transform(iris_w_vecs).limit(5).toPandas()
```

Table 3-11. Output from MinMaxScaler

	...	petal_length	petal_width	class	features	petal_length_scaled
0	...	1.4	0.2	Iris-setosa	[5.1, 3.5, 1.4, 0.2]	[0.22, 0.63, 0.06...
1	...	1.4	0.2	Iris-setosa	[4.9, 3.0, 1.4, 0.2]	[0.17, 0.42, 0.06...
2	...	1.3	0.2	Iris-setosa	[4.7, 3.2, 1.3, 0.2]	[0.11, 0.5, 0.05...
3	...	1.5	0.2	Iris-setosa	[4.6, 3.1, 1.5, 0.2]	[0.08, 0.46, 0.08...
4	...	1.4	0.2	Iris-setosa	[5.0, 3.6, 1.4, 0.2]	[0.19, 0.667, 0.06...

Notice that the `petal_length_scaled` column now has values between 0 and 1. This can help some training algorithms, specifically those that have difficulty combining features of different scales.

StringIndexer

Let's build a model! We will try and predict the class from the other features, and we will use a decision tree. First, though, we must convert our target into index values.

The `StringIndexer Estimator` will turn our class values into indices. We want to do this to simplify some of the downstream processing. It is simpler to implement most training algorithms with the assumption that the target is a number. The `StringIndexer` takes four parameters:

`inputCol`
    The column to be indexed

`outputCol`
    The column containing the indexed values

`handleInvalid`
    The policy for how the model should handle values not seen by the estimator (optional, default = error)

stringOrderType

How to order the values to make the indexing deterministic (optional, default = frequencyDesc)

We will also want an IndexToString Transformer. This will let us map our predictions, which will be indices, back to string values. IndexToString takes three parameters:

inputCol

The column to be mapped

outputCol

The column containing the mapped values

labels

The mapping from index to value, usually generated by StringIndexer

```
from pyspark.ml.feature import StringIndexer, IndexToString

indexer = StringIndexer(inputCol='class', outputCol='class_ix')
indexer_model = indexer.fit(iris_w_vecs)

index2string = IndexToString(
    inputCol=indexer_model.getOrDefault('outputCol'),
    outputCol='pred_class',
    labels=indexer_model.labels
)

iris_indexed = indexer_model.transform(iris_w_vecs)
```

Now we are ready to train our DecisionTreeClassifier. This Estimator has many parameters, so I recommend you become familiar with the APIs. They are all well documented in the PySpark API documentation (*https://oreil.ly/_EOSI*). Table 3-12 shows our results.

```
from pyspark.ml.classification import DecisionTreeClassifier

dt_clfr = DecisionTreeClassifier(
    featuresCol='features',
    labelCol='class_ix',
    maxDepth=5,
    impurity='gini',
    seed=123
)

dt_clfr_model = dt_clfr.fit(iris_indexed)

iris_w_pred = dt_clfr_model.transform(iris_indexed)

iris_w_pred.limit(5).toPandas()
```

Table 3-12. Predictions from DecisionTreeClassifier model

	...	class	features	class_ix	rawPrediction	probability	prediction
0	...	Iris-setosa	[5.1, 3.5, 1.4, 0.2]	0.0	[50.0, 0.0, 0.0]	[1.0, 0.0, 0.0]	0.0
1	...	Iris-setosa	[4.9, 3.0, 1.4, 0.2]	0.0	[50.0, 0.0, 0.0]	[1.0, 0.0, 0.0]	0.0
2	...	Iris-setosa	[4.7, 3.2, 1.3, 0.2]	0.0	[50.0, 0.0, 0.0]	[1.0, 0.0, 0.0]	0.0
3	...	Iris-setosa	[4.6, 3.1, 1.5, 0.2]	0.0	[50.0, 0.0, 0.0]	[1.0, 0.0, 0.0]	0.0
4	...	Iris-setosa	[5.0, 3.6, 1.4, 0.2]	0.0	[50.0, 0.0, 0.0]	[1.0, 0.0, 0.0]	0.0

Now we need to map the predicted classes back to their string form using our
IndexToString (see Table 3-13).

```
iris_w_pred_class = index2string.transform(iris_w_pred)

iris_w_pred_class.limit(5).toPandas()
```

Table 3-13. Predictions mapped to class labels

	...	class	features	class_ix	rawPrediction	probability	prediction	pred_class
0	...	Iris-setosa	[5.1, 3.5, 1.4, 0.2]	0.0	[50.0, 0.0, 0.0]	[1.0, 0.0, 0.0]	0.0	Iris-setosa
1	...	Iris-setosa	[4.9, 3.0, 1.4, 0.2]	0.0	[50.0, 0.0, 0.0]	[1.0, 0.0, 0.0]	0.0	Iris-setosa
2	...	Iris-setosa	[4.7, 3.2, 1.3, 0.2]	0.0	[50.0, 0.0, 0.0]	[1.0, 0.0, 0.0]	0.0	Iris-setosa
3	...	Iris-setosa	[4.6, 3.1, 1.5, 0.2]	0.0	[50.0, 0.0, 0.0]	[1.0, 0.0, 0.0]	0.0	Iris-setosa
4	...	Iris-setosa	[5.0, 3.6, 1.4, 0.2]	0.0	[50.0, 0.0, 0.0]	[1.0, 0.0, 0.0]	0.0	Iris-setosa

How well did our model fit the data? Let's see how many predictions match the true
class.

Evaluators

The evaluation options in MLlib are still limited compared to libraries like scikit-
learn, but they can be useful if you are looking to create an easy-to-run training pipeline that calculates metrics.

In our example, we are trying to solve a multiclass prediction problem, so we will use
the MulticlassClassificationEvaluator.

```
from pyspark.ml.evaluation import MulticlassClassificationEvaluator

evaluator = MulticlassClassificationEvaluator(
    labelCol='class_ix',
    metricName='accuracy'
)

evaluator.evaluate(iris_w_pred_class)

1.0
```

This seems too good. What if we are overfit? Perhaps we should try using cross-validation to evaluate our models. Before we do that, let's organize stages into a pipeline.

Pipelines

Pipelines are a special kind of Estimator that takes a list of Transformers and Estimators and allows us to use them as a single Estimator (see Table 3-14).

```
from pyspark.ml import Pipeline

pipeline = Pipeline(
    stages=[assembler, indexer, dt_clfr, index2string]
)

pipeline_model = pipeline.fit(iris)

pipeline_model.transform(iris).limit(5).toPandas()
```

Table 3-14. Output from full pipeline

	...	class	features	class_ix	rawPrediction	probability	prediction	pred_class
0	...	Iris-setosa	[5.1, 3.5, 1.4, 0.2]	0.0	[50.0, 0.0, 0.0]	[1.0, 0.0, 0.0]	0.0	Iris-setosa
1	...	Iris-setosa	[4.9, 3.0, 1.4, 0.2]	0.0	[50.0, 0.0, 0.0]	[1.0, 0.0, 0.0]	0.0	Iris-setosa
2	...	Iris-setosa	[4.7, 3.2, 1.3, 0.2]	0.0	[50.0, 0.0, 0.0]	[1.0, 0.0, 0.0]	0.0	Iris-setosa
3	...	Iris-setosa	[4.6, 3.1, 1.5, 0.2]	0.0	[50.0, 0.0, 0.0]	[1.0, 0.0, 0.0]	0.0	Iris-setosa
4	...	Iris-setosa	[5.0, 3.6, 1.4, 0.2]	0.0	[50.0, 0.0, 0.0]	[1.0, 0.0, 0.0]	0.0	Iris-setosa

Cross validation

Now that we have a Pipeline and an Evaluator we can create a CrossValidator. The CrossValidator itself is also an Estimator. When we call fit, it will fit our pipe line to each fold of data, and calculate the metric determined by our Evaluator. CrossValidator takes five parameters:

estimator
    The Estimator to be tuned

estimatorParamMaps
    The hyperparameter values to try in a hyperparameter grid search

evaluator
    The Evaluator that calculates the metric

numFolds
    The number of folds to split the data into

seed
   A seed for making the splits reproducible

We will make a trivial hyperparameter grid here, since we are only interested in esti-
mating how well our model does on data it has not seen.

```
from pyspark.ml.tuning import CrossValidator, ParamGridBuilder

param_grid = ParamGridBuilder().\
    addGrid(dt_clfr.maxDepth, [5]).\
    build()
cv = CrossValidator(
    estimator=pipeline,
    estimatorParamMaps=param_grid,
    evaluator=evaluator,
    numFolds=3,
    seed=123
)

cv_model = cv.fit(iris)
```

Now, we can see how the model does when trained on two-thirds and evaluated on
one-third. The avgMetrics in cv_model contains the average value of the designated
metric across folds for each point in the hyperparameter grid tested. In our case,
there is only one point in the grid.

```
cv_model.avgMetrics
```

```
[0.9588996659642801]
```

Keep in mind that 95% accuracy is much more believable than 100%.

There are many other Transformers, Estimators, and Models. We will look into more
as we continue, but for now, there is one more thing we need to discuss—saving our
pipelines.

Serialization of models

MLlib allows us to save Pipelines so that we can use them later. We can also save
individual Transformers and Models, but we will often want to keep all the stages of a
Pipeline together. Generally speaking, we use separate programs for building models
and using models.

```
pipeline_model.write().overwrite().save('pipeline.model')
```

```
! ls pipeline.model/*
```

```
pipeline.model/metadata:
part-00000  _SUCCESS

pipeline.model/stages:
0_VectorAssembler_45458c77ca2617edd7f6
1_StringIndexer_44d29a3426fb6b26b2c9
```

```
2_DecisionTreeClassifier_4473a4feb3ff2cf54b73
3_IndexToString_4157a15742628a489a18
```

NLP Libraries

There are two kinds of NLP libraries, generally speaking: *functionality libraries* and *annotation libraries*.

Functionality Libraries

A *functionality library* is a collection of functions built for specific NLP tasks and techniques. Often, the functions are built without assuming that other functions will be used first. This means that functions like part-of-speech (POS) tagging will also perform tokenization. These libraries are good for research because it is often much easier to implement novel functions. On the other hand, because there is no unifying design, the performance of these libraries is generally much worse than that of *annotation libraries*.

The Natural Language Tool Kit (NLTK) is a great functionality library. It was originally created by Edward Loper. The landmark NLP book *Natural Language Processing with Python (https://oreil.ly/Z319V)* (O'Reilly) was written by Steven Bird, Ewan Klein, and Edward Loper. I strongly recommend that book to anyone learning NLP. There a many useful and interesting modules in NLTK. It is, and will likely remain, the best NLP library for teaching NLP. The functions are not necessarily implemented with runtime performance or other productionization concerns in mind. If you are working on a research project and using a data set manageable on a single machine, you should consider NLTK.

Annotation Libraries

Annotation libraries are libraries in which all the functionality is built around a *document-annotation* model. There are three objects to keep in mind with annotation libraries: document, annotation, and annotator. The idea behind annotation libraries is to augment the incoming data with the results of our NLP functions.

Document
: The document is the representation of the piece of text we wish to process. Naturally, the document must contain the text. Additionally, we often want to have an identifier associated with each document so that we can store our augmented data as structured data. This identifier will often be a title if the texts we are processing have titles.

Annotation
: The annotation is the representation of the output of our NLP functions. For the annotation we need to have a *type* so that later processing knows how to interpret

the annotations. Annotations also need to store their location within the document. For example, let's say the word "pacing" occurs 134 characters into the document. It will have 134 as the start, and 140 as the end. The lemma annotation for "pacing" will have the location. Some annotation libraries also have a concept of document-level annotation that does not have a location. There will be additional fields, depending on the type. Simple annotations like tokens generally don't have extra fields. Stem annotations usually have the stem that was extracted for the range of the text.

Annotator

The annotator is the object that contains the logic for using the NLP function. The annotator will often require configuration or external data sets. Additionally, there are model-based annotators. One of the benefits of an annotation library is that annotators can take advantage of the work done by previous annotators. This naturally creates a notion of a pipeline of annotators.

spaCy

spaCy is an "industrial strength" NLP library. I will give a brief description, but I encourage you to go and read their fantastic documentation. spaCy combines the document model just described with a model for the language being processed (English, Spanish, etc.), which has allowed spaCy to support multiple languages in a way that is easy for developers to use. Much of its functionality is implemented in Python to get the speed of native code. If you are working in an environment that is using only Python, and you are unlikely to run distributed processes, then spaCy is a great choice.

NLP in Other Libraries

There are some non-NLP libraries that have some NLP functionality. It is often in machine learning libraries to support machine learning on text data.

scikit-learn

A Python machine learning library that has functionality for extracting features from text. This functionality is generally of the bag-of-words kind of processing. The way these processes are built allows them to easily take advantage of more NLP-focused libraries.

Lucene

A Java document search framework that has some text-processing functionality necessary for building a search engine. We will use Lucene later on when we talk about information retrieval.

Gensim
> A topic-modeling library (and it performs other distributional semantics techniques). Like spaCy, it is partially implemented in Cython, and like scikit-learn, it allows plug-and-play text processing in its API.

Spark NLP

The *Spark NLP* library was originally designed in early 2017 as an annotation library native to Spark to take full advantage of Spark SQL and MLlib modules. The inspiration came from trying to use Spark to distribute other NLP libraries, which were generally not implemented with concurrency or distributed computing in mind.

Annotation Library

Spark NLP has the same concepts as any other annotation library but differs in how it stores annotations. Most annotation libraries store the annotations in the document object, but Spark NLP creates columns for the different types of annotations.

The annotators are implemented as `Transformers`, `Estimators`, and `Models`. Let's take a look at some examples.

Stages

One of the design principles of Spark NLP is easy interoperability with the existing algorithms in MLlib. Because there is no notion of documents or annotations in MLlib there are transformers for turning text columns into documents and converting annotations into vanilla Spark SQL data types. The usual usage pattern is as follows:

1. Load data with Spark SQL.
2. Create document column.
3. Process with Spark NLP.
4. Convert annotations of interest into Spark SQL data types.
5. Run additional MLlib stages.

We have already looked at how to load data with Spark SQL and how to use MLlib stages in the standard Spark library, so we will look at the middle three stages now. First, we will look at the `DocumentAssembler` (stage 2).

Transformers

To explore these five stages we will again use the `mini_newsgroups` data set (see Table 3-15).

```
from sparknlp import DocumentAssembler, Finisher

# RDD containing filepath-text pairs
texts = spark.sparkContext.wholeTextFiles(path)

schema = StructType([
    StructField('path', StringType()),
    StructField('text', StringType()),
])

texts = spark.createDataFrame(texts, schema=schema)

texts.limit(5).toPandas()
```

Table 3-15. mini_newsgroups data

	path	text
0	file:/.../spark-nlp-book/data/...	Xref: cantaloupe.srv.cs.cmu.edu sci.astro:3522...
1	file:/.../spark-nlp-book/data/...	Newsgroups: sci.space\nPath: cantaloupe.srv.cs...
2	file:/.../spark-nlp-book/data/...	Xref: cantaloupe.srv.cs.cmu.edu sci.space:6146...
3	file:/.../spark-nlp-book/data/...	Path: cantaloupe.srv.cs.cmu.edu!rochester!udel...
4	file:/.../spark-nlp-book/data/...	Newsgroups: sci.space\nPath: cantaloupe.srv.cs...

DocumentAssembler

The `DocumentAssembler` takes five parameters (see Table 3-16):

`inputCol`
> The column containing the text of the document

`outputCol`
> The name of the column containing the newly constructed document

`idCol`
> The name of the column containing the identifier (optional)

`metadataCol`
> The name of a `Map`-type column that represents document metadata (optional)

`trimAndClearNewLines ->`
> Determines whether to remove new line characters and trim strings (optional, default = True)

```
document_assembler = DocumentAssembler()\
    .setInputCol('text')\
```

```
        .setOutputCol('document')\
        .setIdCol('path')

docs = document_assembler.transform(texts)

docs.limit(5).toPandas()
```

Table 3-16. Output from DocumentAssembler

	path	text	document
0	file:/.../spark-nlp-book/data/...	Xref: cantaloupe.srv.cs.cmu.edu sci.astro: 3522...	[(document, 0, 1834, Xref: cantaloupe.srv.cs.c...
1	file:/.../spark-nlp-book/data/...	Newsgroups: sci.space\nPath: cantaloupe.srv.cs...	[(document, 0, 1804, Newsgroups: sci.space Pat...
2	file:/.../spark-nlp-book/data/...	Xref: cantaloupe.srv.cs.cmu.edu sci.space: 6146...	[(document, 0, 1259, Xref: cantaloupe.srv.cs.c...
3	file:/.../spark-nlp-book/data/...	Path: cantaloupe.srv.cs.cmu.edu!rochester! udel...	[(document, 0, 8751, Path: cantaloupe.srv.cs.c...
4	file:/.../spark-nlp-book/data/...	Newsgroups: sci.space\nPath: cantaloupe.srv.cs...	[(document, 0, 1514, Newsgroups: sci.space Pat...

```
docs.first()['document'][0].asDict()

{'annotatorType': 'document',
 'begin': 0,
 'end': 1834,
 'result': 'Xref: cantaloupe.srv.cs.cmu.edu sci.astro:...',
 'metadata': {
  'id': 'file:/.../spark-nlp-book/data/mini_newsg...'
 }
}
```

Annotators

Now we look at stage 3—the annotators. This is the heart of the NLP work. So let's look at some of the `Annotators` available in Spark NLP.

We will look at some commonly used annotators:

- `SentenceDetector`
- `Tokenizer`
- `lemmatizer`
- `PerceptronApproach` (POSTagger)

SentenceDetector

The `SentenceDetector` uses a rule-based algorithm inspired by Kevin Dias's Ruby implementation (*https://oreil.ly/lyQeI*). It takes the following parameters (see Table 3-17):

`inputCols`
A list of columns to sentence-tokenize.

`outputCol`
The name of the new sentence column.

`useAbbreviations`
Determines whether to apply abbreviations at sentence detection.

`useCustomBoundsOnly`
Determines whether to only utilize custom bounds for sentence detection.

`explodeSentences`
Determines whether to explode each sentence into a different row, for better parallelization. Defaults to false.

`customBounds`
Characters used to explicitly mark sentence bounds.

```
from sparknlp.annotator import SentenceDetector

sent_detector = SentenceDetector()\
    .setInputCols(['document'])\
    .setOutputCol('sentences')

sentences = sent_detector.transform(docs)
sentences.limit(5).toPandas()
```

Table 3-17. Output from SentenceDetector

	path	text	document	sentences
0	file:/.../spark-nlp-book/data/...	...	[(document, 0, 1834, Xref: cantaloupe.srv.cs.c...	[(document, 0, 709, Xref: cantaloupe.srv.cs.cm...
1	file:/.../spark-nlp-book/data/...	...	[(document, 0, 1804, Newsgroups: sci.space Pat...	[(document, 0, 288, Newsgroups: sci.space Path...
2	file:/.../spark-nlp-book/data/...	...	[(document, 0, 1259, Xref: cantaloupe.srv.cs.c...	[(document, 0, 312, Xref: cantaloupe.srv.cs.cm...
3	file:/.../spark-nlp-book/data/...	...	[(document, 0, 8751, Path: cantaloupe.srv.cs.c...	[(document, 0, 453, Path: cantaloupe.srv.cs.cm...
4	file:/.../spark-nlp-book/data/...	...	[(document, 0, 1514, Newsgroups: sci.space Pat...	[(document, 0, 915, Newsgroups: sci.space Path...

Tokenizer

A `Tokenizer` is a fundamental `Annotator`. Almost all text-based data processing begins with some form of tokenization. Most classical NLP algorithms expect tokens as the basic input. Many deep learning algorithms are being developed that take characters as basic input. Most NLP applications still use tokenization. The Spark NLP `Tokenizer` is a little more sophisticated than just a regular expression-based tokenizer. It has a number of parameters. The following are some of the basic ones (see Table 3-18 for the results):

inputCols

A list of columns to tokenize.

outputCol

The name of the new token column.

targetPattern

Basic regex rule to identify a candidate for tokenization. Defaults to \S+ which means anything not a space (optional).

prefixPattern

Regular expression (regex) to identify subtokens that come in the beginning of the token. Regex has to start with \A and must contain groups (). Each group will become a separate token within the prefix. Defaults to nonletter characters—for example, quotes or parentheses (optional).

suffixPattern

Regex to identify subtokens that are in the end of the token. Regex has to end with \z and must contain groups (). Each group will become a separate token within the prefix. Defaults to nonletter characters—for example, quotes or parentheses (optional).

```
from sparknlp.annotator import Tokenizer

tokenizer = Tokenizer()\
    .setInputCols(['sentences'])\
    .setOutputCol('tokens')\
    .fit(sentences)

tokens = tokenizer.transform(sentences)
tokens.limit(5).toPandas()
```

Table 3-18. Output from Tokenizer

	path	text	document	sentences	tokens
0	file:/.../spark-nlp-book/data/...	...	...	[(document, 0, 709, Xref: cantaloupe.srv.cs.cm...	[(token, 0, 3, Xref, {'sentence': '1'}), (toke...
1	file:/.../spark-nlp-book/data/...	...	...	[(document, 0, 288, Newsgroups: sci.space Path...	[(token, 0, 9, Newsgroups, {'sentence': '1'}),...
2	file:/.../spark-nlp-book/data/...	...	...	[(document, 0, 312, Xref: cantaloupe.srv.cs.cm...	[(token, 0, 3, Xref, {'sentence': '1'}), (toke...
3	file:/.../spark-nlp-book/data/...	...	...	[(document, 0, 453, Path: cantaloupe.srv.cs.cm...	[(token, 0, 3, Path, {'sentence': '1'}), (toke...
4	file:/.../spark-nlp-book/data/...	...	...	[(document, 0, 915, Newsgroups: sci.space Path...	[(token, 0, 9, Newsgroups, {'sentence': '1'}),...

There are some Annotators that require additional resources. Some require reference data, like the following example, the lemmatizer.

Lemmatizer

The lemmatizer finds the *lemmas* for the tokens. Lemmas are the entry words in dictionaries. For example, "cats" lemmatizes to "cat," and "oxen" lemmatizes to "ox." Loading the lemmatizer requires a dictionary and the following three parameters:

inputCols
> A list of columns to tokenize

outputCol
> The name of the new token column

dictionary
> The resource to be loaded as the lemma dictionary

```
from sparknlp.annotator import Lemmatizer

lemmatizer = Lemmatizer() \
  .setInputCols(["tokens"]) \
  .setOutputCol("lemma") \
  .setDictionary('en_lemmas.txt', '\t', ',')\
  .fit(tokens)

lemmas = lemmatizer.transform(tokens)
lemmas.limit(5).toPandas()
```

Table 3-19 shows the results.

Table 3-19. Output from Lemmatizer

	path	text	document	sentences	tokens	lemma
0	file:/.../spark-nlp-book/data/...	...	...	...	[(token, 0, 3, Xref, {'sentence': '1'}), (toke...	[(token, 0, 3, Xref, {'sentence': '1'}), (toke...
1	file:/.../spark-nlp-book/data/...	...	,,,	...	[(token, 0, 9, Newsgroups, {'sentence': '1'}),...	[(token, 0, 9, Newsgroups, {'sentence': '1'}),...
2	file:/.../spark-nlp-book/data/...	...	...	...	[(token, 0, 3, Xref, {'sentence': '1'}), (toke...	[(token, 0, 3, Xref, {'sentence': '1'}), (toke...
3	file:/.../spark-nlp-book/data/...	...	...	...	[(token, 0, 3, Path, {'sentence': '1'}), (toke...	[(token, 0, 3, Path, {'sentence': '1'}), (toke...
4	file:/.../spark-nlp-book/data/...	...	...	...	[(token, 0, 9, Newsgroups, {'sentence': '1'}), ...	[(token, 0, 9, Newsgroups, {'sentence': '1'}),...

POS tagger

There are also `Annotators` that require models as resources. For example, the POS tagger uses a perceptron model, so it is called `PerceptronApproach`. The `PerceptronApproach` has five parameters:

`inputCols`
  A list of columns to tag

`outputCol`
  The name of the new tag column

`posCol`
  Column of `Array` of POS tags that match tokens

`corpus`
  POS tags delimited corpus; needs "delimiter" in options

`nIterations`
  Number of iterations in training, converges to better accuracy

We will load a pretrained model here (see Table 3-20) and look into training our own model in Chapter 8.

```
from sparknlp.annotator import PerceptronModel

pos_tagger = PerceptronModel.pretrained() \
    .setInputCols(["tokens", "sentences"]) \
    .setOutputCol("pos")
```

```
postags = pos_tagger.transform(lemmas)
postags.limit(5).toPandas()
```

Table 3-20. Output from PerceptronModel POS tagger

	path	...	sentences	tokens	pos
0	file:/.../ spark-nlp-book/data/...	...	[(document, 0, 709, Xref: cantaloupe.srv.cs.cm...	[(token, 0, 3, Xref, {'sentence': '1'}), (toke...	[(pos, 0, 3, NNP, {'word': 'Xref'}), (pos, 4, ...
1	file:/.../ spark-nlp-book/data/...	...	[(document, 0, 288, Newsgroups: sci.space Path...	[(token, 0, 9, Newsgroups, {'sentence': '1'}),...	[(pos, 0, 9, NNP, {'word': 'Newsgroups'}), (po...
2	file:/.../ spark-nlp-book/data/...	...	[(document, 0, 312, Xref: cantaloupe.srv.cs.cm...	[(token, 0, 3, Xref, {'sentence': '1'}), (toke...	[(pos, 0, 3, NNP, {'word': 'Xref'}), (pos, 4, ...
3	file:/.../ spark-nlp-book/data/...	...	[(document, 0, 453, Path: cantaloupe.srv.cs.cm...	[(token, 0, 3, Path, {'sentence': '1'}), (toke...	[(pos, 0, 3, NNP, {'word': 'Path'}), (pos, 4, ...
4	file:/.../ spark-nlp-book/data/...	...	[(document, 0, 915, Newsgroups: sci.space Path...	[(token, 0, 9, Newsgroups, {'sentence': '1'}),...	[(pos, 0, 9, NNP, {'word': 'Newsgroups'}), (po...

Pretrained Pipelines

We saw earlier how we can organize multiple MLlib stages into a `Pipeline`. Using `Pipelines` is especially useful in NLP tasks because there are often many stages between loading the raw text and extracting structured data.

Spark NLP has pretrained pipelines that can be used to process text. This doesn't mean that you do not need to tune pipelines for application. But it is often convenient to begin experimenting with a prebuilt NLP pipeline and find what needs tuning.

Explain document ML pipeline

The `BasicPipeline` does sentence splitting, tokenization, lemmatization, stemming, and POS tagging. If you want to get a quick look at some text data, this is a great pipeline to use (see Table 3-21).

```
from sparknlp.pretrained import PretrainedPipeline

pipeline = PretrainedPipeline('explain_document_ml', lang='en')

pipeline.transform(texts).limit(5).toPandas()
```

Table 3-21. Output from explain_document_ml PretrainedPipeline

	...	sentence	token	spell	lemma	stem	pos
0	...	...	...	[(token, 0, 9, Newsgroups, {'confidence': '0.0...	...	[(token, 0, 9, newsgroup, {'confidence': '0.0'...	[(pos, 0, 9, NNP, {'word': 'Newsgroups'}, [], ...
1	...	...	...	[(token, 0, 3, Path, {'confidence': '1.0'}, []...	...	[(token, 0, 3, path, {'confidence': '1.0'}, []...	[(pos, 0, 3, NNP, {'word': 'Path'}, [], []), (...
2	...	...	...	[(token, 0, 9, Newsgroups, {'confidence': '0.0...	...	[(token, 0, 9, newsgroup, {'confidence': '0.0'...	[(pos, 0, 9, NNP, {'word': 'Newsgroups'}, [], ...
3	...	...	...	[(token, 0, 3, xref, {'confidence': '0.3333333...	...	[(token, 0, 3, pref, {'confidence': '0.3333333...	[(pos, 0, 3, NN, {'word': 'pref'}, [], []), (p...
4	...	...	...	[(token, 0, 3, tref, {'confidence': '0.3333333...	...	[(token, 0, 3, xref, {'confidence': '0.3333333...	[(pos, 0, 3, NN, {'word': 'pref'}, [], []), (p...

You can also use the `annotate` function to process a document without Spark:

```
text = texts.first()['text']

annotations = pipeline.annotate(text)
list(zip(
    annotations['token'],
    annotations['stems'],
    annotations['lemmas']
))[100:120]

[('much', 'much', 'much'),
 ('argument', 'argum', 'argument'),
 ('and', 'and', 'and'),
 ('few', 'few', 'few'),
 ('facts', 'fact', 'fact'),
 ('being', 'be', 'be'),
 ('offered', 'offer', 'offer'),
 ('.', '.', '.'),
 ('The', 'the', 'The'),
 ('summaries', 'summari', 'summary'),
 ('below', 'below', 'below'),
 ('attempt', 'attempt', 'attempt'),
 ('to', 'to', 'to'),
 ('represent', 'repres', 'represent'),
 ('the', 'the', 'the'),
 ('position', 'posit', 'position'),
 ('on', 'on', 'on'),
 ('which', 'which', 'which'),
 ('much', 'much', 'much'),
 ('of', 'of', 'of')]
```

There are many other pipelines, and there is additional information available (*https://oreil.ly/snh_3*).

Now let's talk about how we will perform step 4, converting the annotations into native Spark SQL types using the *Finisher*.

Finisher

The annotations are useful for composing NLP steps, but we generally want to take some specific information out to process. The `Finisher` handles most of these use cases. If you want to get a list of tokens (or stems, or what have you) to use in downstream MLlib stages, the `Finisher` can do this (see Table 3-22). Let's look at the parameters:

`inputCols`
Name of input annotation cols

`outputCols`
Name of finisher output cols

`valueSplitSymbol`
Character separating annotations

`annotationSplitSymbol`
Character separating annotations

`cleanAnnotations`
Determines whether to remove annotation columns

`includeMetadata`
Annotation metadata format

`outputAsArray`
Finisher generates an `Array` with the results instead of string

```
finisher = Finisher()\
    .setInputCols(['tokens', 'lemma'])\
    .setOutputCols(['tokens', 'lemmata'])\
    .setCleanAnnotations(True)\
    .setOutputAsArray(True)

custom_pipeline = Pipeline(stages=[
    document_assembler,
    sent_detector,
    tokenizer,
    lemmatizer,
    finisher
]).fit(texts)

custom_pipeline.transform(texts).limit(5).toPandas()
```

Table 3-22. Output from Finisher

	path	text	tokens	lemmata
0	...	...	[Newsgroups, :, sci.space, Path, :, cantaloupe...	[Newsgroups, :, sci.space, Path, :, cantaloupe...
1	...	...	[Path, :, cantaloupe.srv.cs.cmu.edu!rochester!...	[Path, :, cantaloupe.srv.cs.cmu.edu!rochester!...
2	...	...	[Newsgroups, :, sci.space, Path, :, cantaloupe...	[Newsgroups, :, sci.space, Path, :, cantaloupe...
3	...	...	[Xref, :, cantaloupe.srv.cs.cmu.edu, sci.space...	[Xref, :, cantaloupe.srv.cs.cmu.edu, sci.space...
4	...	...	[Xref, :, cantaloupe.srv.cs.cmu.edu, sci.astro...	[Xref, :, cantaloupe.srv.cs.cmu.edu, sci.astro...

Now we will use the `StopWordsRemover` transformer from Spark MLlib. The results are shown in Table 3-23.

```
from pyspark.ml.feature import StopWordsRemover

stopwords = StopWordsRemover.loadDefaultStopWords('english')

larger_pipeline = Pipeline(stages=[
    custom_pipeline,
    StopWordsRemover(
        inputCol='lemmata',
        outputCol='terms',
        stopWords=stopwords)
]).fit(texts)

larger_pipeline.transform(texts).limit(5).toPandas()
```

Table 3-23. Output from StopWordsRemover

	...	lemmata	terms
0	...	[Newsgroups, :, sci.space, Path, :, cantaloupe...	[Newsgroups, :, sci.space, Path, :, cantaloupe...
1	...	[Path, :, cantaloupe.srv.cs.cmu.edu!rochester!...	[Path, :, cantaloupe.srv.cs.cmu.edu!rochester!...
2	...	[Newsgroups, :, sci.space, Path, :, cantaloupe...	[Newsgroups, :, sci.space, Path, :, cantaloupe...
3	...	[Xref, :, cantaloupe.srv.cs.cmu.edu, sci.space...	[Xref, :, cantaloupe.srv.cs.cmu.edu, sci.space...
4	...	[Xref, :, cantaloupe.srv.cs.cmu.edu, sci.astro...	[Xref, :, cantaloupe.srv.cs.cmu.edu, sci.astro...

Now that we have reviewed Spark and Spark NLP, we are almost ready to start building an NLP application. There is an extra benefit to learning an annotation library—it helps you understand how to structure a pipeline for NLP. This knowledge will be applicable even if you are using other technologies.

The only topic left for us to cover is deep learning, which we cover in the next chapter.

Exercises: Build a Topic Model

One of the easiest things you can do to begin exploring your data set is to create a topic model. To do this we need to transform the text into numerical vectors. We will go into this more in the next part of the book. For now, let's build a pipeline for processing text.

First, we need to split the texts into sentences. Second, we need to tokenize. Next, we need to normalize our words with a `lemmatizer` and the normalizer. After this, we need to finish our pipeline and remove stop words. (So far, everything except the `Normalizer` has been demonstrated in this chapter.) After that, we will pass the information into our topic modeling pipeline.

Check the online documentation (*https://oreil.ly/T7Od8*) for help with the normalizer.

```
# document_assembler = ???
# sent_detector = ???
# tokenizer = ???
# lemmatizer = ???
# normalizer = ???
# finisher = ???
# sparknlp_pipeline = ???

# stopwords = ???
# stopword_remover = ??? # use outputCol='terms'

#text_processing_pipeline = ??? # first stage is sparknlp_pipeline

# from pyspark.ml.feature import CountVectorizer, IDF
# from pyspark.ml.clustering import LDA

# tf = CountVectorizer(inputCol='terms', outputCol='tf')
# idf = IDF(inputCol='tf', outputCol='tfidf')
# lda = LDA(k=10, seed=123, featuresCol='tfidf')

# pipeline = Pipeline(stages=[
#     text_processing_pipeline,
#     tf,
#     idf,
#     lda
# ])

# model = pipeline.fit(texts)

# tf_model = model.stages[-3]
# lda_model = model.stages[-1]

# topics = lda_model.describeTopics().collect()
# for k, topic in enumerate(topics):
#     print('Topic', k)
#     for ix, wt in zip(topic['termIndices'], topic['termWeights']):
```

```
#          print(ix, tf_model.vocabulary[ix], wt)
#      print('#' * 50)
```

Congratulations! You have built your first full Spark pipeline with Spark NLP.

Resources

- Spark API: this is a great resource to have handy. With each new release there can be new additions, so I rely on the API documentation to keep up to date.
  — Scala (*https://oreil.ly/zrnQX*)
  — Java (*https://oreil.ly/obt1N*)
  — Python (*https://oreil.ly/5gbJE*)
  — R (*https://oreil.ly/cVFOA*)
  — Spark SQL programming guide (*https://oreil.ly/0bAmZ*)
  — MLlib programming guide (*https://oreil.ly/EAm60*)
- *Natural Language Processing with Python* (*https://oreil.ly/H6bjk*): this is the book written explaining NLP with NLTK. It is available for free online.
- spaCy (*https://spacy.io*): this library is doing a lot of cool things and has a strong community.
- Spark NLP (*https://oreil.ly/ByTGk*): the website of the Spark NLP library. Here you can find documentation, tutorials, and videos about the library.
- *Foundations of Statistical Natural Language Processing* by Christopher D. Manning and Hinrich Schütze (MIT Press)
  — This is considered a classic for natural language processing. It is an older book, so you won't find information on deep learning. If you want to have a strong foundation in NLP this is a great book to have.
- *Spark: The Definitive Guide* (*https://oreil.ly/rTXvT*) by Matei Zaharia and Bill Chambers (O'Reilly)
  — This is a great resource to have when using Spark.

## CHAPTER 4

Deep Learning Basics

In this chapter we will cover the basics of deep learning. The goal of this chapter is to create a foundation for us to discuss how to apply deep learning to NLP. There are new deep learning techniques being developed every month, and we will cover some of the newer techniques in later chapters, which is why we need this foundation. In the beginning of this chapter we will cover some of the history of the artificial neural network, and we will work through some example networks representing logical operators. This will help us build a solid foundation for thinking about artificial neural networks.

Fundamentally, deep learning is a field of study of *artificial neural networks*, or *ANNs*. The first appearance of artificial neural networks in academic literature was in a paper called *A Logical Calculus of the Ideas Immanent in Nervous Activity*, by Warren S. McCulloch and Walter Pitts in 1943. Their work was an attempt to explain how the brain worked from a cyberneticist perspective. Their work would become the root of modern neuroscience and modern artificial neural networks.

An ANN is a biologically inspired algorithm. *ANNs* are not realistic representations of how a brain learns, although from time to time news stories still hype this. We are still learning many things about how the brain processes information. As new discoveries are made, there is often an attempt to represent real neurological structures and processes in terms of ANNs, like the concept of receptive fields inspiring convolutional neural networks. Despite this, it cannot be overstated how far we are from building an artificial brain.

In 1957, Frank Rosenblatt created the *perceptron* algorithm. Initially, there were high hopes about the *perceptron*. When evaluating, the single layer perceptron does the following:

1. n inputs, $x_1, \ldots, x_n$

2. Each input is multiplied by a weight, $x_i w_i$

3. These products are then summed with the bias term, $s = b + \sum_{i=1}^{n} x_i w_i$

4. This sum is then run through an *activation* function, which returns 0 or 1, $\hat{y} = f(s)$

   - The Heaviside step function, H, is often used

$$H(x): = \begin{cases} 0, & \text{if } x < 0 \\ 1, & \text{if } x > 0 \end{cases}$$

This can also be expressed through linear algebra.

$$\vec{x} = \langle x_1, \ldots, x_n \rangle$$

$$\vec{w} = \langle w_1, \ldots, w_n \rangle$$

$$y = H\left(\vec{x} \cdot \vec{w} + b\right)$$

This can be visualized with the diagram in Figure 4-1.

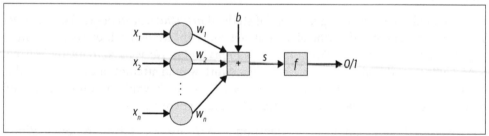

Figure 4-1. Perceptron

In 1969, Marvin Minsky and Seymour Papert showed the limitations of the algorithm. The perceptron could not represent the exclusive "or" operator XOR. The difficulty here is that a simple perceptron cannot solve problems that do not have *linear separability*. In terms of binary classification, a linearly separable problem is one in which the two classes can be separated by a single line, or plane in higher dimensions. To better understand this in terms of neural networks, let's look at some examples.

We will try and create some perceptrons representing logical functions by hand, to explore the XOR problem. Imagine that we want to train networks to perform some basic logical functions. The inputs will be 0s and 1s.

If we want to implement the NOT operator, what would we do? In this case, there is no x_2. We want the following function:

$$NOT(x): = \begin{cases} 0, & \text{if } x = 1 \\ 1, & \text{if } x = 0 \end{cases}$$

This gives us two equations to work with.

$$H(0 \cdot w_1 + b) = 1$$
$$H(1 \cdot w_1 + b) = 0$$

So let's see if we can find values that satisfy these equations.

$$H(0 \cdot w_1 + b) = 1$$
$$0 \cdot w_1 + b > 0$$
$$b > 0$$

So we know b must be positive.

$$H(1 \cdot w_1 + b) = 0$$
$$1 \cdot w_1 + b < 0$$
$$w_1 < -b$$

So w_1 must be a negative number less than $-b$. An infinite number of values fit this, so the perceptron can easily represent NOT.

Now let's represent the OR operator. This requires two inputs. We want the following function:

$$OR(x_1, x_2): = \begin{cases} 1, & \text{if } x_1 = 1, x_2 = 1 \\ 1, & \text{if } x_1 = 1, x_2 = 0 \\ 1, & \text{if } x_1 = 0, x_2 = 1 \\ 0, & \text{if } x_1 = 0, x_2 = 0 \end{cases}$$

We have a few more equations here; let's start with the last case.

$$H(0 \cdot w_1 + 0 \cdot w_2 + b) = 0$$
$$0 \cdot w_1 + 0 \cdot w_2 + b < 0$$
$$b < 0$$

So b must be negative. Now let's handle the second case.

$$H(1 \cdot w_1 + 0 \cdot w_2 + b) = 1$$
$$1 \cdot w_1 + 0 \cdot w_2 + b > 0$$
$$w_1 > -b$$

So w_1 must be larger than $-b$, and so it is a positive number. The same will work for case 3. For case 1, if $w_1 + b > 0$ and $w_2 + b > 0$ then $w_1 + w_2 + b > 0$. So again, there are an infinite number of values. A perceptron can represent OR.

Let's look at XOR now.

$$XOR(x_1, x_2) := \begin{cases} 0, & \text{if } x_1 = 1, x_2 = 1 \\ 1, & \text{if } x_1 = 1, x_2 = 0 \\ 1, & \text{if } x_1 = 0, x_2 = 1 \\ 0, & \text{if } x_1 = 0, x_2 = 0 \end{cases}$$

So we have four equations:

$$H(1 \cdot w_1 + 1 \cdot w_2 + b) = 0$$
$$H(1 \cdot w_1 + 0 \cdot w_2 + b) = 1$$
$$H(0 \cdot w_1 + 1 \cdot w_2 + b) = 1$$
$$H(0 \cdot w_1 + 0 \cdot w_2 + b) = 0$$

Cases 2 to 4 are the same as for OR, so this implies the following:

$$b < 0$$
$$w_1 > -b$$
$$w_2 > -b$$

However, when we look at case 1, it falls apart. We cannot add the two weights, either of which are larger than $-b$ to b and get a negative number. So *XOR* is not representable with the perceptron. In fact, the perceptron can solve only linearly separable classification problems. *Linearly separable problems* are problems that can be solved by drawing a single line (or plane for higher dimensions). *XOR* is not linearly separable.

However, this problem can be solved by having multiple layers, but this was difficult given the computational capability of the time. The limitations of the single-layer perceptron network caused research to turn toward other machine-learning approaches. In the 1980s there was renewed interest when hardware made multilayer perceptron networks more feasible (see Figure 4-2).

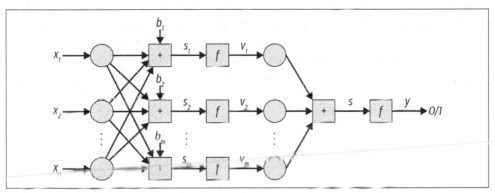

Figure 4-2. Multilayer perceptron

Now that we are dealing with modern neural networks there are some more options for us to consider:

1. The output is not necessarily 0 or 1. It could be real valued, or even a vector of values.

2. There are several activation functions to choose from.

3. Now that we have hidden layers, we will have a matrix of weights between each layer.

Look at how we would calculate the output for a neural network with one hidden layer:

$$\hat{y} = g\left(W^{(2)} \cdot f\left(W^{(1)} \cdot \vec{x} + \vec{b}^{(1)}\right) + \vec{b}^{(2)}\right)$$

We could repeat this for many layers if we wish. And now that we have hidden layers, we're going to have a lot more parameters—so solving for them by hand won't do. We are going to need to talk about *gradient descent* and *backpropagation*.

Gradient Descent

In gradient descent, we start with a *loss function*. The *loss function* is a way of assigning a loss, also referred to as a cost, to an undesired output. Let's represent our model with the function $F\left(\vec{x}; \Theta\right)$, where Θ represents our parameters $\theta_1, \ldots, \theta_k$, and $\vec{x}$ is an input. There are many options for a loss function; let's use squared error for now.

$$SE(\Theta) = \left(y - F\left(\vec{x}; \Theta\right)\right)^2$$

Naturally, the higher the value the worse the loss. So we can also imagine this loss function as a surface. We want to find the lowest point in this surface. To find it, we start from some point and find the slope along each dimension—the gradient ∇. We then want to adjust each parameter so that it decreases the error. So if parameter θ_i has a positive slope, we want to decrease the parameter, and if it has a negative slope we want to increase the parameter. So how do we calculate the gradient? We take the partial derivative for each parameter.

$$\nabla SE(\Theta) = \; < \frac{\partial}{\partial \theta_1} E(\Theta), \ldots, \frac{\partial}{\partial \theta_k} SE(\Theta) >$$

We calculate partial derivatives for \theta_i by holding the other parameters constant and taking the derivative with respect to θ_i. This will give us the slope for each parameter. We can use these slopes to update the parameters by subtracting the slope from the parameter value.

If we overcorrect a parameter we might overshoot the minimal point, but the weaker our updates, the slower we learn from examples. To control the learning rate we use a hyperparameter. I'll use r for this learning rate, but you may also see it represented by other characters (often Greek). The update looks like this:

$$\theta_j = \theta_j - r \frac{\partial}{\partial \theta_j} SE(\Theta)$$

If we do this for each example, training on a million examples will take a prohibitively long time, so let's use an error function based on a batch of examples—a mean squared error.

$$MSE(\Theta) = \frac{1}{n} \sum_{i=1}^{M} SE(\Theta)$$

$$= \frac{1}{n} \sum_{i=1}^{M} \left(y - F\left(\vec{x}_i; \Theta\right) \right)^2$$

$$\theta_j = \theta_j - r \frac{\partial}{\partial \theta_j} MSE(\Theta)$$

$$= \theta_j - r \frac{\partial}{\partial \theta_j} \frac{1}{n} \sum_{i=1}^{M} SE(\Theta)$$

The gradient is a linear operator, so we can distribute it under the sum.

$$\theta_j = \theta_j - r \frac{\partial}{\partial \theta_j} MSE(\Theta)$$

$$= \theta_j - r \frac{1}{n} \sum_{i=1}^{M} \frac{\partial}{\partial \theta_j} \frac{1}{n} SE(\Theta)$$

$$= \theta_j - r \frac{1}{n} \sum_{i=1}^{M} \frac{\partial}{\partial \theta_j} \frac{1}{n} \left(y - F\left(\vec{x}; \Theta\right) \right)^2$$

$$= \theta_j - r \frac{1}{n} \sum_{i=1}^{M} \frac{2}{n} \left(y - F\left(\vec{x}; \Theta\right) \right) \frac{\partial}{\partial \theta_j} F\left(\vec{x}; \Theta\right)$$

This will change if you use a different loss function. We will go over loss functions as we come across them in the rest of the book. The value of $\frac{\partial}{\partial \theta_j} F\left(\vec{x}; \Theta\right)$ will depend on your model. If it is a neural network, it will depend on your activation function.

Backpropagation

Backpropagation is an algorithm for training neural networks. It is essentially an implementation of chain rule from calculus. To talk about backpropagation, we must first talk about forward propagation.

To build a solid intuition, we will proceed with two parallel descriptions of neural networks: mathematical and numpy. The mathematical description will help us understand what is happening on a theoretical level. The numpy description will help us understand how this can be implemented.

We will again be using the Iris data set. This data is really too small for a realistic use of deep learning, but it will help us explore backpropagation. Let's remind ourselves about the Iris data set (see Table 4-1).

```
import numpy as np
import pandas as pd
from sklearn.model_selection import train_test_split
from scipy.special import softmax

df = pd.read_csv('data/iris/iris.data', names=[
    'sepal_length',
    'sepal_width',
    'petal_length',
    'petal_width',
    'class',
])

df.head()
```

Table 4-1. Iris data

	sepal_length	sepal_width	petal_length	petal_width	class
0	5.1	3.5	1.4	0.2	Iris-setosa
1	4.9	3.0	1.4	0.2	Iris-setosa
2	4.7	3.2	1.3	0.2	Iris-setosa
3	4.6	3.1	1.5	0.2	Iris-setosa
4	5.0	3.6	1.4	0.2	Iris-setosa

Now, let's define our network.

We know we will have 4 inputs (the number of our features), so our input layer has a length of 4. There are 3 outputs (the number of our classes), so our output layer must have a length of 3. We do whatever we want for the layers in between, and we will use 6 and 5 for the first and second hidden layers, respectively. A lot of research has gone into how to construct your network. You will likely want to explore research for different use cases and approaches. As is so common in NLP and machine learning in general, one size does not fit all.

```
layer_sizes = [4, 6, 5, 3]
```

We will define our inputs, X, and our labels, Y. We *one-hot encode* the classes. In short, *one-hot encoding* is when we represent a categorical variable as a collection of binary variables. Let's look at the one-hot–encoded DataFrame. The results are in Tables 4-2 and 4-3.

```
X = df.drop(columns=['class'])
Y = pd.get_dummies(df['class'])

X.head()
```

Table 4-2. Iris features matrix

	sepal_length	sepal_width	petal_length	petal_width
0	5.1	3.5	1.4	0.2
1	4.9	3.0	1.4	0.2
2	4.7	3.2	1.3	0.2
3	4.6	3.1	1.5	0.2
4	5.0	3.6	1.4	0.2

```
Y.head()
```

Table 4-3. Iris labels matrix

	Iris-setosa	Iris-versicolor	Iris-virginica
0	1	0	0
1	1	0	0
2	1	0	0
3	1	0	0
4	1	0	0

As we can see, each possible value of the class column has become a column itself. For a given row, if the value of class was, say, iris-versicolor, then the iris-versicolor column will have value 1, and the others will have 0.

In mathematical terms, this is what our network looks like:

$$W^{(1)} = 5 \times 4 \text{ matrix}$$
$$b^{(1)} = 5 \times 1 \text{ vector}$$
$$f_1 = tanh$$
$$W^{(2)} = 6 \times 5 \text{ matrix}$$
$$b^{(2)} = 6 \times 1 \text{ vector}$$
$$f_2 = tanh$$
$$W^{(3)} = 3 \times 5 \text{ matrix}$$
$$b^{(3)} = 3 \times 1 \text{ vector}$$
$$f_3 = tanh$$

There are many ways to initialize parameters. It might seem easy to set all the parameters to 0, but this does not work. If all the weights are 0, then the output of forward propagation is unaffected by the input, making learning impossible. Here, we will be randomly initializing them. If you want to learn about more sophisticated initialization techniques, there are links in the "Resources" on page 100. We can, however, set the bias terms to 0, since they are not associated with an input.

```
np.random.seed(123)
W_1 = np.random.randn(layer_sizes[1], layer_sizes[0])
b_1 = np.zeros((layer_sizes[1], 1))
f_1 = np.tanh
W_2 = np.random.randn(layer_sizes[2], layer_sizes[1])
b_2 = np.zeros((layer_sizes[2], 1))
f_2 = np.tanh
W_3 = np.random.randn(layer_sizes[3], layer_sizes[2])
b_3 = np.zeros((layer_sizes[3], 1))
f_3 = lambda H: np.apply_along_axis(softmax, axis=0, arr=H)

layers = [
    (W_1, b_1, f_1),
    (W_2, b_2, f_2),
    (W_3, b_3, f_3),
]
```

Now, we will implement forward propagation.

Mathematically, this is what our network is doing:

$$X = 3 \times M \ matrix$$
$$H^{(1)} = W^{(1)} \cdot X + b^{(1)}$$
$$V^{(1)} = f_1\left(H^{(1)}\right) = \tanh\left(H^{(1)}\right)$$
$$H^{(2)} = W^{(2)} \cdot V^{(1)} + b^{(2)}$$
$$V^{(2)} = f_2\left(H^{(2)}\right) = \tanh\left(H^{(2)}\right)$$
$$H^{(3)} = W^{(3)} \cdot V^{(2)} + b^{(3)}$$
$$\hat{Y} = f_3\left(H^{(3)}\right) = \text{softmax}\left(H^{(1)}\right)$$

. . .

$$\text{softmax}\left(\vec{x}\right) = \ < \frac{e^{x_j}}{\Sigma_{i=0}^{K} e^{x_i}} >$$

. . .

The following code shows how forward propagation works with an arbitrary number of layers. In this function, X is the input (one example per row). The argument `layers` is a list of weight matrix, bias term, and activation function triplets.

```
def forward(X, layers):
    V = X.T
    Hs = []
    Vs = []
    for W, b, f in layers:
        H = W @ V
        H = np.add(H, b)
        Hs.append(H)
        V = f(H)
        Vs.append(V)
    return V, Hs, Vs
```

Now we need to talk about our *loss function*. As we described previously, the *loss function* is the function we use to calculate how the model did on a given batch of data. We will be using log-loss.

$$L = -\sum_{k}^{K}\left(Y \circ log\left(\widehat{Y}\right)\right)$$

The symbol ∘ represents elementwise multiplication, also known as the *Hadamard product*. The following function safely calculates the log-loss. We need to make sure that our predicted probabilities are between 0 and 1, but neither 0 nor 1. This is why we need the eps argument.

```
def log_loss(Y, Y_hat, eps=10**-15):
    # we need to protect against calling log(0), so we seet an
    # epsilon, and define our predicted probabilities to be between
    # epsilon and 1 - epsilon
    min_max_p = np.maximum(np.minimum(Y_hat, 1-eps), eps)
    log_losses = -np.sum(np.multiply(np.log(min_max_p), Y), axis=0)
    return np.sum(log_losses) / Y.shape[1]
```

```
Y_hat, Hs, Vs = forward(X, layers)
loss = log_loss(Y.T, Y_hat)
loss
```

```
1.4781844247149367
```

Now we see how forward propagation works and how to calculate the loss. To use gradient descent, we need to be able to calculate the gradient of the loss with respect to the individual parameters.

$$\frac{\partial L}{\partial W^{(3)}} = \frac{1}{M}\frac{\partial L}{\partial \widehat{Y}} \cdot \frac{\partial \widehat{Y}}{\partial W^{(3)}}$$

$$= \frac{1}{M}\frac{\partial L}{\partial \widehat{Y}} \cdot \frac{\partial \widehat{Y}}{\partial H^{(3)}} \cdot \frac{\partial H^{(3)}}{\partial W^{(3)}}$$

The combination of log-loss and softmax gives us a friendly expression for $\frac{\partial L}{\partial \hat{Y}} \cdot \frac{\partial \hat{Y}}{\partial H^{(3)}}$.

$$\frac{\partial L}{\partial W^{(3)}} = \frac{1}{M}\left(\hat{Y} - Y\right) \cdot \frac{\partial H^{(3)}}{\partial W^{(3)}}$$

$$= \frac{1}{M}\left(\hat{Y} - Y\right) \cdot V^{(2)T}$$

The gradient for the bias term is derived in the same way. Instead of taking the output from the earlier layer, it is multiplied (dot product) by a vector of all 1s.

$$\frac{\partial L}{\partial b^{(3)}} = \frac{1}{M}\left(\hat{Y} - Y\right) \cdot \vec{1}$$

$$= \frac{1}{M}\sum_{j}^{M} \hat{y}_j - y_j$$

Let's see what this looks like in code. We will use names that parallel the mathematical terms. First we can define $\frac{\partial L}{\partial H^{(3)}}$. We need to remember to transpose Y, so it has the same dimensions as Y_hat.

Let's look at the gradient values for $\frac{\partial L}{\partial W^{(3)}}$ (see Table 4-4).

```
dL_dH_3 = Y_hat - Y.values.T
dH_3_dW_3 = Vs[1]
dL_dW_3 = (1 / len(Y)) * dL_dH_3 @ dH_3_dW_3.T
print(dL_dW_3.shape)
dL_dW_3

(3, 5)
```

Table 4-4. Gradient values for \frac{\partial L}{\partial W^{(3)}}

	0	1	2	3	4
0	0.010773	-0.008965	0.210314	-0.210140	0.207157
1	-0.084970	-0.214219	0.123530	-0.122504	0.126386
2	0.074197	0.223184	-0.333843	0.332644	-0.333543

Now let's calculate the gradient for the bias term (see Table 4-5).

```
dH_3_db_3 = np.ones(len(Y))
dL_db_3 = (1 / len(Y)) * dL_dH_3 @ dH_3_db_3
print(dL_db_3.shape)
dL_db_3

(3,)
```

Table 1 5. Gradient values for \frac{\partial L}{\partial b^{(3)}}

	0
0	-0.210817
1	-0.123461
2	0.334278

Let's look a layer further. To calculate the gradient for the $\frac{\partial L}{\partial W^{(2)}}$, we will need to con-tinue applying the chain rule. As you can see, this derivation gets complicated quickly.

$$\frac{\partial L}{\partial W^{(2)}} = \frac{1}{M}\frac{\partial L}{\partial \hat{Y}} \cdot \frac{\partial \hat{Y}}{\partial W^{(2)}}$$

$$= \frac{1}{M}\frac{\partial L}{\partial \hat{Y}} \cdot \frac{\partial \hat{Y}}{\partial H^{(3)}} \cdot \frac{\partial H^{(3)}}{\partial W^{(2)}}$$

$$= \frac{1}{M}\frac{\partial L}{\partial \hat{Y}} \cdot \frac{\partial \hat{Y}}{\partial H^{(3)}} \cdot \frac{\partial H^{(3)}}{\partial V^{(2)}} \cdot \frac{\partial V^{(3)}}{\partial W^{(2)}}$$

$$= \frac{1}{M}\frac{\partial L}{\partial \hat{Y}} \cdot \frac{\partial \hat{Y}}{\partial H^{(3)}} \cdot \frac{\partial H^{(3)}}{\partial V^{(2)}} \cdot \frac{\partial V^{(2)}}{\partial H^{(2)}} \cdot \frac{\partial H^{(2)}}{\partial W^{(2)}}$$

We know part of this.

$$\frac{\partial L}{\partial W^{(2)}} = \frac{1}{M}(\hat{Y} - Y) \cdot \frac{\partial H^{(3)}}{\partial V^{(2)}} \cdot \frac{\partial V^{(2)}}{\partial H^{(2)}} \cdot \frac{\partial H^{(2)}}{\partial W^{(2)}}$$

$$= \frac{1}{M}(\hat{Y} - Y) \cdot W^{(3)} \cdot \left(1 - V^{(2)} \circ V^{(2)}\right) \cdot V^{(1)T}$$

We can calculate this. Notice here that we need to keep track of intermediate values. Use these values returned from the forward propagation step.

```
dH_3_dV_2 = W_3
dV_2_dH_2 = 1 - np.power(Vs[1], 2)
dH_2_dW_2 = Vs[0]
dL_dH_2 = np.multiply((dL_dH_3.T @ dH_3_dV_2).T, dV_2_dH_2)
dL_dW_2 = (1 / len(Y)) * dL_dH_2 @ dH_2_dW_2.T
print(dL_dW_2.shape)
dL_dW_2

(5, 6)
```

Now we can look at the gradient values, shown in Table 4-6.

Table 4-6. Gradient values for \frac{\partial L}{\partial W^{(2)}}

	0	1	2	3	4	5
0	-0.302449	-0.194403	0.314719	0.317461	0.317539	0.317538
1	0.049117	-0.001843	-0.055560	-0.055613	-0.055634	-0.055636
2	0.000722	0.000503	-0.000734	-0.000747	-0.000747	-0.000747
3	0.003561	0.002604	-0.003723	-0.003732	-0.003732	-0.003732
4	0.016696	-0.006639	-0.017758	-0.018240	-0.018247	-0.018247

For the bias term it is similar (see Table 4-7).

$$\frac{\partial L}{\partial b^{(2)}} = \frac{1}{M}(\hat{Y} - Y) \cdot \frac{\partial H^{(3)}}{\partial V^{(2)}} \cdot \frac{\partial V^{(2)}}{\partial H^{(2)}} \cdot \frac{\partial H^{(2)}}{\partial b^{(2)}}$$

$$= \frac{1}{M}(\hat{Y} - Y) \cdot W^{(3)} \cdot \left(1 - V^{(2)} \circ V^{(2)}\right) \cdot \vec{1}$$

```
dH_2_db_2 = np.ones(len(Y))
dL_db_2 = (1 / len(Y)) * dL_dH_2 @ dH_2_db_2.T
print(dL_db_2.shape)
dL_db_2

(5,)
```

Table 4-7. Gradient values for \frac{\partial L}{\partial b^{(2)}}

	0
0	0.317539
1	-0.055634
2	-0.000747
3	-0.003732
4	-0.018247

I'll leave deriving the next layer as an exercise. It should be straightforward because layer 1 is so similar to layer 2 (see Tables 4-8 and 4-9).

```
dH_2_dV_1 = W_2
dV_1_dH_1 = 1 - np.power(Vs[0], 2)
dL_dH_1 = np.multiply((dL_dH_2.T @ dH_2_dV_1).T, dV_1_dH_1)
dH_1_dW_1 = X.values.T
dL_dW_1 = (1 / len(Y)) * dL_dH_1 @ dH_1_dW_1.T
print(dL_dW_1.shape)
dL_dW_1

(6, 4)
```

Table 4-8. Gradient values for \frac{\partial L}{\partial W^{(1)}}?

	0	1	2	3
0	-1.783060e-01	-1.253225e-01	-5.240050e-02	-7.952154e-03
1	4.773021e-01	3.260914e-01	1.394070e-01	2.328259e-02
2	1.808615e-02	3.469462e-02	-4.649400e-02	-2.300012e-02
3	-7.880986e-04	-5.902413e-04	-3.475747e-05	8.403521e-05
4	4.729628e-16	-2.866947e-16	-1.341379e-16	-2.326840e-17
5	-4.116040e-06	-2.487064e-06	7.311565e-08	4.091940e-07

```
dH_1_db_1 = np.ones(len(Y))
dL_db_1 = (1 / len(Y)) * dL_dH_1 @ dH_1_db_1.T
print(dL_db_1.shape)
dL_db_1

(6,)
```

Table 4-9. Gradient values for \frac{\partial L}{\partial b^{(1)}}

	0
0	-3.627637e-02
1	9.832581e-02
2	7.392729e-03
3	-1.758950e-04
4	-1.066024e-16
5	-1.025423e-06

Now that we have calculated the gradients for our first iteration, let's build a function for doing these calculations.

```
params = [[W_1, W_2, W_3], [b_1, b_2, b_3]]
```

We need a function for calculating our gradients. This method will need the following: the inputs X, the labels Y, the predicted probabilities $\hat{Y}$, the parameters $W^{(i)}$ and $b^{(i)}$, and the intermediate values $V^{(i)}$.

```
def gradients(X, Y, Y_hat, params, Vs):
    Ws, bs = params
```

```
assert len(Ws) == len(bs)
dL_dHs = [None] * len (layers)
dL_dWs = [None] * len (layers)
dL_dbs = [None] * len (layers)
dL_dHs[2] = Y.T - Y_hat
for layer in np.arange(len(layers), 0, -1) - 1:
    dL_dH = dL_dHs[layer]
    dH_dW = Vs[layer - 1] if layer > 0 else X.T
    dL_dW = (1 / len(Y)) * dL_dH @ dH_dW.T
    dH_db = np.ones(len(Y))
    dL_db = (1 / len(Y)) * dL_dH @ dH_db
    dL_dWs[layer] = dL_dW
    dL_dbs[layer] = dL_db.reshape(len(dL_db), 1)
    if layer > 0:
        dH_dV = Ws[layer]
        # just supporting tanh
        dV_dH_next = 1 - np.power(Vs[layer - 1], 2)
        dL_dHs[layer - 1] = \
            np.multiply((dL_dH.T @ dH_dV).T, dV_dH_next)

return dL_dWs, dL_dbs
```

We need a method that will evaluate the model then calculate the loss and gradients.

```
def update(X, Y, params, learning_rate=0.1):
    Ws, bs = params
    Y_hat, Hs, Vs = forward(X, layers)
    loss = log_loss(Y.T, Y_hat)
    dWs, dbs = gradients(X, Y, Y_hat, params, Vs)
    for i in range(len(Ws)):
        Ws[i] += learning_rate * dWs[i]
        bs[i] += learning_rate * dbs[i]
    return Ws, bs, loss
```

Finally, we will have a method for training the network.

```
def train(X, Y, params, learning_rate=0.1, epochs=6000):
    X = X.values
    Y = Y.values
    Ws = [W for W in params[0]]
    bs = [b for b in params[1]]
    for i in range(epochs):
        Ws, bs, loss = update(X, Y, [Ws, bs], learning_rate)
        if i % (epochs // 10) == 0:
            print('epoch', i, 'loss', loss)
    print('epoch', i, 'loss', loss)
    return Ws, bs
```

Let's train our network. The results are shown in Table 4-10.

```
Ws, bs = train(X, Y, params)

epoch 0 loss 1.4781844247149367
epoch 600 loss 0.4520794985146122
epoch 1200 loss 0.29327186345356115
```

```
epoch 1800 loss 0.08517606119594413
epoch 2400 loss 0.057984381652688245
epoch 3000 loss 0.05092154382167823
epoch 3600 loss 0.04729254314395461
epoch 4200 loss 0.044660097961296365
epoch 4800 loss 0.038386971515831474
epoch 5400 loss 0.03735081006838356
epoch 5999 loss 0.036601105223619555

Y_hat, _, _ = forward(X, layers)
Y_hat = pd.DataFrame(Y_hat.T, columns=[c + '_prob' for c in Y.columns])
Y_hat['pred'] = np.argmax(Y_hat.values, axis=1)
Y_hat['pred'] = Y_hat['pred'].apply(Y.columns.__getitem__)
Y_hat['truth'] = Y.idxmax(axis=1)
Y_hat.head()
```

Table 4-10. Predictions from the trained model

	Iris-setosa_prob	Iris-versicolor_prob	Iris-virginica_prob	pred	truth
0	0.999263	0.000737	2.394779e-07	Iris-setosa	Iris-setosa
1	0.998756	0.001244	3.903808e-07	Iris-setosa	Iris-setosa
2	0.999256	0.000744	2.416573e-07	Iris-setosa	Iris-setosa
3	0.998855	0.001145	3.615654e-07	Iris-setosa	Iris-setosa
4	0.999376	0.000624	2.031758e-07	Iris-setosa	Iris-setosa

Let's see the proportion we got right.

```
(Y_hat['pred'] == Y_hat['truth']).mean()
```

```
0.9933333333333333
```

This is good, but we have likely overfit. When we try actual training models, we will need to create train, validation, and test data sets. The train data set will be for learning our parameters (e.g., weights), validation for learning our hyperparameters (e.g., number and sizes of layers), and finally the test data set for understanding how our model will perform on unseen data.

Let's look at the errors our model makes (see Table 4-11).

```
Y_hat[Y_hat['pred'] != Y_hat['truth']]\
  .groupby(['pred', 'truth']).size()
```

```
pred            truth
Iris-virginica  Iris-versicolor    1
dtype: int64
```

Table 4-11. Erroneous predictions

pred	truth	count
Iris-virginica	Iris-versicolor	1

It looks like the only mistake we made was misidentifying an *Iris versicolor* as an *Iris virginica*. So it looks like we have learned from this data—though we most likely have overfit to the data.

Training the model is done in batches. These batches are generally small sets of your training data. There are tradeoffs to the size of the batches: if you pick a smaller batch size, you require less computation. However, you are using less data to perform an update, which may be noisy. If you pick a larger batch size, you get a more reliable update, but this requires more computation and can lead to overfitting. The overfitting is possible because you are using more of your data to calculate the updates.

Once we have these gradients, we can use them to update our parameters and so perform gradient descent. This is a very simplified introduction to a rich and complicated topic. I encourage you to do additional learning on the topic. As we go on, I will cover deep learning topics to the depth necessary to understand how the techniques are implemented. A thorough explanation of deep learning topics is outside the scope of this book.

Now let's look at some developments on top of neural networks.

Convolutional Neural Networks

In 1959 David H. Hubel and Torsten Wiesel conducted experiments on cats that showed the existence of specialized neurons that detected edges, position, and motion. This inspired Kunihiko Fukushima to create the "cognitron" in 1975 and later the "neocognitron" in 1980. This neural network, and others based on it, included early notions of pooling layers and filters. In 1989, the modern *convolutional neural network,* or *CNN,* with weights learned fully by backpropagation, was created by Yann LeCun.

Generally, CNNs are explained with images as an example, but it's just as easy to apply these techniques to one-dimensional data.

Filters

Filters are layers that take a continuous subset of the previous layer (e.g., a block of a matrix) and feed it into a neuron in the next layer. This technique is inspired by the idea of a receptive field in the human eye, where different neurons are responsible for different regions and shapes in vision.

Imagine you have a 6×6 matrix coming into a layer. We can use a filter of size 4×4 to feed into 9 neurons. We do this by doing an element-wise multiplication between a subsection of the input matrix and the filter and then summing the products. In this example we use elements (1,1) to (4,4) with the filter for the first element of the output vector. We then multiply the elements (1,2) to (4,5) with the filter for the second element. We can also change the stride, which is the number of columns/rows for which we move the filter for each output neuron. If we have our 6×6 matrix with 4×4 filter and a stride of 2, we can feed into 4 neurons. With padding, we can add extra rows and columns of 0s to our input matrix, so that the values at the edge get the same treatment as the interior values. Otherwise, elements on the edge are used less than inner elements.

Pooling

Pooling works similarly to filters—except, instead of using weights that must be learned, simple aggregate is used. Max pooling, taking the max of the continuous subset, is the most commonly used. Though, one can use average pooling or other aggregates.

This is often useful for reducing the size of the input data without adding new parameters.

Recurrent Neural Networks

In the initial research into modeling biological neural networks, it has been assumed that memory and learning have some dependence on time. However, none of the techniques covered so far take that into account.

In a multilayer perceptron, we get one example and produce one output. The forward propagation step for one example is not affected by another example. In a *recurrent neural network*, or *RNN*, we need to be aware of the previous, and sometimes later, examples. For example, if I am trying to translate a word, it is important that I know its context.

Now, the most common type of RNN uses *long short-term memory*, or *LSTM*. To understand LSTMs, let's talk about some older techniques.

Backpropagation Through Time

The primary training algorithm for RNNs is *backpropagation through time*, or *BPTT*. This works by *unfolding* the network. Let's say we have a sequence of k items. Conceptually, unfolding works by copying the recurrent part of the network k times. Practically, it works by calculating the partial derivate of each intermediate output with respect to the parameters of the recurrent part of the network.

We will go through BPTT in depth in Chapter 8 when we cover sequence modeling.

Elman Nets

Also known as *simple RNNs*, or *SRNNs*, an Elman network reuses the output of the previous layer. Jeffrey Elman invented the Elman network in 1990. The idea is relatively straightforward. We want the output of the previous example to represent the context. We combine that output with current input, using different weights.

$$V^{(0)} = 0$$
$$1 \leq t \leq T$$
$$V^{(t)} = f_{input}\left(W_{input} \cdot X^{(t)} + U_{input} \cdot V^{(t-1)} + b_{input}\right)$$
$$Y^{(t)} = f_{output}\left(W_{output} \cdot V^{(t)} + b_{output}\right)$$

As you can see, the context is represented by $V^{(t-1)}$. This will provide information from all previous elements in the sequence to some degree. This means that the longer the sequence, the more terms there are in the gradient for the parameters. This can make the parameters change chaotically. To reduce this concern, we could use a much smaller learning rate at the cost of increased training time. We still have the chance of a training run resulting in *exploding* or *vanishing gradients*. Exploding/ vanishing gradients are when the gradients for a parameter increase rapidly or go to 0. This problem can occur in any sufficiently deep network, but RNNs are particularly susceptible.

$$\frac{\partial L}{\partial W_{input}^{(i)}} = \frac{\partial L}{\partial \widehat{Y}} \cdot \ldots \cdot \frac{\partial L}{\partial V^{(i, T)}} \cdot \Pi_{t=2}^{T} \frac{\partial V^{(i, t)}}{\partial V^{(i, t-1)}} \cdot \frac{\partial V^{(i, 1)}}{\partial W_{input}^{(i)}}$$

For long sequences, this could make our gradient go very high or very low quickly.

LSTMs

The LSTM was invented by Sepp Hochreiter and Jürgen Schmidhuber in 1997 to address the exploding/vanishing gradients problem. The idea is that we can learn how long to hold on to information by giving our recurrent units state. We can store an output produced from an element of the sequence and use this to modify the output. This state can also be connected with a notion of forgetting, so we can allow some gradients to vanish when appropriate. Here are the components of the LSTM:

$$v_0 = 0$$

$$c_0 = 0$$

$$1 \le t \le T$$

$$f_t = \sigma\left(W_f \cdot \vec{x}_t + U_f \cdot v^{(t-1)} + b_f\right)$$

$$i_t = \sigma\left(W_i \cdot \vec{x}_t + U_i \cdot v^{(t-1)} + b_i\right)$$

$$o_t = \sigma\left(W_o \cdot \vec{x}_t + U_o \cdot v^{(t-1)} + b_o\right)$$

$$\tilde{c}_t = \tanh\left(W_c \cdot \vec{x}_t + U_c \cdot v^{(t-1)} + b_c\right)$$

$$c_t = f_t \circ c_{t-1} + i_t \circ \tilde{c}_t$$

$$v_t = o_t \circ \tanh\left(c_t\right)$$

There is a lot to unpack here. We will go into more depth, including covering variants, when we get to Chapter 8, in which we present a motivating example.

Exercise 1

Being able to reason mathematically about what is happening in a neural network is important. Derive the updates for the first layer in the network mentioned in this chapter.

$$\frac{\partial L}{\partial w^{(1)}} = \frac{1}{M} \frac{\partial L}{\partial \hat{Y}} \cdot \frac{\partial \hat{Y}}{\partial w^{(1)}}$$

Exercise 2

A common exercise when studying deep learning is to implement a classifier on the Modified National Institute of Standards and Technology (MNST) data set. This classifier takes in an image of a handwritten digit and predicts which digit it represents.

There are thousands of such tutorials available, so I will not retread that overtrodden ground. I recommend doing the TensorFlow tutorial (*https://oreil.ly/PqdTQ*).

Resources

- Andrew Ng's Deep Learning Specialization (*https://oreil.ly/GiBJj*): this course is a great way to become familiar with deep learning concepts.

- TensorFlow tutorials (*https://oreil.ly/dbQ66*): TensorFlow has a number of great resources. Their tutorials are a way to get familiar with deep learning and the TensorFlow API.

- *Deep Learning* (*https://oreil.ly/Z0dPs*), by Ian Goodfellow, Yoshua Bengio, and Aaron Courville (MIT Press): this is a free online book that goes over the theory of deep learning.

- *Natural Language Processing with PyTorch* (*https://oreil.ly/NSFZY*), by Delip Rao and Brian McMahan (O'Reilly)

  — This book covers NLP with PyTorch, which is another popular deep learning library. This book won't cover PyTorch, but if you want to have a good understanding of the field, learning about PyTorch is a good idea.

- *Hands-On Machine Learning with Scikit-Learn, Keras and TensorFlow* (*https://oreil.ly/itu77*), by Aurélien Géron (O'Reilly)

  — This book covers many machine learning techniques in addition to deep learning.

## PART II

Building Blocks

In this part of the book, we will introduce the techniques you'll need for building your own NLP application. Understanding how and why these techniques work will equip you with the tools needed to apply and adapt techniques you learn here and elsewhere to your own application.

First, we will start off with the fundamental text processing tasks.

Building Blocks

## CHAPTER 5

Processing Words

This chapter focuses on the basic word-processing techniques you can apply to get started with NLP, including tokenization, vocabulary reduction, bag-of-words, and N-grams. You can solve many tasks with these techniques plus some basic machine learning. Knowing how, when, and why to use these techniques will help you with simple and complicated NLP tasks. This is why the discussion of the linguistics technique covers implementation. We will focus on working with English for now, though we will mention some things that should be considered when working with other languages. We are focusing on English because it would be very difficult to cover these techniques in depth across different languages.

Let's load the data from the mini_newsgroups again, and then we will explore tokenization.

```
import os

from pyspark.sql.types import *
from pyspark.ml import Pipeline

import sparknlp
from sparknlp import DocumentAssembler, Finisher

spark = sparknlp.start()

space_path = os.path.join('data', 'mini_newsgroups', 'sci.space')
texts = spark.sparkContext.wholeTextFiles(space_path)

schema = StructType([
    StructField('path', StringType()),
    StructField('text', StringType()),
])

texts = spark.createDataFrame(texts, schema=schema).persist()
```

```
## excerpt from mini newsgroups modified for examples
example = '''
Nick's right about this.  It's always easier to obtian forgiveness than
permission.  Not many poeple remember that Britan's Kng George III
expressly forbade his american subjects to cross the alleghany/appalachian
mountains.  Said subjects basically said, "Stop us if you can."  He
couldn't.
'''

example = spark.createDataFrame([('.', example)], schema=schema).persist()
```

Tokenization

Language data, from both text and speech, is sequential data. When working with sequential data, it is vital to understand what your sequences are made up of. On disk and in memory, our text data is a sequence of bytes. We use encodings like UTF-8 to turn these bytes into characters. This is the first step toward interpreting our data as language. This is almost always straightforward because we have agreed-upon standards for encoding characters as bytes. Turning bytes into characters is not enough to get the useful information we want, however. We next need to turn our sequence of characters into words. This is called *tokenization*.

Although we all intuitively understand what a "word" is, defining it linguistically is more difficult. Identifying a word is easy for a human. Let's look at some examples:

1. "monasticism"
2. "globglobism"
3. "xhbkgerj"
4. "-ism"

English speakers will recognize example 1 as a word, example 2 as a possible word, and example 3 as not a possible word; example 4 is trickier. The suffix "-ism" is something we attach to a word, a bound morpheme, but it has been used as an unbound morpheme. Indeed, there are languages that do not traditionally have word boundaries in their writing, like Chinese. So, although we can recognize what is and is not a word when standing alone, it is more difficult to define what is and is not a word in a sequence of words. We can go with the following definition: a sequence of morphemes is a word if splitting it apart or combining it with neighboring morphemes would change the meaning of the sentence.

In English, and other languages that use a delimiter between words, it is common to use regular expressions to tokenize. Let's look at some examples.

First, let's look at a whitespace tokenizer:

```
from pyspark.ml.feature import RegexTokenizer

ws_tokenizer = RegexTokenizer()\
    .setInputCol('text')\
    .setOutputCol('ws_tokens')\
    .setPattern('\\s+')\
    .setGaps(True)\
    .setToLowercase(False)

text, tokens = ws_tokenizer.transform(example)\
    .select("text", "ws_tokens").first()

print(text)
```

Nick's right about this. It's always easier to obtian forgiveness than permission. Not many poeple remember that Britan's Kng George III expressly forbade his American subjects to cross the alleghany/appalachian mountains. Said subjects basically said, "Stop us if you can." He couldn't.

```
print(tokens)
```

["Nick's", 'right', 'about', 'this.', "It's", 'always', 'easier', 'to', 'obtian', 'forgiveness', 'than', 'permission.', 'Not', 'many', 'poeple', 'remember', 'that', "Britan's", 'Kng', 'George', 'III', 'expressly', 'forbade', 'his', 'American', 'subjects', 'to', 'cross', 'the', 'alleghany/appalachian', 'mountains.', 'Said', 'subjects', 'basically', 'said,', '"Stop', 'us', 'if', 'you', 'can."', 'He', "couldn't."]

This leaves a lot to be desired. We can see that we have many tokens that are words with some punctuation attached. Let's add the boundary pattern "\b."

```
b_tokenizer = RegexTokenizer()\
    .setInputCol('text')\
    .setOutputCol('b_tokens')\
    .setPattern('\\s+|\\b')\
    .setGaps(True)\
    .setToLowercase(False)

text, tokens = b_tokenizer.transform(example)\
    .select("text", "b_tokens").first()

print(text)
```

Nick's right about this. It's always easier to obtian forgiveness than permission. Not many poeple remember that Britan's Kng George III expressly forbade his American subjects to cross the alleghany/appalachian mountains. Said subjects basically said, "Stop us if you can." He couldn't.

```
print(tokens)
```

['Nick', "'", 's', 'right', 'about', 'this', '.', 'It', "'", 's', 'always', 'easier', 'to', 'obtian', 'forgiveness', 'than', 'permission', '.', 'Not', 'many', 'poeple', 'remember', 'that', 'Britan', "'", 's', 'Kng', 'George', 'III', 'expressly', 'forbade', 'his', 'American',

```
'subjects', 'to', 'cross', 'the', 'alleghany', '/', 'appalachian',
'mountains', '.', 'Said', 'subjects', 'basically', 'said', ',', '"',
'Stop', 'us', 'if', 'you', 'can', '."', 'He', 'couldn', "'", 't', '.']
```

We have the punctuation separated, but now all the contractions are broken into three tokens—for example, "It's" becomes "It", """, "s". This is less than ideal.

In Spark NLP, the tokenizer is more sophisticated than just single regex. It takes the following parameters (apart from the usual input and output column name parameters):

compositeTokens
These are multitoken words that you may not want to split (e.g., "New York").

targetPattern
This is the basic pattern for defining candidate tokens.

infixPatterns
These are the patterns for separating tokens that are found inside candidate tokens.

prefixPattern
This is the pattern for separating tokens that are found at the beginning of candidate tokens.

suffixPattern
This is the pattern for separating tokens that are found at the end of candidate tokens.

The algorithm works in the following steps:

1. Protect the composite tokens.

2. Create the candidate tokens.

3. Separate out the prefix, infix, and suffix patterns.

Let's see an example.

```
from sparknlp.annotator import Tokenizer

assembler = DocumentAssembler()\
    .setInputCol('text')\
    .setOutputCol('doc')
tokenizer = Tokenizer()\
    .setInputCols(['doc'])\
    .setOutputCol('tokens_annotations')
finisher = Finisher()\
    .setInputCols(['tokens_annotations'])\
    .setOutputCols(['tokens'])\
    .setOutputAsArray(True)
```

```
pipeline = Pipeline()\
    .setStages([assembler, tokenizer, finisher])

text, tokens = pipeline.fit(texts).transform(example)\
    .select("text", "tokens").first()

print(text)
```

Nick's right about this. It's always easier to obtian forgiveness than
permission. Not many poeple remember that Britan's Kng George III
expressly forbade his American subjects to cross the alleghany/appalachian
mountains. Said subjects basically said, "Stop us if you can." He
couldn't.

```
print(tokens)
```

['Nick', "'s", 'right', 'about', 'this', '.', 'It', "'s", 'always',
'easier', 'to', 'obtian', 'forgiveness', 'than', 'permission', '.',
'Not', 'many', 'poeple', 'remember', 'that', 'Britan', "'s", 'Kng',
'George', 'III', 'expressly', 'forbade', 'his', 'American', 'subjects',
'to', 'cross', 'the', 'alleghany/appalachian', 'mountains', '.', 'Said',
'subjects', 'basically', 'said', ',', '"', 'Stop', 'us', 'if', 'you',
'can', '.', '"', 'He', 'could', "n't", '.']

Here we see that the punctuation is separated out, and the contractions are split into two tokens. This matches closely with the intuitive definition of the word.

Now that we have our tokens, we have another thing to contend with—reducing our vocabulary.

Vocabulary Reduction

Most NLP tasks involve turning the text into vectors. Initially, your vectors will have dimension equal to your vocabulary. An implicit assumption to doing this is that the words are orthogonal to each other. In terms of words, this means that "cat," "dog," and "dogs" are all considered equally different. We would like to represent words in a vector space that is somehow related to their meaning, but that is more complicated. We will cover such representations in Chapters 10 and 11. There are simpler ways to tackle this problem, however. If we know that two words are almost the same, or are at least equivalent for our purposes, we can represent them with the same dimension in our vector. This will help classification, regression, and search tasks. So how can we do this? We can use our knowledge of morphology (how words are constructed from smaller words and affixes). We can remove affixes before constructing our vector. The two primary techniques for doing this are *stemming* and *lemmatization*.

Stemming

Stemming is the process of removing affixes and leaving a word stem. This is done according to sets of rules that determine what characters to delete or replace. The first stemming algorithm was created by Julie Beth Lovins in 1968, although there had been earlier work done on the subject. In 1980, Martin Porter created the Porter Stemmer. This is certainly the most well-known stemming algorithm. He later created a domain-specific language and associated tools for writing stemming algorithms called *snowball*. Although people almost always use a predefined stemmer, if you find that there are affixes that are not being removed but should be, or the other way around, consider writing or modifying an existing algorithm.

Lemmatization

Lemmatization is the process of replacing a word with its *lemma* or *head-word*. The lemma is the form of a word that has a full dictionary entry. For example, if you look up "oxen" in a dictionary, it will likely redirect you to "ox." Algorithmically, this is easy to implement but is dependent on the data you use for looking up lemmas.

Stemming Versus Lemmatization

There are pros and cons to both stemming and lemmatization.

- Stemming has the pro of requiring almost no memory, unlike lemmatization, which requires a dictionary.
- Lemmatization is generally quicker, since it is just a hash map lookup.
- Stemming can be easily tuned because it is based on an algorithm instead of a data source.
- Lemmatization returns an actual word, which makes inspecting results easier.

Which method you use will depend on your task and your resource constraints.

Use stemming if:

- You need to tune how much you reduce your vocabulary.
- You have tight memory constraints and fewer time constraints.
- You expect many new or unknown words.

Use lemmatization if:

- You need results of processing exposed to users.
- You have tight time constraints and less restriction on memory.

Let's look at some examples of using stemming and lemmatization in Spark NLP.

```
from sparknlp.annotator import Stemmer, Lemmatizer, LemmatizerModel

assembler = DocumentAssembler()\
    .setInputCol('text')\
    .setOutputCol('doc')
tokenizer = Tokenizer()\
    .setInputCols(['doc'])\
    .setOutputCol('tokens_annotations')
stemmer = Stemmer()\
    .setInputCols(['tokens_annotations'])\
    .setOutputCol('stems_annotations')
# The next line downloads lemmatizer "model". Here, "training"
# is reading the user supplied dictionary
lemmatizer = LemmatizerModel.pretrained()\
    .setInputCols(['tokens_annotations'])\
    .setOutputCol('lemma_annotations')
finisher = Finisher()\
    .setInputCols(['stems_annotations', 'lemma_annotations'])\
    .setOutputCols(['stems', 'lemmas'])\
    .setOutputAsArray(True)

pipeline = Pipeline()\
    .setStages([
        assembler, tokenizer, stemmer, lemmatizer, finisher])
text, stems, lemmas = pipeline.fit(texts).transform(example)\
    .select("text", "stems", "lemmas").first()

print(text)
```

```
Nick's right about this.  It's always easier to obtian forgiveness than
permission.  Not many poeple remember that Britan's Kng George III
expressly forbade his American subjects to cross the alleghany/appalachian
mountains.  Said subjects basically said, "Stop us if you can."  He
couldn't.
```

```
print(stems)
```

```
['nick', "'", 'right', 'about', 'thi', '.', 'it', "'", 'alwai', 'easier',
'to', 'obtian', 'forgiv', 'than', 'permiss', '.', 'not', 'mani', 'poepl',
'rememb', 'that', 'britan', "'", 'kng', 'georg', 'iii', 'expressli',
'forbad', 'hi', 'american', 'subject', 'to', 'cross', 'the',
'alleghany/appalachian', 'mountain', '.', 'said', 'subject', 'basic',
'said', ',', '"', 'stop', 'u', 'if', 'you', 'can', '.', '"', 'he',
'could', "n't", '.']
```

```
print(lemmas)
```

```
['Nick', 'have', 'right', 'about', 'this', '.', 'It', 'have', 'always',
'easy', 'to', 'obtian', 'forgiveness', 'than', 'permission', '.', 'Not',
'many', 'poeple', 'remember', 'that', 'Britan', 'have', 'Kng', 'George',
'III', 'expressly', 'forbid', 'he', 'American', 'subject', 'to', 'cross',
'the', 'alleghany/appalachian', 'mountain', '.', 'Said', 'subject',
```

```
'basically', 'say', ',', '"', 'Stop', 'we', 'if', 'you', 'can', '.', '"',
'He', 'could', 'not', '.']
```

Some examples to note:

- The word "forbade" is stemmed to "forbad" and lemmatized to "forbid."

- The contraction "n't" is not affected by stemming, but lemmatization converts it to "not."

- The word "forgiveness" is stemmed to "forgiv" and it is not affected by lemmatization.

- The word "Britain's" (a possessive) is stemmed to `["britain", "'"]` and lemmatized to `["Britain", "have"]` erroneously.

Note for Non-English Languages

The typology of the language will greatly influence which approach is easier. There are common forms of words that have drastically different meanings. For example, in Spanish we would not want to combine "puerto" ("port") and "puerta" ("door"), but we may want to combine "niño" ("boy") and "niña" ("girl"). This means that reductions will be dependent on the lexical semantics (meaning of the word). This would be near impossible to fully support in a stemming algorithm, so you likely want to lemmatize. On the other hand, if a language has a rich morphology, the lemma dictionary will be very large (the number of forms times the number of words).

Spelling Correction

An often overlooked aspect of vocabulary reduction is misspellings. In text that is not edited or proofread by the author, this can create a very long tail. Worse, there are some mistakes that are so common that the misspelling can actually be a moderately common token, which makes it very hard to remove.

There are two approaches to spelling correction in Spark NLP. *SymmetricDelete* needs a set of correct words to search. This vocabulary can be provided as a dictionary, or by providing a trusted corpus. It is based on the SymSpell project by Wolf Garbe. The other approach is the *Norvig* spelling correction algorithm, which works by creating a simple probability model. This approach also needs a correct vocabulary, but it suggests the most probable word—i.e., the most frequent word in the trusted corpus with a certain edit distance from the given word.

Let's look at the pretrained Norvig spelling correction.

```
from sparknlp.annotator import NorvigSweetingModel
from sparknlp.annotator import SymmetricDeleteModel

# Norvig pretrained
assembler = DocumentAssembler()\
    .setInputCol('text')\
    .setOutputCol('doc')
tokenizer = Tokenizer()\
    .setInputCols(['doc'])\
    .setOutputCol('tokens_annotations')
norvig_pretrained = NorvigSweetingModel.pretrained()\
    .setInputCols(['tokens_annotations'])\
    .setOutputCol('norvig_annotations')
finisher = Finisher()\
    .setInputCols(['norvig_annotations'])\
    .setOutputCols(['norvig'])\
    .setOutputAsArray(True)

pipeline = Pipeline()\
    .setStages([
    assembler, tokenizer, norvig_pretrained, lemmatizer, finisher])
text, norvig = pipeline.fit(texts).transform(example)\
    .select("text", "norvig").first()

print(text)
```

Nick's right about this. It's always easier to obtian forgiveness than
permission. Not many poeple remember that Britan's Kng George III
expressly forbade his American subjects to cross the alleghany/appalachian
mountains. Said subjects basically said, "Stop us if you can." He
couldn't.

```
print(norvig)
```

```
['Nick', "'s", 'right', 'about', 'this', '.', 'It', "'s", 'always',
'easier', 'to', 'obtain', 'forgiveness', 'than', 'permission', '.', 'Not',
'many', 'people', 'remember', 'that', 'Britain', "'s", 'Kng', 'George',
'III', 'expressly', 'forbade', 'his', 'American', 'subjects', 'to',
'cross', 'the', 'alleghany/appalachian', 'mountains', '.', 'Said',
'subjects', 'basically', 'said', ',', '"', 'Stop', 'us', 'if', 'you',
'can', '.', '"', 'He', 'could', "n't", '.']
```

We see that "obtian," "poeple," and "Britan" are all corrected. However, "Kng" is missed, and "american" is converted to "Americana." The latter two mistakes are likely due to capitalization, which makes matching with the probability model more difficult.

Normalization

This is a more heuristic-based cleanup step. If you are processing data scraped from the web, it is not uncommon to have HTML artifacts (tags, HTML encodings, etc.) left behind. Getting rid of these artifacts can reduce your vocabulary by quite a bit. If your task does not require numbers or anything nonalphabetic, for instance, you can also use normalization to remove these.

```
from sparknlp.annotator import Normalizer

assembler = DocumentAssembler()\
    .setInputCol('text')\
    .setOutputCol('doc')
tokenizer = Tokenizer()\
    .setInputCols(['doc'])\
    .setOutputCol('tokens_annotations')
norvig_pretrained = NorvigSweetingModel.pretrained()\
    .setInputCols(['tokens_annotations'])\
    .setOutputCol('norvig_annotations')
lemmatizer = LemmatizerModel.pretrained()\
    .setInputCols(['norvig_annotations'])\
    .setOutputCol('lemma_annotations')
normalizer = Normalizer()\
    .setInputCols(['lemma_annotations'])\
    .setOutputCol('normtoken_annotations')\
    .setLowercase(True)
finisher = Finisher()\
    .setInputCols(['normtoken_annotations'])\
    .setOutputCols(['normtokens'])\
    .setOutputAsArray(True)

sparknlp_pipeline = Pipeline().setStages([
    assembler, tokenizer, norvig_pretrained,
    lemmatizer, normalizer, finisher
])

pipeline = Pipeline()\
    .setStages([
        assembler, tokenizer, norvig_pretrained,
        lemmatizer, normalizer, finisher])
text, normalized = pipeline.fit(texts).transform(example)\
    .select("text", "normtokens").first()

print(text)

Nick's right about this.  It's always easier to obtian forgiveness
than permission.  Not many poeple remember that Britan's Kng
George III expressly forbade his american subjects to cross the
alleghany/appalachian mountains.  Said subjects basically said,
"Stop us if you can."  He couldn't.

print(normalized)
```

```
['nicks', 'right', 'about', 'this', 'itys', 'always', 'easy', 'to',
 'obtain', 'forgiveness', 'than', 'permission', 'not', 'many',
 'people', 'remember', 'that', 'britans', 'kng', 'george', 'iii',
 'expressly', 'forbid', 'he', 'americana', 'subject', 'to', 'cross',
 'the', 'alleghanyappalachian', 'mountain', 'said', 'subject',
 'basically', 'say', 'stop', 'we', 'if', 'you', 'can', 'he',
 'couldnt']
```

Bag-of-Words

Now that we have reduced our vocabulary by combining similar and misspelled words and removing HTML artifacts, we can feel confident that the vocabulary we are working with is a realistic reflection of the content of our documents. The next step is to turn these words into vectors for our model. There are many techniques for doing this, but we will start with the most straightforward approach, called *bag-of-words*. A *bag* (also called a multiset), is a set in which each element has a count. If you are familiar with the Python collection Counter, that is a good way to understand what a bag is. And so, a bag-of-words is the count of the words in our document. Once we have these counts, we turn them into a vector by mapping each unique word to an index.

Let's look at a simple example using Python's Counter.

```python
text = "the cat in the hat"
tokens = text.split()
tokens

['the', 'cat', 'in', 'the', 'hat']

from collections import Counter

counts = Counter(tokens)
counts

Counter({'the': 2, 'cat': 1, 'in': 1, 'hat': 1})

index = {token: ix for ix, token in enumerate(counts.keys())}
index

{'the': 0, 'cat': 1, 'in': 2, 'hat': 3}

import numpy as np

vec = np.zeros(len(index))

for token, count in counts.items():
    vec[index[token]] = count

vec

array([2., 1., 1., 1.])
```

The example we have is for only one document. If we are working on a large corpus, our index will have far more words than we would expect to ever find in a single document. It is not uncommon for corpus vocabularies to number in the tens of thousands or hundreds of thousands, even though a single document will generally have tens to hundreds of unique words. For this reason, we want our vectors to be *sparse*.

A *sparse* vector is one in which only the nonzero values are stored. Sparse vectors are generally implemented as associative arrays, maps, or dictionaries from index to value. For sparse data, like bags-of-words, this can save a great deal of space. However, not all algorithms are implemented in a way that is compatible with sparse vectors.

In Spark, we can use the CountVectorizer to create our bags-of-words.

CountVectorizer

```python
from pyspark.ml.feature import CountVectorizer

assembler = DocumentAssembler()\
    .setInputCol('text')\
    .setOutputCol('doc')
tokenizer = Tokenizer()\
    .setInputCols(['doc'])\
    .setOutputCol('tokens_annotations')
norvig_pretrained = NorvigSweetingModel.pretrained()\
    .setInputCols(['tokens_annotations'])\
    .setOutputCol('norvig_annotations')
lemmatizer = LemmatizerModel.pretrained()\
    .setInputCols(['norvig_annotations'])\
    .setOutputCol('lemma_annotations')
normalizer = Normalizer()\
    .setInputCols(['lemma_annotations'])\
    .setOutputCol('normtoken_annotations')\
    .setLowercase(True)
finisher = Finisher()\
    .setInputCols(['normtoken_annotations'])\
    .setOutputCols(['normtokens'])\
    .setOutputAsArray(True)

sparknlp_pipeline = Pipeline().setStages([
    assembler, tokenizer, norvig_pretrained,
    lemmatizer, normalizer, finisher
])

count_vectorizer = CountVectorizer()\
    .setInputCol('normtokens')\
    .setOutputCol('bows')

pipeline = Pipeline().setStages([sparknlp_pipeline, count_vectorizer])
```

```
model = pipeline.fit(texts)
processed = model.transform(example)
text, normtokens, bow = processed\
    .select("text", "normtokens", 'bows').first()

print(text)
```

Nick's right about this. It's always easier to obtian forgiveness than
permission. Not many poeple remember that Britan's Kng George III
expressly forbade his American subjects to cross the alleghany/appalachian
mountains. Said subjects basically said, "Stop us if you can." He
couldn't.

```
print(normtokens)
```

['nick', 'have', 'right', 'about', 'this', 'it', 'have', 'always', 'easy',
'to', 'obtain', 'forgiveness', 'than', 'permission', 'not', 'many',
'people', 'remember', 'that', 'britain', 'have', 'kng', 'george', 'iii',
'expressly', 'forbid', 'he', 'american', 'subject', 'to', 'cross', 'the',
'alleghanyappalachian', 'mountain', 'said', 'subject', 'basically', 'say',
'stop', 'we', 'if', 'you', 'can', 'he', 'could', 'not']

Let's look at the bag-of-words. This will be a sparse vector, so the elements are indices into the vocabulary and counts of occurrences. For example, 7: 3.0 means that the seventh word in our vocabulary occurs three times in this document.

```
bow
```

SparseVector(5319, {0: 1.0, 3: 2.0, 7: 3.0, 9: 1.0, 10: 1.0, 14: 2.0, 15:
1.0, 17: 1.0, 28: 1.0, 30: 1.0, 31: 2.0, 37: 1.0, 52: 1.0, 67: 1.0, 79:
2.0, 81: 1.0, 128: 1.0, 150: 1.0, 182: 1.0, 214: 1.0, 339: 1.0, 369: 1.0,
439: 1.0, 459: 1.0, 649: 1.0, 822: 1.0, 953: 1.0, 1268: 1.0, 1348: 1.0,
1698: 1.0, 2122: 1.0, 2220: 1.0, 3149: 1.0, 3200: 1.0, 3203: 1.0, 3331:
1.0, 3611: 1.0, 4129: 1.0, 4840: 1.0})

We can get the learned vocabulary from the CountVectorizerModel. This is the list of words. In the previous example, we said that the seventh word occurs three times in a document. Looking at this vocabulary, that means that "have" occurs three times.

```
count_vectorizer_model = model.stages[-1]
```

```
vocab = count_vectorizer_model.vocabulary
print(vocab[:20])
```

['the', 'be', 'of', 'to', 'and', 'a', 'in', 'have', 'for', 'it', 'that',
'i', 'on', 'from', 'not', 'you', 'space', 'this', 'they', 'as']

The drawback to doing this is that we lose the meaning communicated by the arrangement of the words—the syntax. To say that parsing the syntax of natural language is difficult is an understatement. Fortunately, we often don't need all the information encoded in the syntax.

N-Gram

The main drawback to using bag-of-words is that we are making use of only the meanings encoded in individual words and document-wide context. Language encodes a great deal of meaning in local contexts as well. Syntax is hard to model, let alone parse. Fortunately, we can use N-grams to extract some of the context without needing to use a complicated syntax parser.

N-grams, also known as *shingles*, are subsequences of words of length n within a string of words. They allow us to extract information from small windows of context. This gives us a first approximation of the information we can gather from syntax because, although we are looking at local context, there is structural information explicitly extracted. In many applications, N-grams are enough to extract the information necessary.

For low values of n there are special names. For example, 1-grams are called unigrams, 2-grams are called bigrams, and 3-grams are called trigrams. For values higher than 3, they are usually referred to as "number" + grams, like 4-grams.

Let's look at some example N-grams.

```
text = "the quick brown fox jumped over the lazy dog"
tokens = ["the", "quick", "brown", "fox", "jumped", "over", "the", "lazy",
"dog"]
unigrams = [('the',), ('quick',), ('brown',), ('fox',), ('jumped',), ('over',),
('the',), ('lazy',), ('dog',)]
bigrams = [('the', 'quick'), ('quick', 'brown'), ('brown', 'fox'), ('fox', 'jum-
ped'), ('jumped', 'over'), ('over', 'the'), ('the', 'lazy'), ('lazy', 'dog')]
trigrams = [('the', 'quick', 'brown'), ('quick', 'brown', 'fox'), ('brown',
'fox', 'jumped'), ('fox', 'jumped', 'over'), ('jumped', 'over', 'the'),
('over', 'the', 'lazy'), ('the', 'lazy', 'dog')]
```

We still need to determine our n. Generally, n is less than 4. Consider the largest size multiword phrase you think will be important to your application. This will generally depend on the length of your documents and how technical the language is expected to be. In hospital medical records or in long documents with highly technical language, 3, 4, or even 5-grams might be useful. For tweets or short documents with informal language, bigrams should suffice.

Let's look at some examples.

```
from pyspark.ml.feature import NGram

bigrams = NGram()\
    .setN(2)\
    .setInputCol("normtokens")\
    .setOutputCol("bigrams")
trigrams = NGram()\
    .setN(3)\
    .setInputCol("normtokens")\
```

```
        .setOutputCol("trigrams")

pipeline = Pipeline().setStages([sparknlp_pipeline, bigrams, trigrams])
model = pipeline.fit(texts)
processed = model.transform(example)
text, normtokens, bigrams, trigrams = processed\
    .select("text", "normtokens", 'bigrams', 'trigrams').first()

print(text)
```

Nick's right about this. It's always easier to obtian forgiveness than
permission. Not many poeple remember that Britan's Kng George III
expressly forbade his American subjects to cross the alleghany/appalachian
mountains. Said subjects basically said, "Stop us if you can." He
couldn't.

```
print(normtokens)
```

['nick', 'have', 'right', 'about', 'this', 'it', 'have', 'always', 'easy',
'to', 'obtain', 'forgiveness', 'than', 'permission', 'not', 'many',
'people', 'remember', 'that', 'britain', 'have', 'kng', 'george', 'iii',
'expressly', 'forbid', 'he', 'american', 'subject', 'to', 'cross', 'the',
'alleghanyappalachian', 'mountain', 'said', 'subject', 'basically', 'say',
'stop', 'we', 'if', 'you', 'can', 'he', 'could', 'not']

```
print(bigrams)
```

['nick have', 'have right', 'right about', 'about this', 'this it',
'it have', 'have always', 'always easy', 'easy to', 'to obtain',
'obtain forgiveness', 'forgiveness than', 'than permission',
'permission not', 'not many', 'many people', 'people remember',
'remember that', 'that britain', 'britain have', 'have kng', 'kng george',
'george iii', 'iii expressly', 'expressly forbid', 'forbid he',
'he american', 'american subject', 'subject to', 'to cross', 'cross the',
'the alleghanyappalachian', 'alleghanyappalachian mountain',
'mountain said', 'said subject', 'subject basically', 'basically say',
'say stop', 'stop we', 'we if', 'if you', 'you can', 'can he', 'he could',
'could not']

```
print(trigrams)
```

['nick have right', 'have right about', 'right about this',
'about this it', 'this it have', 'it have always', 'have always easy',
'always easy to', 'easy to obtain', 'to obtain forgiveness',
'obtain forgiveness than', 'forgiveness than permission',
'than permission not', 'permission not many', 'not many people',
'many people remember', 'people remember that', 'remember that britain',
'that britain have', 'britain have kng', 'have kng george',
'kng george iii', 'george iii expressly', 'iii expressly forbid',
'expressly forbid he', 'forbid he american', 'he american subject',
'american subject to', 'subject to cross', 'to cross the',
'cross the alleghanyappalachian', 'the alleghanyappalachian mountain',
'alleghanyappalachian mountain said', 'mountain said subject',
'said subject basically', 'subject basically say', 'basically say stop',
'say stop we', 'stop we if', 'we if you', 'if you can', 'you can he',
'can he could', 'he could not']

Visualizing: Word and Document Distributions

Now that we have learned how to extract tokens, we can look at how we can visualize a data set. We will look at two visualizations: word frequencies and word clouds from the space and autos newsgroups. They represent the same information but in different ways.

```
from sparknlp.pretrained import PretrainedPipeline

space_path = os.path.join('data', 'mini_newsgroups', 'sci.space')
space = spark.sparkContext.wholeTextFiles(space_path)

schema = StructType([
    StructField('path', StringType()),
    StructField('text', StringType()),
])

space = spark.createDataFrame(space, schema=schema).persist()

sparknlp_pipeline = PretrainedPipeline(
    'explain_document_ml', lang='en').model

normalizer = Normalizer()\
    .setInputCols(['lemmas'])\
    .setOutputCol('normalized')\
    .setLowercase(True)

finisher = Finisher()\
    .setInputCols(['normalized'])\
    .setOutputCols(['normalized'])\
    .setOutputAsArray(True)

count_vectorizer = CountVectorizer()\
    .setInputCol('normalized')\
    .setOutputCol('bows')

pipeline = Pipeline().setStages([
    sparknlp_pipeline, normalizer, finisher, count_vectorizer])
model = pipeline.fit(space)
processed = model.transform(space)

vocabulary = model.stages[-1].vocabulary
word_counts = Counter()

for row in processed.toLocalIterator():
    for ix, count in zip(row['bows'].indices, row['bows'].values):
        word_counts[vocabulary[ix]] += count

from matplotlib import pyplot as plt
%matplotlib inline
```

```
y = list(range(20))
top_words, counts = zip(*word_counts.most_common(20))

plt.figure(figsize=(10, 8))
plt.barh(y, counts)
plt.yticks(y, top_words)
plt.show()
```

Figure 5-1 shows the word frequencies from the space newsgroup.

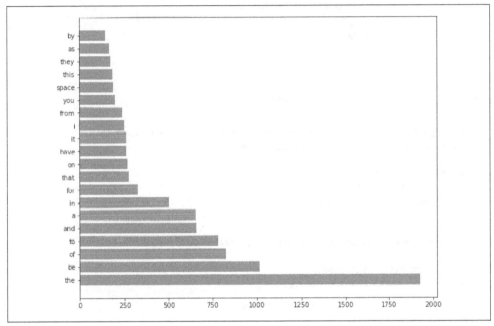

Figure 5-1. Word frequencies for the documents from the space newsgroup

```
from wordcloud import WordCloud

plt.figure(figsize=(10, 8))
wc = WordCloud(colormap='Greys', background_color='white')
im = wc.generate_from_frequencies(word_counts)
plt.imshow(im, interpolation='bilinear')
plt.axis("off")
plt.title('sci.space')

plt.show()
```

Figure 5-2 shows the word cloud from the space newsgroup.

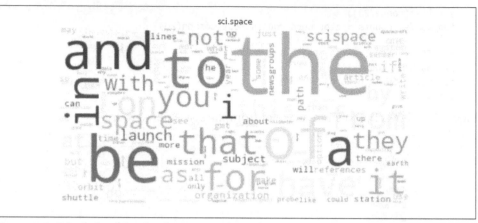

Figure 5-2. Word cloud for the documents from the space newsgroup

```
autos_path = os.path.join('data', 'mini_newsgroups', 'rec.autos')
autos = spark.sparkContext.wholeTextFiles(autos_path)

schema = StructType([
    StructField('path', StringType()),
    StructField('text', StringType()),
])

autos = spark.createDataFrame(autos, schema=schema).persist()

model = pipeline.fit(autos)
processed = model.transform(autos)

vocabulary = model.stages[-1].vocabulary
word_counts = Counter()

for row in processed.toLocalIterator():
    for ix, count in zip(row['bows'].indices, row['bows'].values):
        word_counts[vocabulary[ix]] += count

y = list(range(20))
top_words, counts = zip(*word_counts.most_common(20))

plt.figure(figsize=(10, 8))
plt.barh(y, counts)
plt.yticks(y, top_words)
plt.show()
```

Figure 5-3 shows the word frequencies from the autos newsgroup.

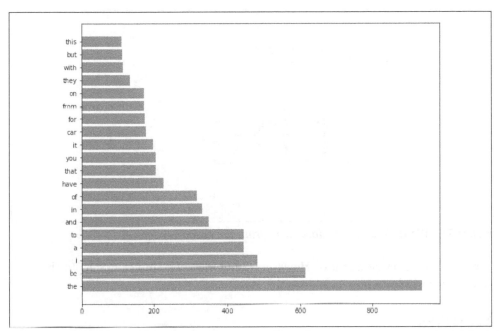

Figure 5-3. Word frequencies for the documents from the autos newsgroup

```
from wordcloud import WordCloud

plt.figure(figsize=(10, 8))
wc = WordCloud(colormap='Greys', background_color='white')
im = wc.generate_from_frequencies(word_counts)
plt.imshow(im, interpolation='bilinear')
plt.axis("off")
plt.title('rec.autos')

plt.show()
```

Figure 5-4 shows the word cloud from the autos newsgroup.

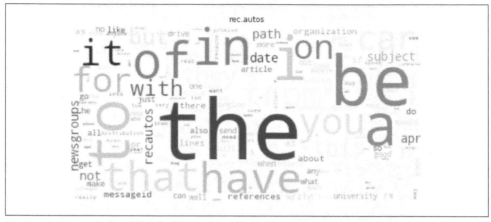

Figure 5-4. Word cloud for the documents from the autos newsgroup

Now we can visualize our text. However, they have such similar words. In the next chapter, we will learn how to address this issue.

Exercises

We've visualized unigrams, but we have a problem with common words. Let's try visualizing N-grams. Try bigrams and trigrams.

Resources

- Google Ngram Viewer (*https://oreil.ly/ja0Sz*): Google offers a way to look at the occurrence of N-grams in books through history.
- Hunspell (*https://oreil.ly/fb_gD*): Hunspell is a very broadly used library for spell-checking and morphological analysis.

## CHAPTER 6

Information Retrieval

In the previous chapter we came across common words that made it difficult to characterize a corpus. This is a problem for different kinds NLP tasks. Fortunately, the field of information retrieval has developed many techniques that can be used to improve a variety of NLP applications.

Earlier, we talked about how text data exists, and more is being generated every day. We need some way to manage and search through this data. If there is an ID or title, we can of course have an index on this data, but how do we search by content? With structured data, we can create logical expressions and retrieve all rows that satisfy the expressions. This can also be done with text, though less exactly.

The foundation of information retrieval predates computers. Information retrieval focuses on how to find specific pieces of information in a larger set of information, especially information in text data. The most common type of task in information retrieval is search—in other words, document search.

The following are the components of a document search:

Query q
A logical statement describing the document or kind of document you are looking for

Query term q_t
A term in the query, generally a token

Corpus of documents D
A collection of documents

Document d
A document in D with terms t_d that describe the document

Ranking function r(q, D)

A function that ranks the documents in D according to *relevance* to the query q

Result R

The ranked list of documents

Before we get into how to implement these components, we need to consider a technical problem. How can we quickly access documents based on the information within them? If we have to scan every document, then we could not search large collections of documents. To solve this problem we use an *inverted index*.

Inverted Indices

Originally, *indexing* was a means of organizing and labeling information in a way that made retrieving it easier. For example, libraries use indexing to organize and find books. The Dewey Decimal Classification system is a way to index books based on their subject matter. We can also have indices based on titles, authors, publication dates, and so on. Another kind of index can often be found at the back of a book. This is a list of concepts in the book and pages on which to find them.

The *index* in *inverted index* is slightly different than the traditional index; instead, it takes inspiration from the mathematical concept of indexing—that is, assigning indices to an element of a set. Recall our set of documents D. We can assign a number to each document, creating mapping from integers to documents, i -> d.

Let's create this index for our DataFrame. Normally, we would store an inverted index in a data store that allows for quick lookups. Spark DataFrames are not for quick lookups. We will introduce the tools used for search.

Building an Inverted Index

Let's look at how we can build an inverted index in Spark. Here are the steps we will follow:

1. Load the data.
2. Create the index: i -> d*
   - Since we are using Spark, we will generate this index on the rows.
3. Process the text.
4. Create the inverted index from terms to documents: t_d -> i*

Step 1

We will be creating an inverted index for the mini_newsgroups data set.

```
import os

from pyspark.sql.types import *
from pyspark.sql.functions import collect_set
from pyspark.sql import Row
from pyspark.ml import Pipeline

import sparknlp
from sparknlp import DocumentAssembler, Finisher
from sparknlp.annotator import *

spark = sparknlp.start()

path = os.path.join('data', 'mini_newsgroups', '*')
texts = spark.sparkContext.wholeTextFiles(path)

schema = StructType([
    StructField('path', StringType()),
    StructField('text', StringType()),
])

texts = spark.createDataFrame(texts, schema=schema).persist()
```

Step 2

Now we need to create the index. Spark assumes the data is distributed, so to assign an index, we need to use the lower-level RDD API. The zipWithIndex will sort the data on the workers and assign the indices.

```
rows_w_indexed = texts.rdd.zipWithIndex()
(path, text), i = rows_w_indexed.first()

print(i)
print(path)
print(text[:200])

0
file:/home/alext/projects/spark-nlp-book/data/mini_...
Xref: cantaloupe.srv.cs.cmu.edu sci.astro:35223 sci.space:61404
Newsgroups: sci.astro,sci.space
Path: cantaloupe.srv.cs.cmu.edu!das-news.harvard.edu!...
```

Now that we have created the index, we need to create a DataFrame like we did previously, except now we need to add our index into our Rows. Table 6-1 shows the result.

```
indexed = rows_w_indexed.map(
    lambda row_index: Row(
        index=row_index[1],
        **row_index[0].asDict())
)
(i, path, text) = indexed.first()

indexed_schema = schema.add(StructField('index', IntegerType()))
```

```
indexed = spark.createDataFrame(indexed, schema=indexed_schema)\
    .persist()

indexed.limit(10).toPandas()
```

Table 6-1. Indexed documents

	path	text	index
0	file:/.../spark-nlp-book/data/m...	Newsgroups: rec.motorcycles\nFrom: lisa@alex.c...	0
1	file:/.../spark-nlp-book/data/m...	Path: cantaloupe.srv.cs.cmu.edu!das-news.harva...	1
2	file:/.../spark-nlp-book/data/m...	Newsgroups: rec.motorcycles\nPath: cantaloupe....	2
3	file:/.../spark-nlp-book/data/m...	Xref: cantaloupe.srv.cs.cmu.edu rec.motorcycle...	3
4	file:/.../spark-nlp-book/data/m...	Path: cantaloupe.srv.cs.cmu.edu!das-news.harva...	4
5	file:/.../spark-nlp-book/data/m...	Path: cantaloupe.srv.cs.cmu.edu!magnesium.club...	5
6	file:/.../spark-nlp-book/data/m...	Newsgroups: rec.motorcycles\nPath: cantaloupe....	6
7	file:/.../spark-nlp-book/data/m...	Newsgroups: rec.motorcycles\nPath: cantaloupe....	7
8	file:/.../spark-nlp-book/data/m...	Path: cantaloupe.srv.cs.cmu.edu!rochester!udel...	8
9	file:/.../spark-nlp-book/data/m...	Path: cantaloupe.srv.cs.cmu.edu!crabapple.srv....	9

Each document d is a collection of terms, t_d. So our index is the mapping from integers to collections of terms.

An inverted index, on the other hand, is the mapping from terms t_d to integers, inv-index: t_d -> i, j, k, ... This allows us to quickly look up what documents contain a given term.

Step 3

Now let's process the text (see Table 6-2).

```
from sparknlp.pretrained import PretrainedPipeline

assembler = DocumentAssembler()\
    .setInputCol('text')\
    .setOutputCol('document')
tokenizer = Tokenizer()\
    .setInputCols(['document'])\
    .setOutputCol('token')
lemmatizer = LemmatizerModel.pretrained()\
    .setInputCols(['token'])\
    .setOutputCol('lemma')
normalizer = Normalizer()\
    .setInputCols(['lemma'])\
    .setOutputCol('normalized')\
    .setLowercase(True)
finisher = Finisher()\
    .setInputCols(['normalized'])\
    .setOutputCols(['normalized'])\
    .setOutputAsArray(True)
```

```
pipeline = Pipeline().setStages([
    assembler, tokenizer,
    lemmatizer, normalizer, finisher
]).fit(indexed)

indexed_w_tokens = pipeline.transform(indexed)

indexed_w_tokens.limit(10).toPandas()
```

Table 6-2. Documents with normalized tokens

	path	text	index	normalized
0	file:/.../spark-nlp-book/data/m...	...	0	[newsgroups, recmotorcycles, from, lisaalexcom...
1	file:/.../spark-nlp-book/data/m...	...	1	[path, cantaloupesrvcscmuedudasnewsharvardedun...
2	file:/.../spark-nlp-book/data/m...	...	2	[newsgroups, recmotorcycles, path, cantaloupes...
3	file:/.../spark-nlp-book/data/m...	...	3	[xref, cantaloupesrvcscmuedu, recmotorcyclesha...
4	file:/.../spark-nlp-book/data/m...	...	4	[path, cantaloupesrvcscmuedudasnewsharvardeduo
5	file:/.../spark-nlp-book/data/m...	...	5	[path, cantaloupesrvcscmuedumagnesiumclubcccmu...
6	file:/.../spark-nlp-book/data/m...	...	6	[newsgroups, recmotorcycles, path, cantaloupes...
7	file:/.../spark-nlp-book/data/m...	...	7	[newsgroups, recmotorcycles, path, cantaloupes...
8	file:/.../spark-nlp-book/data/m...	...	8	[path, cantaloupesrvcscmuedurochesterudelbogus...
9	file:/.../spark-nlp-book/data/m...	...	9	[path, cantaloupesrvcscmueducrabapplesivcscmue...

Because we are using a small data set, we will move out of Spark for the purposes of this example. We will collect our data into pandas and use our index field as our DataFrame index.

```
doc_index = indexed_w_tokens.select('index', 'path', 'text').toPandas()
doc_index = doc_index.set_index('index')
```

Step 4

Now, let us create our inverted index. We will use Spark SQL to do this. The result is shown in Table 6-3.

```
SELECT term, collect_set(index) AS documents
FROM (
    SELECT index, explode(normalized) AS term
    FROM indexed_w_tokens
)
GROUP BY term
ORDER BY term

inverted_index = indexed_w_tokens\
    .selectExpr('index', 'explode(normalized) AS term')\
    .distinct()\
    .groupBy('term').agg(collect_set('index').alias('documents'))\
    .persist()
```

```
inverted_index.show(10)
```

Table 6-3. Inverted index (mapping from term to document index)

	term	documents
0	aaangel.qdeck.com	[198]
1	accumulation	[857]
2	adventists	[314]
3	aecfb.student.cwru.edu	[526]
4	again...hmmm	[1657]
5	alt.binaries.pictures	[815]
6	amplifier	[630, 624, 654]
7	antennae	[484, 482]
8	apr..gordian.com	[1086]
9	apr..lokkur.dexter.mi.us	[292]

This is our inverted index. We can see that the term "amplifier" occurs in documents 630, 624, and 654. With this information, we can quickly find all documents that contain particular terms.

Another benefit is that this inverted index is based on the size of our vocabulary, not on the amount of text in our corpus, so it is not *big data*. The inverted index grows only with new terms and document indices. For very large corpora, this can still be a large amount of data for a single machine. In the case of the mini_newsgroups data set, however, it is easily manageable.

Let's see how big our inverted index is.

```
inverted_index.count()

42624
```

For us, since we have such a small number of documents, the inverted index has more entries than the index. Word frequencies follow Zipf's law—that is, the frequency of a word is inversely proportional to its rank when sorted. As a result, the most-used English words are already in our inverted index. This can be further constrained by not tracking words that don't occur at least a certain number of times.

```
inverted_index = {
    term: set(docs)
    for term, docs in inverted_index.collect()
}
```

Now we can begin our most basic ranking function—*simple Boolean search*. In this case, let's look up all the documents that contain the words "language" or "information."

```
lang_docs = inverted_index['language']
print('docs', ('{}, ' * 10).format(*list(lang_docs)[:10]), '...')
print('number of docs', len(lang_docs))

docs 1926, 1937, 1171, 1173, 1182, 1188, 1830, 808, 1193, 433,  ...
number of docs 44

info_docs = inverted_index['information']
print('docs', ('{}, ' * 10).format(*list(info_docs)[:10]), '...')
print('number of docs', len(info_docs))

docs 516, 519, 520, 1547, 1035, 1550, 1551, 17, 1556, 22,  ...
number of docs 215

filter_set = list(lang_docs | info_docs)
print('number of docs in filter set', len(filter_set))

number of docs in filter set 246

intersection = list(lang_docs & info_docs)
print('number of docs in intersection set', len(intersection))

number of docs in intersection set 13
```

Let's print out lines from our filter set. Here, the filter set is the result set, but generally, the filter set is ranked by r(q, D), which results in the result set.

Let's look at the lines in which we see the occurrences, to get an idea about our result set.

```
k = 1
for i in filter_set:
    path, text = doc_index.loc[i]
    lines = text.split('\n')
    print(path.split('/')[-1], 'length:', len(text))
    for line_number, line in enumerate(lines):
        if 'information' in line or 'language' in line:
            print(line_number, line)
    print()
    k += 1
    if k > 5:
        break

178813 length: 1783
14 >>    Where did you get this information?  The FBI stated ...

104863 length: 2795
14 of information that I received, but as my own bad mouthing) ...

104390 length: 2223
51 ... appropriate disclaimer to outgoing public information,

178569 length: 11735
60  confidential information obtained illegally from law ...
64  ... to allegations of obtaining confidential information from
86  employee and have said they simply traded information with ...
```

```
 91   than truthful" in providing information during an earlier ...
125   and Department of Motor Vehicles information such as ...
130   Bullock also provided information to the South African ...
142   information.
151   exchanged information with the FBI and worked with ...
160   information in Los Angeles, San Francisco, New York, ...
168   some confidential information in the Anti-Defamation ...
182   police information on citizens and groups.
190   ... spying operations, which collected information on more than
209   information to police, journalists, academics, government ...
211   information illegally, he said.
215   identity of any source of information," Foxman said.

104616 length: 1846
 45 ... an appropriate disclaimer to outgoing public information,
```

Now that we have our result set, how should we rank our results? We could just count the number of occurrences of our search term, but that would be biased toward long documents. Also, what happens if our query includes a very common word like "the"? If we just use the counts, common words like "the" will dominate our results. In our result set, the one with the most occurrences of the query terms has the longest text. We could say that the more terms found in the document, the more relevant the document is, but this has problems too. What do we do with one-term queries? In our example, only one document has both. Again, if our query has a common word— for example, "the cat in the hat"—should "the" and "in" have the same importance as "cat" and "hat"? To solve this problem, we need a more flexible model for our documents and queries.

Vector Space Model

In the previous chapter, we introduced the concept of vectorizing documents. We talked about creating binary vectors, where 1 means that the word is present in the document. We can also use the counts.

When we convert a corpus to a collection of vectors, we are implicitly modeling our language as a vector space. In this vector space, each dimension represents one term. This has many benefits and drawbacks. It is a simple way to represent our text in a manner that allows machine learning algorithms to work with it. It also allows us to represent the vectors sparsely. On the other hand, we lose the information contained in the word order. This process also creates high dimensional data sets, which can be problematic to some algorithms.

Let's calculate the vectors for our data set. In the previous chapter, we used the Count Vectorizer for this. We will build the vectors in Python, but the way we will build them will help us understand how libraries implement vectorization.

```
class SparseVector(object):

    def __init__(self, indices, values, length):
        # if the indices are not in ascending order, we need
        # to sort them
        is_ascending = True
        for i in range(len(indices) - 1):
            is_ascending = is_ascending and indices[i] < indices[i+1]
        if not is_ascending:
            pairs = zip(indices, values)
            sorted_pairs = sorted(pairs, key=lambda x: x[0])
            indices, values = zip(*sorted_pairs)
        self.indices = indices
        self.values = values
        self.length = length

    def __getitem__(self, index):
        try:
            return self.values[self.indices.index(index)]
        except ValueError:
            return 0.0

    def dot(self, other):
        assert isinstance(other, SparseVector)
        assert self.length == other.length
        res = 0
        i = j = 0
        while i < len(self.indices) and j < len(other.indices):
            if self.indices[i] == other.indices[j]:
                res += self.values[i] * other.values[j]
                i += 1
                j += 1
            elif self.indices[i] < other.indices[j]:
                i += 1
            elif self.indices[i] > other.indices[j]:
                j += 1
        return res

    def hadamard(self, other):
        assert isinstance(other, SparseVector)
        assert self.length == other.length
        res_indices = []
        res_values = []
        i = j = 0
        while i < len(self.indices) and j < len(other.indices):
            if self.indices[i] == other.indices[j]:
                res_indices.append(self.indices[i])
                res_values.append(self.values[i] * other.values[j])
                i += 1
                j += 1
            elif self.indices[i] < other.indices[j]:
                i += 1
```

```
                elif self.indices[i] > other.indices[j]:
                    j += 1
            return SparseVector(res_indices, res_values, self.length)

        def sum(self):
            return sum(self.values)

        def __repr__(self):
            return 'SparseVector({}, {})'.format(
                dict(zip(self.indices, self.values)), self.length)
```

We need to make two passes over all the documents. In the first pass, we will get our vocabulary and the counts. In the second pass we will construct the vectors.

```
from collections import Counter

vocabulary = set()
vectors = {}

for row in indexed_w_tokens.toLocalIterator():
    counts = Counter(row['normalized'])
    vocabulary.update(counts.keys())
    vectors[row['index']] = counts

vocabulary = list(sorted(vocabulary))
inv_vocabulary = {term: ix for ix, term in enumerate(vocabulary)}
vocab_len = len(vocabulary)
```

Now that we have this information, we need to go back over our word counts and construct actual vectors.

```
for index in vectors:
    terms, values = zip(*vectors[index].items())
    indices = [inv_vocabulary[term] for term in terms]
    vectors[index] = SparseVector(indices, values, vocab_len)

vectors[42]
```

```
SparseVector({56: 1, 630: 1, 678: 1, 937: 1, 952: 1, 1031: 1, 1044: 1,
1203: 1, 1348: 1, 1396: 5, 1793: 1, 2828: 1, 3264: 3, 3598: 3, 3753: 1,
4742: 1, 5907: 1, 7990: 1, 7999: 1, 8451: 1, 8532: 1, 9570: 1, 11031: 1,
11731: 1, 12509: 1, 13555: 1, 13772: 1, 14918: 1, 15205: 1, 15350: 1,
15475: 1, 16266: 1, 16356: 1, 16865: 1, 17236: 2, 17627: 1, 17798: 1,
17931: 2, 18178: 1, 18329: 2, 18505: 1, 18730: 3, 18776: 1, 19346: 1,
19620: 1, 20381: 1, 20475: 1, 20594: 1, 20782: 1, 21831: 1, 21856: 1,
21907: 1, 22560: 1, 22565: 2, 22717: 1, 23714: 1, 23813: 1, 24145: 1,
24965: 3, 25937: 1, 26437: 1, 26438: 1, 26592: 1, 26674: 1, 26679: 1,
27091: 1, 27109: 1, 27491: 2, 27500: 1, 27670: 1, 28583: 1, 28864: 1,
29636: 1, 31652: 1, 31725: 1, 31862: 1, 33382: 1, 33923: 1, 34311: 1,
34451: 1, 34478: 1, 34778: 1, 34904: 1, 35034: 1, 35635: 1, 35724: 1,
36136: 1, 36596: 1, 36672: 1, 37048: 1, 37854: 1, 37867: 3, 37872: 1,
37876: 3, 37891: 1, 37907: 1, 37949: 1, 38002: 1, 38224: 1, 38225: 2,
38226: 3, 38317: 3, 38856: 1, 39818: 1, 40870: 1, 41238: 1, 41239: 1,
41240: 1, 41276: 1, 41292: 1, 41507: 1, 41731: 1, 42384: 2}, 42624)
```

Let's look at some of the words that occur the most.

```
vocabulary[3598]

'be'

vocabulary[37876]

'the'
```

As we discussed previously, there are many drawbacks to using only the counts for a search. The concern is that words that are generally common in English will have more impact than the less common words. There are a couple strategies for addressing this. First, let's look at the simplest solution—removing the common words.

Stop-Word Removal

These common words we are looking to remove are called *stop words*. This term was coined in the 1950s by Hans Peter Luhn, a pioneer in information retrieval. Default stop-word lists are available, but it is often necessary to modify generic stop-word lists for different tasks.

```
from pyspark.ml.feature import StopWordsRemover

sw_remover = StopWordsRemover() \
    .setInputCol("normalized") \
    .setOutputCol("filtered") \
    .setStopWords(StopWordsRemover.loadDefaultStopWords("english"))

filtered = sw_remover.transform(indexed_w_tokens)

from collections import Counter

vocabulary_filtered = set()
vectors_filtered = {}

for row in filtered.toLocalIterator():
    counts = Counter(row['filtered'])
    vocabulary_filtered.update(counts.keys())
    vectors_filtered[row['index']] = counts

vocabulary_filtered = list(sorted(vocabulary_filtered))
inv_vocabulary_filtered = {
    term: ix
    for ix, term in enumerate(vocabulary_filtered)
}
vocab_len_filtered = len(vocabulary)

for index in vectors:
    terms, values = zip(*vectors_filtered[index].items())
    indices = [inv_vocabular_filteredy[term] for term in terms]
    vectors_filtered[index] = \
        SparseVector(indices, values, vocab_len_filtered)
```

```
vectors[42]
```

```
SparseVector({630: 1, 678: 1, 952: 1, 1031: 1, 1044: 1, 1203: 1, 1348: 1,
1793: 1, 2828: 1, 3264: 3, 4742: 1, 5907: 1, 7990: 1, 7999: 1, 8451: 1,
8532: 1, 9570: 1, 11031: 1, 11731: 1, 12509: 1, 13555: 1, 13772: 1,
14918: 1, 15205: 1, 15350: 1, 16266: 1, 16356: 1, 16865: 1, 17236: 2,
17627: 1, 17798: 1, 17931: 2, 18178: 1, 18505: 1, 18776: 1, 20475: 1,
20594: 1, 20782: 1, 21831: 1, 21856: 1, 21907: 1, 22560: 1, 22565: 2,
22717: 1, 23714: 1, 23813: 1, 24145: 1, 25937: 1, 26437: 1, 26438: 1,
26592: 1, 26674: 1, 26679: 1, 27109: 1, 27491: 2, 28583: 1, 28864: 1,
29636: 1, 31652: 1, 31725: 1, 31862: 1, 33382: 1, 33923: 1, 34311: 1,
34451: 1, 34478: 1, 34778: 1, 34904: 1, 35034: 1, 35724: 1, 36136: 1,
36596: 1, 36672: 1, 37048: 1, 37872: 1, 37891: 1, 37949: 1, 38002: 1,
38224: 1, 38225: 2, 38226: 3, 38856: 1, 39818: 1, 40870: 1, 41238: 1,
41239: 1, 41240: 1, 41276: 1, 41731: 1}, 42624)
```

```
vocabulary[3264]
```

```
'bake'
```

```
vocabulary[38226]
```

```
'timmons'
```

The words "bake" and "timmons" seem more informative. You should explore your data when determining what words should be included in the stop-word list.

It may seem like a daunting task to list all the words we don't want. However, recalling what we discussed about morphology, we can narrow down what we want to remove. We want to remove unbound function morphemes.

A fluent speaker of a language, who knows these basics of morphology, is able to create a reasonably good list. However, this still leaves two concerns. What if we need to keep some common words? What if we want to remove some common lexical morphemes? You can modify the list, but that still leaves one last concern. How do we handle queries like "fictional cats"? The word "fictional" is less common than "cats," so it makes sense that the former should be more important in determining what documents are returned. Let's look at how we can implement this using our data.

Inverse Document Frequency

Instead of manually editing our vocabulary, we can try and weight the words. We need to find some way of weighting the words using their "commonness." One way to define "commonness" is by identifying the number of documents in our corpus that contain the word. This is generally called *document frequency*. We want words with high document frequency to be down-weighted, so we are interested in using inverse document frequency (IDF).

We take these values and multiply them by the *term frequencies*, which are the frequencies of words in a given document. The result of multiplying inverse document frequency by term frequency gives us the TF.IDF.

$$tf(t, d) = \text{the number of times } t \text{ occurs in } d$$
$$df(t) = \text{the number of documents } t \text{ occurs in}$$
$$idf(t) = \frac{\text{the number of documents}}{df(t)}$$

There are many different flavors of TF.IDF. The most common kind is smoothed logarithmic.

$$tf(t, d) = log(1 + \text{the number of times } t \text{ occurs in } d)$$
$$df(t) = \text{the number of documents } t \text{ occurs in}$$
$$idf(t) = log\left(\frac{\text{the number of documents}}{1 + df(t)}\right)$$

Let's calculate this with our vectors. We actually already have the term frequency, so all we need to do is calculate the idf, transform the values with log, and multiply tf and idf.

```python
idf = Counter()

for vector in vectors.values():
    idf.update(vector.indices)

for ix, count in idf.most_common(20):
    print('{:5d} {:20s} {:d}'.format(ix, vocabulary[ix], count))
```

```
11031 date                 2000
15475 from                 2000
23813 messageid            2000
26438 newsgroups           2000
28583 path                 2000
36672 subject              2000
21907 lines                1993
27897 organization         1925
37876 the                  1874
 1793 apr                  1861
 3598 be                   1837
38317 to                   1767
27500 of                   1756
   56 a                    1730
16266 gmt                  1717
18329 i                    1708
18730 in                   1695
 1396 and                  1674
15166 for                  1474
17238 have                 1459
```

We can now make idf a SparseVector. We know it contains all the words, so it actually won't be sparse, but this will help us implement the next steps.

```
indices, values = zip(*idf.items())
idf = SparseVector(indices, values, vocab_len)

from math import log

for index, vector in vectors.items():
    vector.values = list(map(lambda v: log(1+v), vector.values))

idf.values = list(map(lambda v: log(vocab_len / (1+v)), idf.values))

tfidf = {index: tf.hadamard(idf) for index, tf in vectors.items()}

tfidf[42]

SparseVector({56: 2.2206482367540246, 630: 5.866068667810157,
678: 5.793038323439593, 937: 2.7785503981772224, 952: 5.157913986067814,
...,
41731: 2.4998956290056062, 42384: 3.8444034764394415}, 42624)
```

Let's look at the TF.IDF values for "be" and "the." Let's also look at one of the terms with a higher TF.IDF than these common words.

```
tfidf[42][3598] # be

4.358148273729854

tfidf[42][37876] # the

4.3305185461380855

vocabulary[17236], tfidf[42][17236]

('hausmann', 10.188396765921954)
```

Let's look at the document to get an idea of why this word is so important.

```
print(doc_index.loc[42]['text'])

Path: cantaloupe.srv.cs.cmu.edu!das-news.harvard...
From: timmbake@mcl.ucsb.edu (Bake Timmons)
Newsgroups: alt.atheism
Subject: Re: Amusing atheists and agnostics
Message-ID: <timmbake.735285604@mcl>
Date: 20 Apr 93 06:00:04 GMT
Sender: news@ucsbcsl.ucsb.edu
Lines: 32

Maddi Hausmann chirps:

>timmbake@mcl.ucsb.edu (Bake Timmons) writes: >

...

>"Killfile" Keith Allen Schneider = Frank "Closet Theist" O'Dwyer = ...

= Maddi "The Mad Sound-O-Geek" Hausmann
```

```
...whirrr...click...whirrr

--
Bake Timmons, III
...
```

We can see the document is talking about some person named "Maddi Hausman."

In Spark

Spark has stages for calculating TF.IDF in MLlib. If you have a column that contains arrays of strings, you can use either `CountVectorizer`, which we are already familiar with, or `HashingTF` to get the `tf` values. `HashingTF` uses the *hashing trick*, in which you decide on a vector space beforehand, and hash the words into that vector space. If there is a collision, then those words will be counted as the same. This lets you trade off between memory efficiency and accuracy. As you make your predetermined vector space larger, the output vectors become larger, but the chance of collisions decreases.

Now that we know how to turn a document into a vector, in the next chapter we can explore how we can use that vector in classic machine learning tasks.

Exercises

Now that we have calculated the TF.IDF values, let's build a search function. First, we need a function to process the query.

```
def process_query(query, pipeline):
    data = spark.createDataFrame([(query,)], ['text'])
    return pipeline.transform(data).first()['normalized']
```

Then we need a function to get the filter set.

```
def get_filter_set(processed_query):
    filter_set = set()
    # find all the documents that contain any of the terms
    return filter_set
```

Next, we need a function that will compute the score for the document.

```
def get_score(index, terms):
    return # return a single score
```

We also want a function for displaying results.

```
def display(index, score, terms):
    hits = [term for term in terms if term in vocabulary and tfidf[index]
[inv_vocabulary[term]] > 0.]
    print('terms', terms, 'hits', hits)
    print('score', score)
```

```
        print('path', path)
        print('length', len(doc_index.loc[index]['text']))
```

Finally, we are ready for our search function.

```
def search(query, pipeline, k=5):
    processed_query = process_query(query, pipeline)
    filter_set = get_filter_set(processed_query)
    scored = {index: get_score(index, processed_query) for index in filter_set}
    display_list = list(sorted(filter_set, key=scored.get, reverse=True))[:k]
    for index in display_list:
        display(index, scored[index], processed_query)

search('search engine', pipeline)
```

You should be able to implement get_filter_set and get_score easily using examples in this chapter. Try out a few queries. You will likely notice that there are two big limitations here. There is no N-gram support, and the ranker is biased toward longer documents. What could you modify to fix these problems?

Resources

- *An Introduction to Information Retrieval* (*https://oreil.ly/KFZa_*), by Christopher D. Manning, Prabhakar Raghavan, and Hinrich Schütze: this book covers many important aspects of information retrieval. Two of its three authors are also authors of *Foundations of Statistical Natural Language Processing*.
- Apache Lucene (*https://oreil.ly/zM92X*): this is the most-used open source search engine. Often, one of the search platforms built on top of Lucene are used, Apache Solr (*https://oreil.ly/mn5OF*) or Elasticsearch (*https://oreil.ly/gSR6U*).
- *Lucene in Action*, 2nd ed., by Michael McCandless, Erik Hatcher, and Otis Gospodnetic (Manning Publications)
  - A guide to implementing searches using Lucene
- *Elasticsearch: The Definitive Guide* (*https://oreil.ly/81xh0*), by Clinton Gormley and Zachary Tong (O'Reilly)
  - A guide to implementing searches using Elasticsearch
- *Learning to Rank for Information Retrieval*, by Tie-Yan Liu (Springer)
  - Learning to rank, building machine learning–based rankers, is an important part of modern search engines. Tie-Yan Liu is one the most important contributors to the field of learning to rank.

## CHAPTER 7

Classification and Regression

The most common machine learning tasks performed on documents are *classification* and *regression*. From determining insurance billing codes for a clinical note (classification) to predicting the popularity of a social media post (regression), most document-level machine learning tasks fall into one of these categories, with classification being the much more common of the two.

When beginning a machine learning task, it is very informative to try and manually label some documents, even if there are already labels in the data set. This will help you understand what content in the language of the documents can be used in your task. When labeling, note what you look for. For example, particular words or phrases, certain sections of the document, and even document length can be useful.

In a chapter about classification and regression, you might expect most of the discussion to be about different modeling algorithms. With NLP, most of the work is in the featurization. Many of the general techniques for improving models will work with NLP, assuming you have created good features. We will go over some of the considerations for tuning modeling algorithms, but most of this chapter focuses on how to featurize text for classification and regression.

We'll discuss the bag-of-words approach, regular expression-based features, and feature selection. After this, we will talk about how to iterate when building a model on text data.

Let's load and process the mini_newsgroups data, so we can see examples of how to create these features.

```
import os
import re

import matplotlib.pyplot as plt
import numpy as np
```

```
import pandas as pd

from pyspark.sql.types import *
from pyspark.sql.functions import expr
from pyspark.sql import Row
from pyspark.ml import Pipeline

import sparknlp
from sparknlp import DocumentAssembler, Finisher
from sparknlp.annotator import *

%matplotlib inline

spark = sparknlp.start()
```

We will build a classifier to identify which newsgroup a document is from. The newsgroup is mentioned in the header of the documents, so let's remove those to be more sporting.

```
HEADER_PTN = re.compile(r'^[a-zA-Z-]+:.*')

def remove_header(path_text_pair):
    path, text = path_text_pair
    lines = text.split('\n')
    line_iterator = iter(lines)
    while HEADER_PTN.match(next(line_iterator)) is not None:
        pass
    return path, '\n'.join(line_iterator)

path = os.path.join('data', 'mini_newsgroups', '*')
texts = spark.sparkContext.wholeTextFiles(path).map(remove_header)

schema = StructType([
    StructField('path', StringType()),
    StructField('text', StringType()),
])

texts = spark.createDataFrame(texts, schema=schema) \
    .withColumn('newsgroup', expr('split(path, "/")[7]')) \
    .persist()

texts.groupBy('newsgroup').count().collect()

[Row(newsgroup='comp.windows.x', count=100),
 Row(newsgroup='misc.forsale', count=100),
 Row(newsgroup='rec.sport.hockey', count=100),
 Row(newsgroup='rec.sport.baseball', count=100),
 Row(newsgroup='talk.politics.guns', count=100),
 Row(newsgroup='comp.os.ms-windows.misc', count=100),
 Row(newsgroup='talk.politics.misc', count=100),
 Row(newsgroup='comp.sys.ibm.pc.hardware', count=100),
 Row(newsgroup='comp.graphics', count=100),
 Row(newsgroup='soc.religion.christian', count=100),
 Row(newsgroup='comp.sys.mac.hardware', count=100),
```

```
 Row(newsgroup='talk.religion.misc', count=100),
 Row(newsgroup='talk.politics.mideast', count=100),
 Row(newsgroup='rec.motorcycles', count=100),
 Row(newsgroup='rec.autos', count=100),
 Row(newsgroup='alt.atheism', count=100),
 Row(newsgroup='sci.electronics', count=100),
 Row(newsgroup='sci.space', count=100),
 Row(newsgroup='sci.med', count=100),
 Row(newsgroup='sci.crypt', count=100)]
```

```
print(texts.first()['path'])
print(texts.first()['newsgroup'])
print(texts.first()['text'])
```

```
file:/home/.../spark-nlp-book/data/mini_newsgroups/...
rec.motorcycles
Can anyone recommend a good place for reasonably priced bike paint
jobs, preferably but not essentially in the London area.

Thanks

Lisa Rowlands
--
Alex Technologies Ltd           CP House
                                97-107 Uxbridge Road
Tel:  +44 (0)81 566 2307        Ealing
Fax:  +44 (0)81 566 2308        LONDON
email: lisa@alex.com            W5 5LT
```

```
assembler = DocumentAssembler()\
    .setInputCol('text')\
    .setOutputCol('document')
sentence = SentenceDetector() \
    .setInputCols(["document"]) \
    .setOutputCol("sentences")
tokenizer = Tokenizer()\
    .setInputCols(['sentences'])\
    .setOutputCol('token')
lemmatizer = LemmatizerModel.pretrained()\
    .setInputCols(['token'])\
    .setOutputCol('lemma')
normalizer = Normalizer()\
    .setCleanupPatterns([
        '[^a-zA-Z.-]+',
        '^[^a-zA-Z]+',
        '[^a-zA-Z]+$',
    ])\
    .setInputCols(['lemma'])\
    .setOutputCol('normalized')\
    .setLowercase(True)
finisher = Finisher()\
    .setInputCols(['normalized'])\
    .setOutputCols(['normalized'])\
    .setOutputAsArray(True)
```

```
pipeline = Pipeline().setStages([
    assembler, sentence, tokenizer,
    lemmatizer, normalizer, finisher
]).fit(texts)

processed = pipeline.transform(texts).persist()

print(processed.count()) # number of documents

2000
```

Bag-of-Words Features

In the previous chapter we discussed document vectors built with TF.IDF. These features are the most common kinds of features used in document classification and regression. There is some difficulty in using features like this, however. Depending on the size of your corpus, you could potentially have more than a hundred thousand features, where any example will have only a few hundred to a few thousand nonzero features. This can be handled by creating a sparse representation of your feature matrix, where 0 values are omitted. However, not all training algorithms support sparse matrices. This is where the vocabulary reduction techniques we discussed in Chapter 5 become important.

If you have already reduced your vocabulary, but you still need to reduce the number of your features, it is time to consider using a restricted vocabulary. For example, when working with clinical data, it might be best to restrict your vocabulary to medical terminology. This can be done by using external resources like the Unified Medical Language Service (UMLS). If you are working in other domains, consider curating a wordlist. Curated vocabularies can be a filter for your features. There are some pros and cons to such vocabularies, though. They are not biased by the information in your data set, so they will not contribute to overfitting. Conversely, there may be features that are unlikely to show up in a generalized curated list that are genuinely useful. This is why it is important for you to label some examples during iterations of your model building. If you have filtered your vocabulary, you can sample the erroneously classified examples for additions to your vocabulary.

The extension of this manual feature selection is trying to combine parts of the vocabulary into a smaller set of features. This can be done with regular expressions.

Let's look at an example of bag-of-words in Spark (see Table 7-1).

```
from pyspark.ml.feature import CountVectorizer, IDF

count_vectorizer = CountVectorizer(
    inputCol='normalized', outputCol='tf', minDF=10)
idf = IDF(inputCol='tf', outputCol='tfidf', minDocFreq=10)

bow_pipeline = Pipeline(stages=[count_vectorizer, idf])
```

```
bow_pipeline = bow_pipeline.fit(processed)

bows = bow_pipeline.transform(processed)

bows.limit(5).toPandas()[['tf', 'tfidf']]
```

Table 7-1. TF and TF.IDF values per document per term

	tf	tfidf
0	(1.0, 0.0, 0.0, 0.0, 1.0, 0.0, 0.0, 1.0, 0.0, ...	(0.07307056787648658, 0.0, 0.0, 0.0, 0.1507415...
1	(21.0, 10.0, 16.0, 2.0, 9.0, 9.0, 28.0, 12.0, ...	(1.5344819254062183, 0.915192734288196, 2.1079...
2	(1.0, 5.0, 2.0, 2.0, 4.0, 0.0, 3.0, 1.0, 0.0, ...	(0.07307056787648658, 0.457596367144098, 0.263...
3	(4.0, 5.0, 4.0, 2.0, 6.0, 2.0, 3.0, 1.0, 0.0, ...	(0.2922822715059463, 0.457596367144098, 0.5269...
4	(6.0, 2.0, 2.0, 0.0, 2.0, 1.0, 3.0, 3.0, 2.0, ...	(0.4384234072589195, 0.1830385468576392, 0.263...

Regular Expression Features

Let's say you are trying to separate short stories into genres. For this example, we have only three genres in our corpus: science fiction, fantasy, and horror. We can create specific features to help us classify. If we have word lists, we can combine them into a single feature. There are a couple of ways to do this.

- Use bag-of-words features and create a feature that is the result of aggregating the TF.IDF values of the features with sum or max.
- Create a new feature by creating a new token. You can preprocess the documents, adding a tag to any document that contains a word from the vocabulary. You can then calculate TF.IDF for this tag.

We can add other kinds of features. For example, it is common in science fiction to refer to rare and fictional minerals—for example, dilithium (both a real substance and a fictional mineral in *Star Trek*) and adamantium (a fictional alloy in Marvel comics). We could create a regular expression that looks for the common endings to these minerals.

```
(lith|ant|an)ium
```

Discovering which of these features will help us classify is a task on which the data scientist and the domain expert should collaborate. The data scientist can find features that are potentially helpful to the model. The domain expert can identify which features are actually related to the problem and which are spuriously correlated with the target variable.

These features are useful for a first version of a model, but they have some serious drawbacks. If you wish to build a similar model on text in another language, it is very likely that you will not be able to reuse regular expression features.

Let's use the `RegexMatcher` from Spark NLP for finding matches in the text of the document.

```
%%writefile scifi_rules.tsv
\w+(lith|ant|an)ium,mineral
(alien|cosmic|quantum|dimension(al)?),space_word

regex_matcher = RegexMatcher() \
    .setOutputCol("regex") \
    .setExternalRules('./scifi_rules.tsv', ',')
```

Because the `RegexMatcher` works on the raw text, it does not need the other stages. Normally, you would extract the regex matches along with other text-based features. The results are shown in Table 7-2.

```
regex_finisher = Finisher()\
    .setInputCols(['regex'])\
    .setOutputCols(['regex'])\
    .setOutputAsArray(True)

regex_rule_pipeline = Pipeline().setStages([
    assembler, regex_matcher, regex_finisher
]).fit(texts)

regex_matches = regex_rule_pipeline.transform(texts)

regex_matches.orderBy(expr('size(regex)').desc())\
    .limit(5).toPandas()[['newsgroup', 'regex']]
```

Table 7-2. Matches from the scifi_rules in the documents

	newsgroup	regex
0	talk.politics.guns	[alien, alien, alien, alien, alien, alien, alien]
1	comp.graphics	[dimensional, dimension, dimensional, dimension]
2	sci.space	[cosmic, cosmic, cosmic]
3	sci.med	[dimensional, alien, dimensional]
4	sci.space	[quantum, quantum, cosmic]

There are a few ways in which these can be turned into features. You can create binary features—in other words, the value is 1 if any of the regexes match. You can also use the number of matches as a feature.

Now that we have introduced two of the most common classic NLP features, let's talk about how we reduce our dimensions.

Feature Selection

Once you have determined a set of features, often a mix of bag-of-words and regular expressions, you may find that you have a very high dimensional feature space. This will depend very much on the sort of language used in the corpus. In highly technical corpora, it is not uncommon to have more features than examples. If you look at the distribution, you will see that they are distributed by a power law.

We can use the Spark `StopWordsRemover` to remove words like "the" and "of," like we discussed in Chapter 6.

```
from pyspark.ml.feature import StopWordsRemover

sw_remover = StopWordsRemover() \
    .setInputCol("normalized") \
    .setOutputCol("filtered") \
    .setStopWords(StopWordsRemover.loadDefaultStopWords("english"))
```

Finally, we turn this into a pipeline. It is important to include your text processing steps in your pipeline. This will let you explore hyperparameters of your machine learning model alongside NLP parameters. This gets more important the more complex your NLP preprocessing becomes. We will also include our bag-of-words stages.

```
count_vectorizer = CountVectorizer(inputCol='filtered',
    outputCol='tf', minDF=10)
idf = IDF(inputCol='tf', outputCol='tfidf', minDocFreq=10)

pipeline = Pipeline() \
    .setStages([
        assembler,
        sentence,
        tokenizer,
        lemmatizer,
        normalizer,
        finisher,
        sw_remover,
        count_vectorizer,
        idf
    ]) \
    .fit(texts)
```

Now that we have our pipeline constructed, we transform our texts.

```
features = pipeline.transform(texts).persist()

features.printSchema()

root
 |-- path: string (nullable = true)
 |-- text: string (nullable = true)
 |-- newsgroup: string (nullable = true)
 |-- normalized: array (nullable = true)
```

```
|    |-- element: string (containsNull = true)
|-- filtered: array (nullable = true)
|    |-- element: string (containsNull = true)
|-- tf: vector (nullable = true)
|-- tfidf: vector (nullable = true)
```

In Spark MLlib, the features are stored in a single vector-valued column. This is much more efficient than creating a column for each of the features, but it does make interacting with the data more complicated. To deal with this, we will be pulling the data into a pandas `DataFrame`. We can do this because our data is small and can fit in memory. This would not work on a larger data set.

Now that we have a fitted `CountVectorizerModel`, we can look at the vocabulary it found. The words are sorted by document frequency.

```
pipeline.stages
```

```
[DocumentAssembler_e20c28c687ac,
 SentenceDetector_3ac13139f56d,
 REGEX_TOKENIZER_543fbefa0fa3,
 LEMMATIZER_c62ad8f355f9,
 NORMALIZER_0177fbaed772,
 Finisher_4074048574cf,
 StopWordsRemover_2e502cd57d60,
 CountVectorizer_0d555c85604c,
 IDF_a94ab221196d]
```

```
cv_model = pipeline.stages[-2]
```

```
len(cv_model.vocabulary)
```

```
3033
```

This is a modest vocabulary size. We will see larger sizes when we get to Part III of this book.

Let's look at our top 10 words by document frequency.

```
cv_model.vocabulary[:10]
```

```
['write', 'one', 'use', 'get', 'article', 'say', 'know', 'x',
 'make', 'dont']
```

Let's look at the distribution of mean term frequency. We will create a histogram of mean term frequency, as seen in Figure 7-1.

```
tf = features.select('tf').toPandas()
tf = tf['tf'].apply(lambda sv: sv.toArray())
mean_tf = pd.Series(tf.mean(), index=cv_model.vocabulary)

plt.figure(figsize=(12, 8))
mean_tf.hist(bins=10)
plt.show()
```

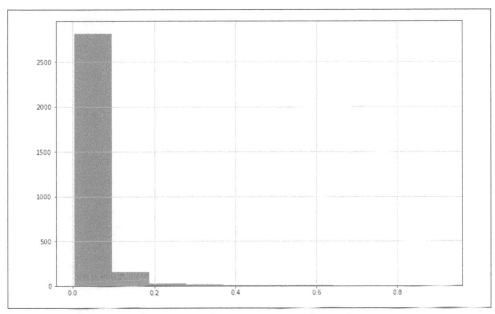

Figure 7-1. Histogram of mean term frequency per word over the corpus

We can see that this looks like a power law distribution. Let's plot the log of the ranks versus the log of the mean term frequency, as seen in Figure 7-2.

```
plt.figure(figsize=(12, 8))
ranks = np.arange(len(mean_tf)) + 1
plt.plot(np.log10(ranks), np.log10(mean_tf.values))
plt.show()
```

This is normally what you see with a vocabulary distribution. Notice, that even though we removed the most common words, and dropped very rare words, by setting minDF to 10, we still have the expected distribution.

Now that we have our features and have assured ourselves that we have not disturbed the expected distribution of words, how can we reduce the number of features? We could try and add more words to our stop-word list, or we could increase our minDF to remove more rare words. But let's think about a more principled way to approach this. Many of the more well-known techniques for reducing the number of features, for example looking at the univariate predictive power of each feature, will not work well with text. The strength of bag-of-words features is their interactions. So we may throw away features that are not powerful on their own but could be very powerful in combination. The high dimensionality means that we can't explore all the possible interactions. So what can we do?

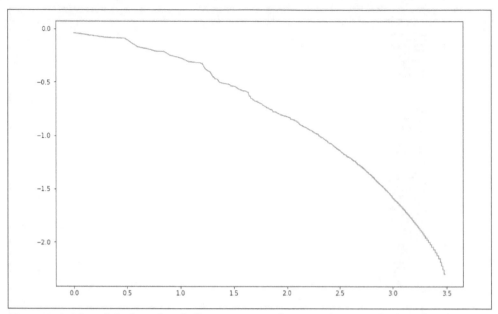

Figure 7-2. Plot of the log of rank (by mean term frequency) versus the log of mean term frequency

We can use a dictionary of words or phrases that domain experts have selected as important to the problem. We can also build a tree-based model, for example, random forest, and use the feature importances to select a subset of features. This can work because the random forest model is nonlinear and can discover interactions—so, a word that is important only in combination.

We will look at other techniques for reducing dimensionality in Chapters 10 and 11. Now, let's discuss the modeling of text using TF.IDF features.

Modeling

Once you have converted your text into a feature vector, things start to look more like a regular machine learning problem, with some exceptions. The following are the most important things to keep in mind:

- There are many sparse features.
- These features are not independent of each other.
- We have lost a massive part of language by losing the ordering of words.

Fortunately, none of these are showstoppers. Even if an algorithm makes assumptions that are violated by these facts, it can still be effective. We will discuss some popular algorithms here, and we will try out these algorithms in the exercises in this chapter.

Naïve Bayes

Naïve Bayes gets its name from its *naïve* assumption that all the features are mutually independent. It then estimates the probability of a class conditioned on the feature values. We know, from linguistics and common sense, that words are not independent of each other. But naïve Bayes is actually a popular baseline for text classification. The reason naïve Bayes is so popular is that the probability that it produces is similar to TF.IDF:

$$P\big(class\,\big|\,\text{term}_1, \text{term}_2, \ldots, \text{term}_N\big) = \frac{P(class)\Pi_{i=1}^{N} P\big(\text{term}_i\,\big|\,class\big)}{\Sigma_{k=1}^{K} P\big(class_k\big)\Pi_{i=1}^{N} P\big(\text{term}_i\,\big|\,class_k\big)}$$

If a term is common in all classes, it will not contribute much to this value. However, if a term is unique to the documents in a particular class it will be an important feature for naïve Bayes. This is similar to how IDF reduces the importance of words that are common to many documents.

Linear Models

Linear models like linear regression and logistic regression assume that their predictors are independent of each other. One way we could get around this is to look at interactions. However, that will not work in our case because we have a very high dimensional space. If you plan on using a linear model, you will likely want to put more effort in your featurization. Specifically, you will want to be more aggressive in reducing the number of features.

Decision/Regression Trees

Decision and regression trees can learn nonlinear relationships, and they don't have any assumptions of independence. They can be adversely affected by the sparse features. Variables with less inherent entropy, like words that are relatively uncommon, are less likely to be picked for splitting by splitting criteria like information gain. This means that any nonsparse features will be favored over sparse features. Also, words with higher variance, often meaning higher document frequency, can be favored over words with lower document frequency. This can be mitigated, for example, by being more aggressive with stop-word removal. If you are using random forest or gradient boosted trees, you can mitigate some of the difficulties mentioned previously.

Another great aspect of tree-based models is the ability to easily interpret the output of the model. Because you can see which features are being selected, you can easily check if the learning algorithm is making a sensible model.

Deep Learning Algorithms

Neural networks are great at learning complex functions, but they do require quite a bit of data. The data needed goes up quickly with the number of parameters. If you are using the bag-of-words approach, the number of parameters for the first layer will be the size of your vocabulary times the size of the first hidden layer. This is already quite large. This means that you are spending a lot of time learning intermediate representations for words—which can also lead to overfitting. It is often a good idea to use word embeddings, which we will discuss in Chapter 11, so that your classification or regression model has far fewer parameters to learn.

Always keep in mind what you want from your data when doing NLP, or machine learning in general. Training and deploying deep learning models is often more complicated than with classical machine learning models. Always try the simplest thing first.

Iteration

The most important part of any classification or regression project is your iteration cycle, as seen in Figure 7-3.

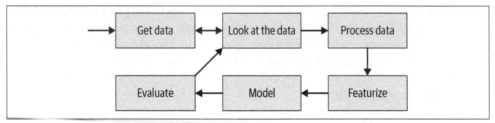

Figure 7-3. How to iterate on NLP classification and regression problems

If you have done machine learning in the past, most of this will look familiar. There are some differences when working with text data that we should keep in mind, so let's go over the following steps.

1. Get data.

   This is often the most time-consuming part of such a project. Hopefully, the data you work with is well-maintained and well-documented. Whether it is or not, you must validate the data.

2. Look at the data.

   Whether working with structured or unstructured data, we generally need to do some work to prepare our data for modeling. With structured data, this often means removing invalid values or normalizing a field. With text data this is a little more murky. There may be business logic that dictates a minimum or maximum length. Or perhaps there are certain documents you want to remove based on metadata. Outside of business logic, you should check the encodings of your documents and convert them to a common encoding (e.g., UTF-8).

You also want to create a hold-out set. Even if you are using a form of cross-validation instead of a train-test split, it's important to keep a completely untouched hold-out. It is easy to overfit to text data.

3. Process the data.

Whether working with structured or unstructured data, we generally need to do some work to prepare our data for modeling. In structured data, this often means removing invalid values or normalizing a field. With text data this is a little more murky. There may be business logic that dictates a minimum or maximum length. Or perhaps there are certain documents you want to remove based on metadata. Outside of business logic, you should check the encodings of your documents and convert them to a common encoding (e.g., UTF-8).

You also want to create a hold-out set. Even if you are using a form of cross-validation instead of a train-test split, it's important to keep a completely untouched hold-out. It is often easy to overfit to text data.

4. Featurize.

Now that you have your data processed and ready, you can create feature vectors. After creating features, you should do some basic exploratory analysis of the features. You look at the vocabulary distribution like we did previously. You can also use topic models for this, which we will cover in Chapter 10. Topic models can give you insights for deciding how to create your model and, as a side benefit, will help you catch errors.

Because NLP featurization is often more complicated than featurization with structured data, you will want to have your featurization stages in the same pipeline as your modeling. This will help optimize model hyperparameters alongside featurization parameters.

5. Model.

You need to decide on which algorithm you want to use. As with general machine learning tasks, you will want to set a baseline. Popular models for setting baselines for text-based classification and regression problems are logistic regression, naïve Bayes, and decision trees. Once you have your features, and you have decided on an algorithm, you can train your model.

6. Evaluate.

Looking at the data is important to understanding what is happening with your model, but looking at metrics is just as important. You should iterate using cross-validation or on a dedicated validation set. Your hold-out set must be saved until you think you are ready to go to production.

7. Review.

It's important to get fresh eyes on as much of your pipeline as possible.

- Review your code: data processing code can be difficult to review if someone does not have familiarity with the data. If you can't find someone who has context to review your code, having thorough documentation becomes important.

- Review your data: you can review your data with a subject-matter expert. Also, consider reviewing with someone who is fully unfamiliar with the data.

- Review your features: the features you've created should make sense. If this is the case, you should review these features with a domain expert. If the features are too abstract to easily tie back to the domain, it might be worthwhile to review the theory behind your features with someone who has experience building similar models.

- Review your model: when working on a modeling project, it's easy to get lost in the details. It's important to review your rationale for the chosen algorithm, as well as the output.

- Review your metrics: as with any machine learning project, you should be able to give clear interpretation of your metrics—especially the metric you make business decisions on. If you have a hard time finding a good metric, you may not have the best approach to the problem. Sometimes, a classification problem is better framed as ranking problem.

- Review your documentation: you should make sure that your whole pipeline is well documented. This is necessary if you want to have reproducibility.

Now that you have validated your baseline model, it's time to make a decision. Is the baseline good enough for production? If so, ship it. Otherwise, it's time to look at the data again. Now you have your cycle set up, and you can start to improve your metrics.

Now we have a framework for building text-based classifiers and regressors. There is no singular technique that makes working with the sparse, high dimensional text easier. You should rely on domain experts to help inform your choices. This chapter covered generic ideas and rules; we will look at more concrete applications in Part III of this book. One issue with the bag-of-words approach is that we lose an important part of language—syntax. We can capture some of that with N-grams, but what happens if we want to classify pieces in the text? In the next chapter, we explore how to build sequence models.

Exercises

Let's build a classifier to predict the newsgroup that a document belongs to. We will start out with the pipeline we built previously in this chapter, and we will use a naïve Bayes classifier.

Use the Spark MLlib Guide (*https://oreil.ly/k4O1H*) as a reference to try new things.

```
train, test = texts.randomSplit([0.8, 0.2], seed=123)

stopwords = set(StopWordsRemover.loadDefaultStopWords("english"))

sw_remover = StopWordsRemover() \
    .setInputCol("normalized") \
    .setOutputCol("filtered") \
    .setStopWords(list(stopwords))

count_vectorizer = CountVectorizer(inputCol='filtered',
    outputCol='tf', minDF=10)
idf = IDF(inputCol='tf', outputCol='tfidf', minDocFreq=10)

text_processing_pipeline = Pipeline(stages=[
        assembler,
        sentence,
        tokenizer,
        lemmatizer,
        normalizer,
        finisher,
        sw_remover,
        count_vectorizer,
        idf
    ])


from pyspark.ml.feature import IndexToString, StringIndexer
from pyspark.ml.classification import *
from pyspark.ml.tuning import *
from pyspark.ml.evaluation import *

label_indexer = StringIndexer(inputCol='newsgroup', outputCol='la-
bel').fit(texts)
naive_bayes = NaiveBayes(featuresCol='tfidf')
prediction_deindexer = IndexToString(inputCol='prediction', output-
Col='pred_newsgroup',
                                    labels=label_indexer.labels)

pipeline = Pipeline(stages=[
    text_processing_pipeline, label_indexer, naive_bayes, prediction_deindexer
])

model = pipeline.fit(train)

train_predicted = model.transform(train)
test_predicted = model.transform(test)
```

We are using F1-score, which is the harmonic mean of precision and recall.

```
evaluator = MulticlassClassificationEvaluator(metricName='f1')

print('f1', evaluator.evaluate(train_predicted))

f1 0.946056760284357

print('f1', evaluator.evaluate(test_predicted))

f1 0.6508170558829952
```

It looks like we are doing much better on the training data than on the testing data—perhaps we are overfitting. Experiment, and see how well you can do on the test set.

## CHAPTER 8

Sequence Modeling with Keras

So far, we have looked at documents as bags-of-words. This is a common, easily achievable approach for many NLP tasks. However, this approach produces a low-fidelity model of language. The order of words is essential to the encoding and decoding of meaning in language, and to incorporate this, we will need to model sequences.

When people refer to *sequences* in a machine learning context, they are generally talking about sequences of data in which data points are not independent of the data points around them. We can still use features derived from the data point, as with general machine learning, but now we can also use the data and labels from the nearby data points. For example, if we are trying to determine if the token "produce" is being used as a noun or verb, knowing what words are around it will be very informative. If the token before it is "might," that indicates "produce" is a verb. If "the" is the preceding token, that indicates it is a noun. These other words give us context.

What if "to" precedes "produce"? That could still indicate either a noun or a verb. We need to look back further. This gives us the concept of windows—the amount of context we want to capture. Many algorithms have a fixed amount of context that is decided as a hyperparameter. There are some algorithms, for example LSTMs, that can learn how long to *remember* the context.

Sequence problems come from different domains, and in different data formats. In this book we are working with text data, which is a sequence of characters, or words, or even messages. Working with voice data is inherently a sequence problem. Economics, physics, and medicine also have many sequence problems. The statistics and behavior of this data is generally very different among these disparate fields, but there are many techniques in common.

One of the common techniques used for sequence modeling is a family of machine learning algorithms called *graphical models*. Graphical models can be used to model probabilistic structures. This is what allows us to capture context. When building the graphical models, we have to decide how much context to capture. How much context we want to capture is based on the specifics of the problem. There are also models that let us learn how much context to use. The algorithm needed to learn a graphical model differs depending on the model chosen. Some can be learned with gradient descent; others have their own learning algorithms.

In this chapter, we will go over some of the popular algorithms for learning sequences, such as hidden Markov models, conditional random fields, and recurrent neural networks. Let's start out with sentence segmentation and hidden Markov models.

Sentence Segmentation

One of the first sequence-modeling problems most learn is the *sentence-boundary detection*, or *SBD* problem, in which we want to determine where a sentence boundary is. This seems like a problem that could be solved by a regular expression. We can simply say that every ".", "?", and "!" are sentence boundaries. We can add something to check for acronyms—perhaps we can check if the previous character is capitalized and the character after the next whitespace is not. This will still miss some situations with acronyms—for example, two acronyms following each other like "U.S. D.O.S."

What if our text is not so regularly formatted? If our text has many lists, as is common in technical communications, there may not be sentence-ending punctuation at the end of each item. However, we don't want to call all the items in a list the same sentence. We could make more and more complicated regular expressions, or we could build a model.

There are some pros and cons to help us in deciding when to use a regular expression for SBD and when to use a model. Using a regular expression is easy to do, if you ignore some exceptions. If you are in a situation where using a model on text will be difficult, it is best to just use a regular expression. On the other hand, SBD models are somewhat generalizable. That being said, if you use an SBD model built on newspapers to process clinical text, it will produce more errors than you would expect.

(Hidden) Markov Models

Hidden Markov model, or *HMM* is a popular model for dealing with sequence data. To understand it, we need to discuss Markov models and the Markov property.

The Markov property relates to a stochastic (random) process. In a stochastic process, a random variable for time t, X_t, can be dependent on all previous variables in the sequence, $X_{t-1}, X_{t-2}, \ldots, X_0$. If X_t is only dependent on the previous variable, X_{t-1}, then we say it has the Markov property. This simplifies problems greatly. This is an unrealistic assumption in language. However, like we saw in the previous chapter with independence assumptions of naïve Bayes and logistic regression, unrealistic assumptions don't necessarily produce a bad model. We can also ease the Markov property and say that X_t is dependent on the last k variables.

We can also use the relationship between the sequence we wish to model and an observable sequence. Now we can estimate the probability of a particular state as:

$$P[y_i = k | x_i = c] \approx P[y_i = k | y_{i-1} = k'] \cdot P[y_{i-1} = k'] \cdot P[x_i = c | y_i = k]$$

We can calculate the *transition* probability $P[y_i = k | y_{i-1} = k']$, the *initial* probability $P[y_0 = k]$, and the *emission* probability $P[x_i = c | y_i = k]$ directly from the data if we have labels. Once we have this, how do we predict the hidden states, y_i? We use the *Viterbi* algorithm.

Let's look at an example. We will be using the Brown corpus available with NLTK.

```
from collections import defaultdict, Counter

import numpy as np
import pandas as pd

import sparknlp

spark = sparknlp.start()

from nltk.corpus import brown
sentences = brown.sents()
```

The corpus is already split into sentences, so we will have to detokenize the data in order to get training data. Fortunately, this also provides us with labels. We will label the last character of a sentence with E, and everything else will be labeled S.

```
def detokenize(sentence):
    text = ''
    for token in sentence:
        if text and any(c.isalnum() for c in token):
            text += ' '
        text += token
    return text

word_counts = Counter()
raw = []
labels = []
for fid in brown.fileids():
        sentences = brown.sents(fid)
        word_counts.update(
            [t for s in sentences for t in s if t.isalpha()])
        sentences = [detokenize(s) for s in sentences]
        raw.append(' '.join(sentences))
        labels.append('S'.join([
```

```
                ('S' * (len(s) - 1)) + 'E'
                for s in sentences
            ]))

    word_counts = pd.Series(word_counts)
```

Now, let us define our training algorithm. If you note the equations defined previously, we will be doing repeated multiplication of probabilities; this creates a danger of *underflow*. Underflow is a limitation of floating-point numbers. Floating-point numbers can represent only so much precision. So, if a number approaches too close to 0, the floating-point representation may round to 0. For example, when implementing naïve Bayes, instead of multiplying probabilities, we will add log-probabilities. This is to avoid underflow when multiplying many numbers that are less than 1.

We will need the set of observations, the characters in the text, the set of states, whether or not a character marks a sentence ending, and the log probabilities. We will need to have the log probability for initial states. In this modeling problem the initial state will always be "S." We will need the emission log probabilities—the log probability of a character given a state. And finally, we need the transition log probability, which is the log probability of a state given a previous state.

```
class HMM(object):
    def __init__(self, obs_set, state_set, initial_log, emission_log,
                 transition_log):
        self.obs_set = obs_set
        self.state_set = state_set
        self.initial_log = initial_log
        self.emission_log = emission_log
        self.transition_log = transition_log
```

To calculate these things, we need to track total possible observations, states, and the counts we will use to calculate the log-probabilities.

```
def training_data():
    data_dict = {}
    data_dict['obs_set'] = set()
    data_dict['state_set'] = set()
    data_dict['transition_ct'] = defaultdict(Counter)
    data_dict['emission_ct'] = defaultdict(Counter)
    data_dict['initial_ct'] = Counter()
    return data_dict
```

Now we need to have a function that will update this data as we traverse over the data set.

```
def update_state(data_dict, ob_seq, st_seq):
    assert len(ob_seq) == len(st_seq)
    data_dict['initial_ct'][st_seq[0]] += 1
    for i in range(1, len(st_seq)):
        ob = ob_seq[i]
```

```
        st = st_seq[i]
        data_dict['obs_set'].add(ob)
        data_dict['state_set'].add(st)
        data_dict['transition_ct'][ob_seq[i-1]][ob] += 1
        data_dict['emission_ct'][st][ob] += 1
```

Now that we have the counts and the total set of observations and states, we can calculate the sums we will need for the log probabiltics.

```
def calculate_sums(data_dict):
    data_dict['transition_sums'] = {
        st: np.sum(list(data_dict['transition_ct'][st].values()))
        for st in data_dict['state_set']
    }
    data_dict['initial_sum'] = np.sum(
        list(data_dict['initial_ct'].values()))
    data_dict['emission_sums'] = {
        st: np.sum(list(data_dict['emission_ct'][st].values()))
        for st in data_dict['state_set']
    }
```

Once we have the counts and the sums, we can calculate the log probabilties.

```
def calculate_log_probs(data_dict, eps):
    data_dict['transition_log'] = {
        prev_st: {
            # log P[y_i = k | y_i-1 = k']
            st: (np.log(data_dict['transition_ct'][prev_st][st] + \
                eps) - \
                np.log(data_dict['transition_sums'][prev_st] + \
                eps))
            for st in data_dict['state_set']
        }
        for prev_st in data_dict['state_set']
    }

    data_dict['initial_log'] = {
            # log P[y_0 = k]
        st: (np.log(data_dict['initial_ct'][st] + eps) - \
            np.log(data_dict['initial_sum'] + eps))
        for st in data_dict['state_set']
    }

    data_dict['emission_log'] = {
        st: {
            # log P[x_i = c | y_i = k]
            ob: (np.log(data_dict['emission_ct'][st][ob] + eps) - \
                np.log(data_dict['emission_sums'][st] + eps))
            for ob in data_dict['obs_set']
        }
        for st in data_dict['state_set']
    }
```

Finally, we have our `train` method to tie everything together.

```
def train(observations, states, eps=1e-8):
    # initialize
    data_dict = training_data()

    # traverse data and count all transitions, initials, and
    # emissions
    for ob_seq, st_seq in zip(observations, states):
        update_state(data_dict, ob_seq, st_seq)

    calculate_sums(data_dict)

    calculate_log_probs(data_dict, eps)

    return HMM(list(data_dict['obs_set']), list(data_dict['state_set']),
               data_dict['initial_log'], data_dict['emission_log'],
               data_dict['transition_log'])

model = train(raw, labels)
```

Now, given a piece of text, we need to calculate the most probable sequence of states. We can use these predicted states to split a piece of text into sentences. For doing this, we will use the *Viterbi* algorithm. This algorithm will let us efficiently traverse the set of possible sequences.

```
def viterbi(y, model):
    # probabilities for the initial states
    path_logs = [{
        st: model.initial_log[st] + model.emission_log[st][y[0]]
        for st in model.state_set
    }]
    path_preds = [{st: '' for st in model.state_set}]

    for i in range(1, len(y)):
        curr_log = {}
        curr_preds = {}
        for st in model.state_set:
            # find the most probable previous state that
            # would lead to st
            curr_log[st] = -np.inf
            curr_preds[st] = ''
            for prev_st in model.state_set:
                # log probability
                local_log = path_logs[i-1][prev_st] + \
                    model.transition_log[prev_st][st] + \
                    model.emission_log[st][y[i]]
                if curr_log[st] < local_log:
                    curr_log[st] = local_log
                    curr_preds[st] = prev_st
        path_logs.append(curr_log)
        path_preds.append(curr_preds)
```

```
        # Now we work backwards. Find the most probable final
        # state, and work back to the beginning.
        terminal_log = -np.inf
        curr_st = ''
        for st in model.state_set:
            if terminal_log < path_logs[-1][st]:
                terminal_log = path_logs[-1][st]
                curr_st = st
        preds = curr_st
        for i in range(len(y)-1, 0, -1):
            curr_st = path_preds[i][curr_st]
            preds = curr_st + preds
        return preds
```

Now that we can make predictions, we can build our own sentence splitter.

```
def split(text, model):
    state_seq = viterbi(text, model)
    sentences = []
    start = 0
    for end in range(1, len(text)):
        if state_seq[end] == 'E':
            sentences.append(text[start:end+1])
            start = end+1
    sentences.append(text[start:])
    return sentences
```

Let's see how it does.

```
example = raw[0]

print('\n###\n'.join(split(example, model)[:10]))

The Fulton County Grand Jury said Friday an investigation of
Atlanta's recent primary election produced`` no evidence'' that
any irregularities took place.
###
The jury further said in term-
###
end presentments that the City Executive Committee, which had over-
###
all charge of the election,`` deserves the praise and thanks of the
City of Atlanta'' for the manner in which the election was
conducted.
###
The September-
###
October term jury had been charged by Fulton Superior Court Judge
Durwood Pye to investigate reports of possible`` irregularities''
in the hard-
###
fought primary which was won by Mayor-
###
nominate Ivan Allen Jr.
```

```
###
.
###
`` Only a relative handful of such reports was received'', the jury
said,`` considering the widespread interest in the election, the
number of voters and the size of this city''.
```

Not great, but this is a simple model built from the data—not from manually encoded heuristics. There are several ways we could improve this. We can add more emission features because we are assuming they are independent of each other. We should look at the data to understand why the model thinks hyphens are ends of sentences.

This model is simple, but we already had plenty of labels. Getting labels like this can be a time-consuming process. You can use the *Baum-Welch* algorithm to learn transition and emission probabilities on a partially labeled or unlabeled data set.

Let's look at how Spark NLP does sentence detection. The algorithm is based on Kevin Dias's `pragmatic_segmenter`, originally implemented in Ruby. Let's compare how it does to how our simple HMM does.

```python
example_df = spark.createDataFrame([(example,)], ['text'])

from sparknlp import DocumentAssembler, Finisher
from sparknlp.annotator import SentenceDetector

from pyspark.ml import Pipeline

assembler = DocumentAssembler()\
    .setInputCol('text')\
    .setOutputCol('document')
sent_detector = SentenceDetector()\
    .setInputCols(['document'])\
    .setOutputCol('sentences')
finisher = Finisher()\
    .setInputCols(['sentences'])\
    .setOutputCols(['sentences'])\
    .setOutputAsArray(True)

pipeline = Pipeline().setStages([
    assembler, sent_detector, finisher
]).fit(example_df)

sentences = pipeline.transform(example_df)

print('\n###\n'.join(sentences.first()['sentences'][:10]))

The Fulton County Grand Jury said Friday an investigation of
Atlanta's recent primary election produced`` no evidence'' that
any irregularities took place.
###
The jury further said in term-end presentments that the City
Executive Committee, which had over-all charge of the election,``
deserves the praise and thanks of the City of Atlanta'' for the
```

```
manner in which the election was conducted.
###
The September-October term jury had been charged by Fulton Superior
Court Judge Durwood Pye to investigate reports of possible``
irregularities'' in the hard-fought primary which was won by
Mayor-nominate Ivan Allen Jr..
###
`` Only a relative handful of such reports was received'', the jury
said,`` considering the widespread interest in the election, the
number of voters and the size of this city''.
###
The jury said it did find that many of Georgia's registration and
election laws`` are outmoded or inadequate and often ambiguous''.
###
It recommended that Fulton legislators act`` to have these laws
studied and revised to the end of modernizing and improving them''.
###
The grand jury commented on a number of other topics, among them
the Atlanta and Fulton County purchasing departments which it
said`` are well operated and follow generally accepted practices
which inure to the best interest of both governments''.
###
Merger proposed However, the jury said it believes`` these two
offices should be combined to achieve greater efficiency and reduce
the cost of administration''.
####
The City Purchasing Department, the jury said,`` is lacking in
experienced clerical personnel as a result of city personnel
policies''.
###
It urged that the city`` take steps to remedy'' this problem.
```

It definitely does better than the HMM. The `pragmatic_segmenter` is quite complex. We could build a more complex model, though. This is a good lesson that in some situations heuristics may be preferable to a model. When you are working on your NLP application, always try the simplest solution first. Look at what goes wrong and then make improvements.

Section Segmentation

There are some documents that are more like a collection of documents. A clinical encounter is recorded as a collection of notes, perhaps from different providers. Legal text is broken into different sections, each with different kinds of content and functions. Narrative text is often broken into chapters or scenes. These different sections may require different treatments, or even different models. For example, we may not want to use the same models on an admission note as we do on a radiological exam, even if they are part of the same visit.

Although sections are incredibly important, they are not actually a part of *language* per se. They are an artifact of the document formatting that the text is recorded in. There may still be meaning in the different kinds of sections, and even in their placement. This means that we often can't generalize our techniques outside of a given corpus. Fortunately, regular expressions are even more effective on this problem than sentence-boundary detection.

Part-of-Speech Tagging

Parts of speech are word categories that govern how words are combined to form phrases and sentences. These can be very valuable, especially in a process that involves extracting information from the text. You are likely familiar with the most common parts of speech. In NLP, the categories are a little more complicated.

The following are common parts of speech:

- Verbs: "know," "try," "call"
- Nouns: "cat," "banana," "happiness"
- Adjectives: "big," "red," "quick"
- Adverbs: "well," "now," "quickly"
- Prepositions: "of," "behind," "with"

Most part-of-speech tagging data comes from the University of Pennsylvania Treebank, or it is similarly formatted. This data set has a much larger set of parts-of-speech:

- CC: Coordinating conjunction ("and")
- CD: Cardinal number ("one," "1")
- DT: Determiner ("an," "the")
- EX: Existential "there" ("there are")
- FW: Foreign word ("zeitgeist")
- IN: Preposition or subordinating conjunction ("of," "because")
- JJ: Adjective ("happy," "fun")
- JJR: Adjective, comparative ("happier")
- JJS: Adjective, superlative ("happiest")
- LS: List item marker ("a)")
- MD: Modal ("can," "might")
- NN: Noun, singular or mass ("cat," "knowledge")

- NNS: Noun, plural ("cats")
- NNP: Proper noun, singular ("Sarah")
- NNPS: Proper noun, plural ("Hungarians")
- PDT: Predeterminer ("half" in "It is half the price.")
- POS: Possessive ending (possessive "'s")
- PRP: Personal pronoun ("I," "they")
- PRP\$: Possessive pronoun ("my," "their")
- RB: Adverb ("quickly," "well")
- RBR: Adverb, comparative ("quicker," "better")
- RBS: Adverb, superlative ("quickest," "best")
- RP: Particle (varies, but infinitive "to," "off" in "It's a write-off")
- SYM: Symbol (x in mathematical context)
- TO: to (sometimes a separate category just for infinitive "to")
- UH: Interjection ("uh")
- VB: Verb, base form (after infinitive "to," "call," "know")
- VBD: Verb, past tense ("called," "knew")
- VBG: Verb, gerund or present participle ("calling," "knowing")
- VBN: Verb, past participle ("called," "known")
- VBP: Verb, non–third-person singular present ("call," "know")
- VBZ: Verb, third-person singular present ("calls," "knows")
- WDT: Wh-determiner ("which")
- WP: Wh-pronoun ("who")
- WP\$: Possessive wh-pronoun ("whose")
- WRB: Wh-adverb ("when")

Understanding the linguistics behind these lexical categories will help us understand how to extract them, as well as how to use them. Let's look a little at how humans identify parts of speech.

Humans decode the part of speech from morphological and syntactic clues. This is why we can determine the parts of speech of nonsense words. Let's look at part of "Jabberwocky," the poem by Lewis Carroll.

> 'Twas brillig, and the slithy toves
> Did gyre and gimble in the wabe:
> All mimsy were the borogoves,
> And the mome raths outgrabe.

"Beware the Jabberwock, my son!
The jaws that bite, the claws that catch!
Beware the Jubjub bird, and shun
The frumious Bandersnatch!"

He took his vorpal sword in hand;
Long time the manxome foe he sought—
So rested he by the Tumtum tree
And stood awhile in thought.

Fluent English speakers will be able to tell you that "brillig" and "vorpal" are adjectives, "gyre" and "gimble" are verbs, and "toves" and "Jabberwock" are nouns. It's not as easy to do this with every category. If you make up your own subordinating conjunction, people may have a hard time identifying it.

I went there cloom they told me to.

This sentence seems wrong. The reason is that we are used to learning new words in some categories and not in others. If we can create words in a category, it is considered an *open category*; those we cannot easily add to are called *closed categories*. This is on a spectrum, though. Pronouns are not as open as nouns, but it is not uncommon for languages to innovate new pronouns. For example, "y'all" is no more than two or three centuries old.

Knowing that there are some categories that are more or less fixed, and some that are fully open, we can tell that our models are learning two kinds of prediction. Lexical cues are useful for closed categories, and contextual cues are useful for open categories.

Let's take a look at how Spark NLP does POS tagging. In Spark NLP, a perceptron is used. We can train a model on the brown corpus, but first we must save the data in a particular format. Each token-tag pair must be joined by an underscore '_'. Each sentence worth of tagged tokens goes on one line. For example:

```
The_AT mayor's_NN$ present_JJ term_NN of_IN office_NN expires_VBZ
Jan._NP 1_CD ._.
He_PPS will_MD be_BE succeeded_VBN by_IN Ivan_NP Allen_NP Jr._NP
,_, who_WPS became_VBD a_AT candidate_NN in_IN the_AT Sept._NP
13_CD primary_NN after_CS Mayor_NN-TL Hartsfield_NP announced_VBD
that_CS he_PPS would_MD not_* run_VB for_IN reelection_NN ._.

from sparknlp.training import POS

with open('tagged_brown.txt', 'w') as out:
    for fid in brown.fileids():
        for sent in brown.tagged_sents(fid):
            for token, tag in sent:
                out.write('{}_{} '.format(token, tag))
            out.write('\n')

tag_data = POS().readDataset(spark, 'tagged_brown.txt', '_', 'tags')
```

Now we can build our pipeline and train our model.

```
from sparknlp.annotator import Tokenizer, PerceptronApproach

assembler = DocumentAssembler()\
    .setInputCol('text')\
    .setOutputCol('document')
sent_detector = SentenceDetector()\
    .setInputCols(['document'])\
    .setOutputCol('sentences')
tokenizer = Tokenizer() \
    .setInputCols(['sentences']) \
    .setOutputCol('tokens')

pos_tagger = PerceptronApproach() \
    .setNIterations(1) \
    .setInputCols(["sentences", "tokens"]) \
    .setOutputCol("pos") \
    .setPosCol("tags")

finisher = Finisher()\
    .setInputCols(['tokens', 'pos'])\
    .setOutputCols(['tokens', 'pos'])\
    .setOutputAsArray(True)

pipeline = Pipeline().setStages([
    assembler, sent_detector, tokenizer, pos_tagger, finisher
])

pipeline = pipeline.fit(tag_data)
```

Let's look at how it did on the first sentence.

```
tag_data.first()['text']

'The Friday an investigation of primary election produced evidence
any irregularities took place .'

tag_data_first = tag_data.first()['tags']
txformed_first = pipeline.transform(tag_data).first()

for i in range(len(tag_data_first)):
    word = tag_data_first[i]['metadata']['word']
    true_pos = tag_data_first[i]['result']
    pred_pos = txformed_first['pos'][i]
    print('{:20s} {:5s} {:5s}'.format(word, true_pos, pred_pos))

The                  AT    AT
Friday               NR    NR
an                   AT    AT
investigation        NN    NN
of                   IN    IN
primary              NN    JJ
election             NN    NN
produced             VBD   VBN
```

```
evidence          NN    NN
any               DTI   DTI
irregularities    NNS   NNS
took              VBD   VBD
place             NN    NN
```

The model has learned this data set well. In fact, "primary" being a noun or adjective can both be true, depending on how you parse the sentence.

There are other techniques for part-of-speech tagging, such as *conditional random fields*.

Conditional Random Field

If hidden Markov models are sequential naïve Bayes, then *conditional random fields (CRFs)* can be thought of as sequential logistic regression. CRFs are another popular technique for part-of-speech tagging. CRFs have a few benefits over HMMs. They allow for more complex features because they make fewer assumptions on the relationships between features and labels. In Spark NLP, CRFs are one approach used for part-of-speech tagging, in addition to using RNNs. CRFs are learned using gradient descent like logistic regression, but they are run using algorithms like the *Viterbi* algorithm.

Chunking and Syntactic Parsing

Now that we have the parts of speech for individual tokens, we must consider combining them. Many NLP tasks involve finding entities in the text. Often, these entities are referenced using more than one-word phrases. This means that we have to understand how to combine tagged tokens in phrases, which are generally known as chunks.

Similar to sentence-boundary detection, we can do this with a heuristic, but there will be errors that we'll need a model to avoid. The heuristics are relatively simple—if two adjacent tokens have the same or similar tags, combine them into a single phrase. For example, the words "fan blade" are both nouns, so they can be combined into a single noun phrase. We can combine certain known structures, like some verb-preposition combinations, such as "knock off," into a single verb or noun. Heuristics won't cover more complex syntactic structures. For example, the verb "knock off" inserts its object between "knock" and "off," so if you are trying to normalize your vocabulary, the infinitive "to knock off" won't be combined with the inflected form "knocked X off." There may also be certain syntactic structures you are interested in, like knowing who did what to whom.

To extract these more complex syntactic structures, we need a syntactic parser. These models turn sequences into tree structures. The tokens then become *constituents* in larger phrases. Language is very complicated, but fortunately, straightforward structures are generally more common than complex ones.

Before using a syntactic parser, make sure that you are certain that you need it. They are often generally complex models that are resource-intensive to train and use. It's probably best if you try to solve your problem with heuristics first, and if that is not sufficient, consider a syntactic parser.

An additional caveat about syntactic parsers is that labeling is a difficult task. Anyone who is fluent in a language can reliably split text into sentences. Most people can learn parts of speech well enough to label data in a few minutes. Syntactic parsing is a significantly more complex labeling task.

Language Models

Another classic application of sequence modeling is language modeling. A *language model* is a model of process that generates language. This is called a generative model, as opposed to a discriminative model, which is used for distinguishing the difference between things. Of course, the actual process by which human language is generated is incredibly complex, and is still being explored by neurologists, psychologists, and philosophers. In NLP, language models make simplifying assumptions—for example, that the text generation process can be learned from text alone.

There are many uses for language models. We can use them for feature generation with other models. For example, a neural-network-based language model can be used to feed into other layers used for sequence labeling. Language models are also used for text generation and summarization.

Some of the techniques covered in this chapter can be used to create a language model. For example, we could use a CRF to predict a sequence of words. We could also use a Markov model to predict a sequence of words by learning the transition probabilities. This would not be a *hidden* Markov model, because there are no hidden states here. We would likely need a larger context window than just the previous token. Fortunately, we can relax the assumption that the language generation has the Markov property. Once we start doing this, however, our model quickly becomes much more complex. This is related to the complication of syntax that made syntactic parsers so challenging.

Currently, RNNs (recurrent neural networks) are the most popular approach to building language models. We introduced RNNs in Chapter 4, but now let's look into more detail about how they work.

Recurrent Neural Networks

We will build a model that can generate English words. To do this we will use an LSTM. Following are the equations that define it:

$$v_0 = 0$$

$$c_0 = 0$$

$$1 \le t \le T$$

$$f_t = \sigma\left(W_f \cdot \vec{x}_t + U_f \cdot v^{(t-1)} + b_f\right)$$

$$i_t = \sigma\left(W_i \cdot \vec{x}_t + U_i \cdot v^{(t-1)} + b_i\right)$$

$$o_t = \sigma\left(W_o \cdot \vec{x}_t + U_o \cdot v^{(t-1)} + b_o\right)$$

$$\tilde{c}_t = \tanh\left(W_c \cdot \vec{x}_t + U_c \cdot v^{(t-1)} + b_c\right)$$

$$c_t = f_t \circ c_{t-1} + i_t \circ \tilde{c}_t$$

$$v_t = o_t \circ \tanh(c_t)$$

The idea behind the LSTM is that it will maintain state as you progress through the sequence. It will learn when to update its state through the training process. The input, x_t, is combined with the previous state, v_t, using four different sets of weights. The first set, W_f, U_f, b_f, represents forgetting, controlling how much prior information affects the state of the cell. The second set, W_i, U_i, b_i, represents input to the cell, controlling how much the current example affects the state of the cell. The third set, W_o, U_o, b_o, represents output of the cell, controlling how much the new cell state affects the output of the LSTM. And finally, W_c, U_c, b_c, represents memory of the current state, controlling what is remembered from the current input and stored in the cell.

In order to pass in our characters, we will need to vectorize them first.

```
from keras.models import Model, Sequential
from keras.layers import *
import keras.utils as ku
import keras.preprocessing as kp

from scipy.special import expit as sigmoid, softmax
```

Let's take only the words that occur frequently. Also, we will mark the end of each word. This will let our model predict when a word should end.

```
vocab = word_counts[word_counts > 100]
vocab = list(w + '#' for w in vocab.index)
```

We will build two lookups, c2i for mapping characters to indices, and i2c for mapping indices back to characters. We will also use ? as a symbol for unknown characters.

```
UNK = '?'
c2i = {UNK: 0}

for word in vocab:
    for c in word:
        c2i.setdefault(c, len(c2i))

i2c = {ix: c for c, ix in c2i.items()}
alphabet_size = len(i2c) + 1
```

Now let's define some utility functions for converting data.

```
def texts_to_sequences(texts):
    return [[c2i.get(c, c2i[UNK]) for c in t] for t in texts]

def sequences_to_texts(seqs):
    return [''.join([i2c.get(ix, UNK) for ix in s]) for s in seqs]
```

Here, we specify the maximum context as 10. We could potentially not do so, but that could lead to some technical difficulties. The implementation of sequence modeling expects to know the maximum length of the sequences. Without fixing the size of the window, the length of the longest word will determine this length. Because long words are much more rare than short ones, most of our sequences will need to be padded. This padding does not help us learn the likely sequences. So there is a trade-off: the larger the window the more context your model has to predict the next item in the sequence. On the other hand, it also increases computational complexity. It's best to realistically consider how large the context is in your data. In English, the median length of vocabulary words is 6 letters. If you take into account word frequency, the median is 4. Indeed, 10 is the 95th percentile of word length considering word frequency. This means that very rarely will information from more than 10 characters away help in predicting the next character.

```
seqs = texts_to_sequences(vocab)

w = 10
X = []
Y = []
for seq in seqs:
    for k in range(1, min(w, len(seq))):
        X.append(seq[:k])
        Y.append(seq[k])
    for k in range(0, len(seq) - w):
        X.append(seq[k:k+w])
        Y.append(seq[k+w])
X = kp.sequence.pad_sequences(X, maxlen=w, padding='pre')
Y = ku.to_categorical(Y, num_classes=alphabet_size)
```

Now we build our model. You may notice the Embedding layer here. This will reduce the dimensionality of our input. Instead of having the width of the input to LSTM be the size of our alphabet, it will be 5. We will learn more about embeddings in Chapter 11.

```
units = 20

model = Sequential()
model.add(Embedding(alphabet_size, 5, input_length=w))
model.add(LSTM(units, unroll=True))
model.add(Dense(alphabet_size, activation='softmax'))

print(model.summary())

Model: "sequential_1"
```

Layer (type)	Output Shape	Param #
embedding_1 (Embedding)	(None, 10, 5)	250
lstm_1 (LSTM)	(None, 20)	2080
dense_1 (Dense)	(None, 50)	1050

```
Total params: 3,380
Trainable params: 3,380
Non-trainable params: 0
```

None

There are 3,380 parameters to be learned. Unsurprisingly, most of them are in the LSTM—the most complex part of our network. Now, let's train our network.

```
model.compile(
    loss='categorical_crossentropy', optimizer='adam',
    metrics=['accuracy'])
model.fit(X, Y, epochs=300, verbose=1)

Epoch 1/300
5688/5688 [==============================] - 1s 224us/step -
  loss: 3.1837 - acc: 0.1790
Epoch 2/300
5688/5688 [==============================] - 0s 79us/step -
  loss: 2.7894 - acc: 0.1834
...
Epoch 299/300
5688/5688 [==============================] - 0s 88us/step -
  loss: 1.7275 - acc: 0.4524
Epoch 300/300
5688/5688 [==============================] - 0s 84us/step -
  loss: 1.7267 - acc: 0.4517

<keras.callbacks.History at 0x7fbf5e94d438>
```

Now that we have a model of the character sequences, we can actually use it to generate words. All we need is a seed character.

```
def generate_word(seed_char, model):
    text = seed_char
    for _ in range(100):
        # encode the current text
        encoded = texts_to_sequences([text])[0]
        # pad the sequence
        encoded = kp.sequence.pad_sequences(
            [encoded], maxlen=w, padding='pre', truncating='pre')
        # predict the next index
        pred = model.predict_classes(encoded, verbose=0)
        # convert the index
        pred = sequences_to_texts([pred])[0]
        # if the model predicts the end of the word, exit
        if pred == '#':
            break
        text += pred
    return text

alphabet = 'ABCDEFGHIJKLMNOPQRSTUVWXYZ'

for c in alphabet:
    print(c, '->', generate_word(c, model), end=', ')
    c = c.lower()
    print(c, '->', generate_word(c, model))
```

```
A -> And, a -> an
B -> Breng, b -> beation
C -> Court, c -> court
D -> Dear, d -> dear
E -> Englent, e -> exter
F -> Fer, f -> fort
G -> Gearth, g -> groud
H -> Her, h -> hort
I -> In, i -> indedant
J -> Jome, j -> jorter
K -> Kenglert, k -> kear
l -> Lexter, l -> land
M -> Mand, m -> mearth
N -> Not, n -> near
O -> One, o -> on
P -> Pling, p -> provest
Q -> Qexter, q -> quale
R -> Rhong, r -> rear
S -> Some, s -> state
T -> Ther, t -> ther
U -> Ued, u -> under
V -> Vexter, v -> vering
W -> Watere, w -> wate
X -> Xexter, x -> xowe
```

```
Y -> Yot, y -> yurn
Z -> Zexter, z -> zelous
```

This looks interesting. Some of these are even real words, like "Her," "land," and "state." The principles for doing this with words is the same. The number of dimensions increases, so we must be mindful of memory usage.

Let's look at how these work. First, let's extract our layers.

```
embedding = model.layers[0]
lstm = model.layers[1]
dense = model.layers[2]
```

After this, we want to extract the weights. The Keras library does not store each of the weights of the LSTM layer separately, so we will have to split them out.

```
# embedding layers don't have a bias term, so
# we only get one here
W_e = embedding.get_weights()[0]

W, U, b = lstm.get_weights()

# The W_* weights are concatenated along the second axis
W_i = W[:, :units]
W_f = W[:, units: units * 2]
W_c = W[:, units * 2: units * 3]
W_o = W[:, units * 3:]

# The U_* weights are concatenated along the second axis
U_i = U[:, :units]
U_f = U[:, units: units * 2]
U_c = U[:, units * 2: units * 3]
U_o = U[:, units * 3:]

# The b_* weights are also concatenated
b_i = b[:units]
b_f = b[units: units * 2]
b_c = b[units * 2: units * 3]
b_o = b[units * 3:]

# Finally, the output weights
W_d, b_d = dense.get_weights()
```

Let's see what we should expect when we try and predict the next character after "recurren."

```
text = ['recurren']
encoded = texts_to_sequences(text)
encoded = kp.sequence.pad_sequences(
    encoded, maxlen=w, padding='pre')
pred = model.predict_classes(encoded)
pred = sequences_to_texts([pred])
pred
```

```
['t']
```

This makes sense because this would make the word "recurrent." Now, let's see if we can calculate this for ourselves. First, we must create our inputs.

```
X = ['recurren']
X = texts_to_sequences(X)
X = kp.sequence.pad_sequences(encoded, maxlen=w, padding='pre')
X = np.eye(alphabet_size)[X.reshape(-1)].T
X.shape

(50, 10)
```

Now, we can convert our 50-dimensional sparse vectors into much more dense 5-dimensional vectors using the embedding layer.

```
V_e = np.dot(W_e.T, X).T
V_e.shape

(10, 5)
```

Let's run this through the LSTM. This code is mostly parallel to the previous equations, the exception being that we store the values in h_* variables before sending them through the activation functions. This is done to keep the lines of code from being too long.

```
v_t = np.zeros(units)
c_t = np.zeros(units)
for v_e in V_e:
    h_f = np.dot(W_f.T, v_e) + np.dot(U_f.T, v_t) + b_f
    f_t = sigmoid(h_f)
    h_i = np.dot(W_i.T, v_e) + np.dot(U_i.T, v_t) + b_i
    i_t = sigmoid(h_i)
    h_o = np.dot(W_o.T, v_e) + np.dot(U_o.T, v_t) + b_o
    o_t = sigmoid(h_o)
    h_cc = np.dot(W_c.T, v_e) + np.dot(U_c.T, v_t) + b_c
    cc_t = np.tanh(h_cc)
    c_t = np.multiply(f_t, c_t) + np.multiply(i_t, cc_t)
    v_t = np.multiply(o_t, np.tanh(c_t))

v_t.shape

(20,)
```

We will take the last output and pass it through the dense layer to get our prediction.

```
h_d = np.dot(W_d.T, v_t) + b_d
pred = softmax(h_d)
pred

array([5.82594437e-14, 1.42019430e-13, 6.24594676e-05, 7.96185826e-03,
       1.44256098e-01, 8.38904616e-02, 2.30058043e-03, 1.34377453e-02,
       2.41413353e-02, 8.99782631e-03, 3.62877644e-04, 7.10518831e-04,
       4.20883844e-05, 1.14326228e-01, 4.10492247e-01, 1.37839318e-03,
       1.71264211e-03, 1.74333516e-03, 2.45791054e-03, 3.24176673e-04,
```

```
9.32490754e-05, 7.62545395e-14, 9.35015496e-05, 1.53205409e-01,
2.67653674e-02, 1.24012713e-03, 5.49467572e-14, 3.55922084e-11,
8.92650636e-14, 9.91368315e-14, 8.16121572e-14, 2.14432828e-18,
9.12657866e-14, 3.24019025e-06, 9.51441183e-14, 8.55035544e-14,
8.72065395e-14, 7.73119241e-14, 9.14113806e-14, 1.08231855e-13,
3.22887102e-07, 8.59110640e-14, 1.10092976e-13, 8.71172907e-14,
1.04723547e-13, 7.06023940e-14, 8.18420309e-14, 1.21049563e-13,
8.37730240e-14, 1.04719426e-13])
```

We just need to find the index with the highest value, so we use `argmax`.

```
i2c[pred.argmax()]
```

```
't'
```

Finally, we have our prediction. Let's look at some of the runners-up.

```
top5 = sorted(enumerate(pred), key=lambda x: x[1], reverse=True)[:5]
```

```
for ix, p in top5:
    print(i2c[ix], p)
```

```
t 0.5984201360888022
e 0.12310572070859592
# 0.08221461341991843
c 0.043372692317500176
l 0.037207052073704866
```

We can speculate as to why the other characters might be predicted. The character "g" could be predicted based on how similar the input string is to "recurring." As we discussed previously, most words are not as long as "recurren," so predicting the end of the word also makes sense. The character "c" is part of the word "recurrence." And the character "s" is a common letter in English, so it will often show up with a high probability.

Modeling sequences is a central part of modern NLP. In the bag-of-words approach, we lose all the information communicated by syntax. Now that we can model language as a sequence, we can look at how to extract information from the sequences.

Exercise: Character N-Grams

Modify the language model RNN to use character N-grams. So, the sequences should be `recurrent -> 2-gram -> [re, cu, rr, en, t#]`.

Remember that you may want to update w to reflect how much context you need.

Exercise: Word Language Model

Take the poem "Jabberwocky" and build a language model from that.

1. Your sequences will be lines in the poem—for example, ["'Twas brillig, and the slithy toves," "Did gyre and gimble in the wabe:"]. Use a Spark NLP pipeline to process the text and extract the list of tokens.

2. Your encoding code will need to change, `c2i`, `i2c`, `texts_to_sequences`, and `sequences_to_texts` will need to be updated to work with words.

3. `generate_word` will need to be updated to generate lines instead.

Resources

- *The Penn Treebank: An Overview*, by Ann Taylor, Mitchell Marcus, and Beatrice Santorini (Springer): this is an overview of the Penn Treebank data set, which is one of the most widely used NLP data sets.

- *Long Short-Term Memory in Recurrent Neural Networks* (*https://oreil.ly/ipKJM*), by Felix Gers: the PhD dissertation describing LSTMs. It's a little dense, as expected in a dissertation, but if you are interested in the mathematical underpinnings it's a must-read.

- *Probabilistic Graphical Models: Principles and Techniques*, by Daphne Koller and Nir Friedman (MIT Press): this is a textbook for probabilistic graphical models like HMMs and CRFs.

CHAPTER 9

Information Extraction

When working with text, we generally want to extract some meaning. Many tasks involve extracting events or entities from the text. We may also want to find all the places in a document that reference a particular person. We may want to find what happened in a particular place. These tasks are called *information extraction.*

Information extraction tasks are focused on entities (nouns and noun phrases) and events (verb phrases including their subjects and objects). This is different than part-of-speech tasks in which, instead of needing to tag everything, we need to identify only the "important" pieces of the text. However, the techniques used to extract this information are generally the same as those used in sequence modeling.

By far, the most common type of information extraction is named-entity recognition. This is the task of finding references to specific entities.

Named-Entity Recognition

Named-entity recognition (NER) is the task of finding specific things (nouns) in text. Often, the desired named entities are proper nouns, but there are other things we may wish to extract as well. Let's look at some of the common types of nouns that are extracted.

To fully understand the linguistics behind named-entity recognition, we need to define some terms:

Referring expression or R-expression
> A word or phrase that refers to an actual or conceptual thing. This is broken into different types based on how specific the R-expression is and how it is specified.

Referent
> The actual or conceptual thing that an R-expression refers to.

Definiteness and Indefiniteness

This refers to how specific the referent is. If an R-expression is definite, there is a particular referent. There are different kinds of indefiniteness, but languages differ on what kinds are distinguished.

Deixis

An R-expression whose referent can be resolved only with contextual information.

Let's look at some examples.

- "Cows" in "Cows eat grass" is an example of an *indefinite noun*. In English, there is no required indefinite article, though "some" can be used.

- "France" in "France is in Europe" is an example of a *proper noun*. A proper noun is, by its nature, definite. In English, most proper nouns don't use a definite article. There are some exceptions—mostly geographical regions and bodies of water, like "The Arctic" and "The Gobi." There are some other exceptions, mainly non–proper-noun phrases that are proper in context—for example, sports teams like "the Cowboys."

- "The Sun" in "The Sun is shining" is an example of a *definite noun*. In English, definite nouns that are not proper nouns require the definite article "the."

- The "that" in "Are you going to eat that" is an example of *deixis*. In context, the referent is a specific food item, but without the context it's impossible to resolve the reference.

- "I" and "here" in "I am here" are also examples of *deixis*. This sentence can be interpreted as a tautology, but it is still common. This is due to the deictic center being different for "I" and "here." "I" has the speaker or writer as the deictic center, while "here" has some location introduced earlier as the deictic center.

- The "tomorrow" in "The next episode airs tomorrow" is an example of *deixis* used as an adverb.

As you can see, this is a complicated aspect of language. Fortunately, when doing NER, we restrict what entities we are looking for. Commonly, NER models identify people, places, organizations, and times. These models are generally looking for proper nouns. We will refer to this as *generic NER*. Another common NER task is finding particular concepts—for example, clinical procedures. This task is made easier by being focused on a particular set of vocabulary. A fluent speaker of a language can generally identify whether a noun is proper, but identifying domain-specific categories requires a domain expert. We will refer to this as *domain-specific NER*.

We can approach either general or domain-specific NER with the sequence-modeling techniques we discussed in Chapter 8. Let's look at how to construct our data. The general notion is that we want to turn this into a classification task in which the classes are "inside a named entity" or "outside a named entity." The basic classes are O, which is the class for tokens outside of a named entity. B-PER, I-PER, B-LOC, and I-LOC are the classes for tokens in a named entity phrase whose referent is a person (B-PER, I-PER) or location (B-LOC, I-LOC). Sometimes, there are more classes. It's common to also have B-* classes for beginning named-entity phrases. Let's look at some examples, with results in Tables 9-1 and 9-2.

"King Arthur went to Camelot."

Table 9-1. NER tags and tokens

token	class
King	B-PER
Arthur	I-PER
went	O
to	O
Camelot	B-LOC
.	O

In clinical text, instead of looking for persons or locations, we are more interested in procedures (B-PROC, I-PROC).

"The patient received a bone scan"

Table 9-2. NER tags in a clinical sentence

token	class
The	O
patient	O
received	O
a	O
bone	B-PROC
scan	I-PROC

With these labels, you can approach modeling similarly to how you performed part-of-speech tagging.

If you are doing domain-specific NER, you can use a curated set of terminology to find the occurrences in the document without a model. Let's look at some ways we can implement this. Let's look at the Brown corpus again. We will look for occurrences of stop words in text.

```
from collections import defaultdict, Counter
from random import sample, seed
from time import time
```

```
from nltk.corpus import brown
from nltk.corpus import stopwords

en_stopwords = set(stopwords.words('english'))
```

Let's define some functions that will help us.

```
brown_fileids = brown.fileids()

def detokenize(sentence):
    """
    This will let us look at the raw text,
    not split into sentences or tokens.
    """
    text = ''
    for token in sentence:
        if text and any(c.isalnum() for c in token):
            text += ' '
        text += token
    return text

def get_sample_files(k):
    """
    This will give us a sample of the documents
    """
    sample_files = []
    for fid in sample(brown_fileids, k):
        tokens = []
        for sent in brown.sents(fid):
            tokens.extend(sent)
        sample_files.append((fid, detokenize(tokens)))
    return sample_files

def get_match_counts(texts, search_fn, *args):
    """
    This will run the given search function, search_fn
    on the texts. Additional arguments are passed as
    *args
    """
    references = defaultdict(Counter)
    for fid, text in texts:
        for term, begin, end in search_fn(text, *args):
            references[term][fid] += 1
    return references
```

Let's create some samples of documents so we can see how long it takes to find matches.

```
seed(123)

raw_10 = [(fid, tokens) for fid, tokens in get_sample_files(10)]
raw_50 = [(fid, tokens) for fid, tokens in get_sample_files(50)]
raw_100 = [(fid, tokens) for fid, tokens in get_sample_files(100)]
raw_500 = [(fid, tokens) for fid, tokens in get_sample_files(500)]
```

Let's try the simple naïve approach. For each position in the text, we will try and match each term in our vocabulary to one of our search terms.

```python
def simple_match(text, vocabulary):
    text = text.lower()
    for term in vocabulary:
        for i in range(len(text) - len(term) + 1):
            j = i+len(term)
            end_of_word = j == len(text) or not text[j].isalpha()
            begin_of_word = i == 0 or not text[i-1].isalpha()
            if begin_of_word and \
                end_of_word and \
                term == text[i:i+len(term)]:
                yield (term, i, j)

timing = []
for texts in [raw_10, raw_50, raw_100]:
    start = time() # milliseconds
    references = get_match_counts(texts, simple_match, en_stopwords)
    timing.append((len(texts), int(time() - start) * 1000))
    print('the', sum(references['the'].values()))
    print('about', sum(references['about'].values()))
    print('wouldn\'t', sum(references['wouldn\'t'].values()))
    print('{} documents in {} ms'.format(*timing[-1]))
```

Let's see how long it takes to process documents using the naïve approach.

```
the 1404
about 34
wouldn't 2
10 documents in 6000 ms
the 6876
about 177
wouldn't 15
50 documents in 30000 ms
the 13962
about 380
wouldn't 40
100 documents in 60000 ms
```

That is quite slow. Let's look at the time complexity of the naïve approach.

If the size of a document is N characters, and M is the sum of the lengths of the vocabulary, this approach has O(MN) complexity. Your timing may be worse, but this is because we are also building the dictionary of references.

There are many wasted checks in this approach. If we are at an 's', we don't need to check for "about." It would be better if we could limit the number of vocabulary items that we need to consider. We can do this with a *trie*.

A *trie* is a data structure that lets us store many sequences in a tree. A trie stores each sequence as a path in the tree. Let's look at an example.

```python
def build_trie(sequences, empty=lambda: ''):
    """
    This will build our trie. We include the path in
    each node to make explaining the trie easier, even
    though this increases our memory footprint.
    """
    trie = {'<path>': empty()}
    for seq in sequences:
        curr = trie
        path = empty()
        for elem in seq:
            path += elem
            curr = curr.setdefault(elem, {'<path>': path})
        curr['<END>'] = True
    return trie


def traverse(trie, empty=lambda: ''):
    """
    This is breadth-first traversal. This will traverse
    the trie one layer at a time.
    """
    queue = [trie]
    while len(queue) > 0:
        head = queue[0]
        path = head['<path>']
        queue = queue[1:] + list(
            node
            for key, node in head.items()
            if not key[0] == '<'
        )
        yield (path, head)


def traverse_depth_first(trie, empty=lambda: ''):
    """
    This is depth-first traversal. This will traverse
    the trie one path at a time.
    """
    stack = [trie]
    while len(stack) > 0:
        head = stack[0]
        path = head['<path>']
        stack = list(
            node
            for key, node in head.items()
            if not key[0] == '<'
        ) + stack[1:]
        yield (path, head)
```

Let's look at the trie with a simple vocabulary.

```python
trie = build_trie(['cat', 'catharsis', 'dog', 'destiny'])

print('Breadth-first traversal')
```

```
for path, _ in traverse(trie):
    print(path)

print()

print('Depth-first traversal')
for path, _ in traverse_depth_first(trie):
    print(path)
```

Breadth-first traversal

c
d
ca
do
de
cat
dog
des
cath
...
destiny
catharsi
catharsis

Depth first traversal

c
ca
cat
cath
...
catharsis
d
do
dog
de
...
destiny

Now that we have this data structure, we can use it to search the text. The gist of the algorithm is to iterate over the text and use the characters from the text to traverse the trie. Let's look at the code.

```
def trie_match(text, trie):
    text = text.lower()
    curr = trie
    # for each character in text
    for i in range(len(text)):
        j = i # begin traversing the trie from text[i]
        begin_of_word = i == 0 or not text[i-1].isalpha()
        if not begin_of_word:
            continue
```

```
        while j < len(text) and text[j] in curr:
            # move down the trie
            curr = curr[text[j]]
            # check if we are not in the middle of a word
            end_of_word = j == len(text) - 1 or not text[j+1].isalpha()
            # if we are at the end of a word and we are currently at
            # an entry, emit a match
            if end_of_word and '<END>' in curr:
                term = curr['<path>']
                yield (term, j-len(term)+1, j+1)
            j += 1
        # when we run out of matching characters or reach the
        # end of the trie, reset and move on to the next character
        curr = trie
```

Let's time the trie-based approach.

```
en_stopwords_trie = build_trie(en_stopwords)
timing = []
for texts in [raw_10, raw_50, raw_100, raw_500]:
    start = time() # milliseconds
    references = get_match_counts(texts, trie_match, en_stopwords_trie)
    timing.append((len(texts), int((time() - start) * 1000)))
    print('the', sum(references['the'].values()))
    print('about', sum(references['about'].values()))
    print('wouldn\'t', sum(references['wouldn\'t'].values()))
    print('{} documents in {} ms'.format(*timing[-1]))
```

```
the 1404
about 34
wouldn't 2
10 documents in 38 ms
the 6876
about 177
wouldn't 15
50 documents in 186 ms
the 13962
about 380
wouldn't 40
100 documents in 371 ms
the 70003
about 1817
wouldn't 129
500 documents in 1815 ms
```

This is much faster. This is a classic trade-off in NLP. To improve speed we increase our memory footprint, in addition to the time necessary to precompute our trie. There are more complex algorithms, like the Aho-Corasick, which uses extra links in the trie to reduce the time spent backtracking.

If you have a constrained vocabulary, a dictionary search—like our previous trie-matching algorithms—can get a lot of information from the document. It is limited by not being able to recognize anything that is not in the curated vocabulary. To decide what approach is best for your project, consider the following:

- Do you have a domain-specific NER requirement? Or is it general NER?
  - If you need general NER, you need to build a model.
- Do you have a curated vocabulary? Do you have labeled text?
  - If you have both, you probably want to create a model to potentially recognize new terms. If you have neither, consider which one would be easier to create.

Once we have our entities, we may want to connect them to external data. For example, let's say that we are looking for mentions of pharmaceuticals in clinical notes. We may want to associate the named entities (drugs) with information from a drug database. How we do this matching will depend on how we are doing the NER. Because this is a domain-specific NER task, we can use either a dictionary-search approach or a model approach. If we have such a database, it can actually be used to create our curated vocabulary. This makes it straightforward to associate recognized drug names with their metadata in our database. If we are using a model approach, things can be a little murkier, since models can recognize names that may not exactly occur in our database. One way we can approach this task is to search for the drug name in our database that is *closest* to the found drug name.

In Spark NLP, there are two ways to do NER. One strategy uses CRFs, and the other is deep learning based. Both approaches take word embeddings as inputs, so we will see examples in Chapter 11 when we discuss word embeddings.

All these approaches to NER miss a class of reference. These approaches identify only direct references. None of them can identify what pronouns to refer to. For example:

> The coelacanth is a living fossil. The ancient fish was discovered off the coast of South Africa.

The "ancient fish" won't be identified as the same thing as "coelacanth."

We can solve this problem with *coreference resolution*.

Coreference Resolution

We previously discussed R-expressions and referents. A coreference is when two R-expressions share a referent. This can be valuable in text if we are trying to understand what is being said about our named entities. Unfortunately, this is a difficult problem.

Humans understand coreference through a number of syntactic and lexical rules. Let's look at some examples.

He knows him.
He knows himself.

In the first sentence, we know that there are two people involved, whereas in the second there is only one. The reason for this is in a subfield of syntax called government and binding. A reflexive pronoun, like "himself," must refer back to something in its clause. For example, look the following nongrammatical sentence.

They were at the mall. *We saw themselves.

Although we can guess that "themselves" refers to the same group to which "they" refers, it seems odd. This is because the reflexive nature tried to bind itself to the other entity in the sentence, "We." Nonreflexives must not be bound in their clause.

Pronominal references aren't the only type of coreference. There are often many ways to refer to an entity. Let's look at an example.

Odysseus, known to the Romans as Ulysses, is an important character in the works of Homer. He is most well known for the adventures he had on his way home from the Trojan War.

In this sentence, Odysseus is referred to five times. In linguistics, it is common to give a subscript to indicate coreference. Let's look at the same sentence marked for coreference.

Odysseus$_i$, known to the Romans as Ulysses$_i$, is an important character in the works of Homer. He$_i$ is most well known for the adventures he$_i$ had on his$_i$ way home from the Trojan War.

Now that we understand coreference, how do we extract it from text? It is a difficult problem. Adoption of deep learning techniques have been slower for this task than the others because it is not often attempted. It is possible to approach this with a rule-based approach. If you parse the sentence into a syntax tree, you can use syntactic rules to identify which R-expressions share a referent. There is a big problem with this, however. It will work only on text with regular syntax. So this approach will work well on newspapers but very poorly on Twitter and clinical notes. An additional downside to this is that the rules require someone who has a strong knowledge of the syntax of the language for which we are building our rules.

The machine learning approach can be treated as a sequence-modeling problem. We must try and identify, for a given R-expression, whether it is the same as a previous R-expression or if it has a new referent. There are a number of data sets available out there that we can practice on.

Now that we have talked about how to get the R-expressions and how to identify coreferents, we can talk about what to do next.

Assertion Status Detection

Imagine we are looking for patients who exhibited a particular symptom when taking a drug—for example, dizziness. If we look for just any clinical report mentioning dizziness, we will find many mentions like the following.

> No dizziness.
> I have prescribed a drug that may cause dizziness. Patient denies dizziness.

Surely, these are not the patients we are looking for. Understanding how the speaker or author is using the information is as important as understanding what is being referred to in the information. This is called the *assertion status task* in the clinical setting. There are uses for it in other styles of communication, like legal documents and technical specifications.

Let's look at it from the linguistic point of view. When we see "false positives" like in the previous "dizziness" example, it is because the statement is in the wrong *mood* or in the wrong *polarity*.

Polarity is whether a statement is affirmative or negative. *Mood* is a feature of a statement that indicates how the speaker or author feels about the statement. All languages have ways of indicating these things, but they differ greatly from language to language. In English, we use adverbs to express doubt, but in some other languages it is expressed in the morphology. Let's see some examples of polarity and mood.

1. The patient did not have difficulty standing.

2. The movie may come out in April.

3. I would have liked the soup if it were warmer.

The first example is an example of *negation* (negative polarity), the second is an example of the *speculative* mood, and the third is an example of the *conditional*. Negation is a feature of all languages, but how it is expressed varies considerably—even between dialects of the same language. You have likely heard of the rule about double negation in English; that is, that a double negative makes a positive.

> I don't have nothing ~ I have something

This is not always the case, however. Consider the following example:

> You're not unfriendly.

Here, the verb is negated by "not," and the predicate is negated by the "un-" prefix. The meaning of this sentence is certainly not "You are friendly," though. Natural language is much more ambiguous than formal logic. In certain dialects of English, double negation can serve to intensify the statement, or it can even be required. In these dialects, "I don't have nothing" means the same as "I have nothing."

Similarly, the speculative case is also ambiguous. How you treat such statements will depend on the application you are building. If you are building something that extracts movie release dates, you may very well want to include a speculative statement. On the other hand, considering the medical example with "may cause dizziness," we likely would not want to include the phrase describing this patient in the set of patients who suffer from dizziness. An additional factor to consider is hedged speech. If someone wishes to soften a statement, they can use the speculative mood or other similar moods. This is a pragmatic effect that can appear to change the semantics.

> You may want to close the window ~ [pragmatically] Close the window
> You might feel a pinch ~ [pragmatically] You will feel a pinch
> You could get your own fries ~ [pragmatically] You should get your own fries

Finally, let's consider the third example, "I would have liked the soup if it were warmer." This sentence has at least two interpretations. One interpretation is, "I would have also liked the soup if it were warmer." The other, and perhaps the more likely, interpretation is, "I did not like the soup because it was not warm enough." This is an example of implied negation. Another common source of implied negation is phrases like "too X to Y," which implies a negation on "Y."

> The patient is in too much pain to do their physical therapy.

This communicates that "the patient did not do their physical therapy" and also gives the reason. Clinical terminology contains many special ways to refer to negation. This is why Wendy Chapman et al. developed the *negex* algorithm. It is a rule-based algorithm that identifies what sections of a sentence are negated depending on the type of cues.

The different cues or triggers signify beginnings and ends of negated scopes, and they prevent negex from incorrectly identifying nonnegated words as negated. Let's look at some examples. We will first show the original sentence, and then the sentence with the cues italicized and the negated words struck through.

1. The patient denies dizziness but appears unstable when standing.

   - The patient *denies* ~~dizziness~~ **but** appears unstable when standing.

2. The test was negative for fungal infection.

   - The test was *negative for* ~~fungal infection~~.

3. The XYZ test ruled the patient out for SYMPTOM.

   - The XYZ test *ruled the patient out for* ~~SYMPTOM~~.

4. Performed XYZ test to rule the patient out for SYMPTOM.

   - Performed XYZ test to *rule the patient out for* SYMPTOM.

In examples 1 and 2, we see that the negation was not signaled by a normal grammatical negative like "not." Instead, there are clinical-specific cues, "denies" and "negative for." Also, note that the negation was terminated by "but" in the first example. In examples 3 and 4, cues are made to rule out false positives. In example 4, the results of the test are not actually discussed.

We've seen how the polarity and mood of verbs can affect entities in the sentence, but is there a way to get out more information? In the next section we will briefly discuss the idea of extracting relationships and facts from text.

Relationship Extraction

Relationship extraction is perhaps the most difficult task in information extraction. This is because we could spend a lot of research and computation time trying to extract more and more fine-grained information. So we should always understand exactly what kind of relationships we want to extract before trying something so challenging.

Let's consider the scenario in which we are trying to extract statements from clinical documents. The nature of these documents limits the kinds of entities that may appear.

- The patient
- Conditions (diseases, injuries, tumors, etc.)
- Body parts
- Procedures
- Drugs
- Tests and results
- Family and friends of the patient (in family history and social history sections)

There can be other entities, but these are common. Let's say our application is supposed to extract all the entities and make statements. Let's look at an example.

```
CHIEF COMPLAINT
Ankle pain

HISTORY OF PRESENT ILLNESS:
The patient is 28 y/o man who tripped when hiking. He struggled back to his
car, and immediately came in. Due to his severe ankle pain, he thought the
right ankle may be broken.

EXAMINATION:
An x-ray of right ankle ruled out fracture.

IMPRESSION:
```

```
The right ankle is sprained.

RECOMMENDATION:
- Take ibuprofen as needed
- Try to stay off right ankle for one week

The patient ...
  is 28 y/o man
  has severe ankle pain
  tripped when hiking
  struggled back to his car
  immediately came in
The right ankle ...
  may be broken
  is sprained
The x-ray of right ankle ...
  rules out fracture
Ibuprofen ...
  is recommended
  take as needed
Try to stay off right ankle ...
  is recommended
  is for one week
```

To perform relationship extraction using this data, there are a number of steps we need to take. We will need all the basic text processing, section segmenting, NER, and coreference resolution. This is just for processing the document. Creating the output would also require some text generation logic. However, we may be able to combine a syntactic parser and some rules to get some of this done. As described in the previous chapter, a syntactic parser will transform sentences into a hierarchical structure. Let's look at some of the sentences.

The patient is 28 y/o man who tripped when hiking.

```
(ROOT
  (S
    (NP (DT The) (NN patient))
    (VP (VBZ is)
      (NP
        (NP (ADJP (CD 28) (JJ y/o)) (NN man))
        (SBAR
          (WHNP (WP who))
          (S
            (VP (VBN tripped)
              (SBAR
                (WHADVP (WRB when))
                (S
                  (VP (VBZ hiking)))))))))
    (. .)))
```

This looks complicated, but it is relatively straightforward. Most sentences can be described in a simple tree structure.

```
(ROOT
  (S
    (NP (NNS SUBJECT))
    (VP (VBP VERB)
      (NP (NN OBJECT)))
    (. .)))
```

Embedded *wh*-clauses can inherit their subjects. For example, let's take the following sentence:

The man who wears a hat.

In the wh-clause "who wears a hat," "who" is coreferent with "The man." In the following sentence we see a clause with no explicit subject:

The man went to the store while wearing a hat.

The subject "wearing" is "The man." The actual syntax behind identifying the subject of an embedded clause can get complicated. Fortunately, such complicated sentences are less common in the terse English found in clinical notes. This means that we can group sentences by the entity that is their subject.

```
PATIENT
    The patient is 28 y/o man who tripped when hiking.
        who tripped when hiking
    He struggled back to his car, and immediately came in.
    he thought the right ankle may be broken.

RIGHT ANKLE
    the right ankle may be broken
    The right ankle is sprained.

X-RAY
    An x-ray of right ankle ruled out fracture.

IBUPROFEN
    Take ibuprofen as needed
```

This gets us most of the sentences we are interested in. In fact, if we make embedded sentences their own sentences and split conjoined verbs, we get all but one of the statements about the patient. The remaining statement, "has severe ankle pain," will be more difficult. We would need to turn something of the form (NP (PRP$ his) (JJ severe) (NN ankle) (NN pain))) into (ROOT (S (NP (PRP He)) (VP (VBZ has) (NP (JJ severe) (JJ ankle) (NN pain))) (. .))) Converting noun phrases with possessives into "have" statements is a simple rule. We have glossed over the coreference resolution here. We can simply say that any third-person singular pronoun outside of family history or social history is the patient. We can also create special rules for different sections—for example, anything mentioned in a recommendation section gets a statement "is recommended." These simplifying approaches can get us most of the statements. We still need something to recognize "Try to stay off right ankle" as a treatment.

Let's use NLTK and CoreNLP to look at what is actually parsed.

```
text_cc = ['Ankle pain']

text_hpi = [
    'The patient is 28 y/o man who tripped when hiking.',
    'He struggled back to his car, and immediately came in.',
    'Due to his severe ankle pain, he thought the right ankle may be broken.']

text_ex = ['An x-ray of right ankle ruled out fracture.']

text_imp = ['The right ankle is sprained.']

text_rec = [
    'Take ibuprofen as needed',
    'Try to stay off right ankle for one week']
```

First, let's start our CoreNLPServer and create our parser.

```
from nltk.parse.corenlp import CoreNLPServer
from  nltk.parse.corenlp import CoreNLPParser

server = CoreNLPServer(
    'stanford-corenlp-3.9.2.jar',
    'stanford-corenlp-3.9.2-models.jar',
)

server.start()
parser = CoreNLPParser()

parse_cc = list(map(lambda t: next(parser.raw_parse(t)), text_cc))
parse_hpi = list(map(lambda t: next(parser.raw_parse(t)), text_hpi))
parse_ex = list(map(lambda t: next(parser.raw_parse(t)), text_ex))
parse_imp = list(map(lambda t: next(parser.raw_parse(t)), text_imp))
parse_rec = list(map(lambda t: next(parser.raw_parse(t)), text_rec))
```

Each parsed sentence is represented as a tree. Let's take a look at the first sentence in the "History of Present Illness" section (as shown in Figure 9-1).

```
parse_hpi[0]
```

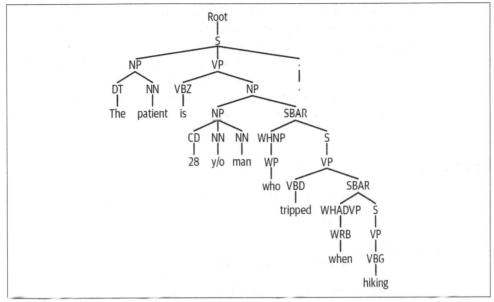

Figure 9-1. Parse of "The patient is 28 y/o. . ."

We can traverse the tree via the indices. For example, we can get the subject-noun phrase by taking the first *child* of the sentence (as shown in Figure 9-2).

```
parse_hpi[0][0][0]
```

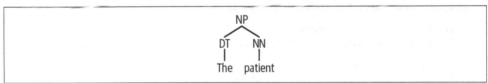

Figure 9-2. Subject of first HPI sentence

The leaves of the tree are the tokens:

```
parse_hpi[0][0][0][0][0]
```

```
'The'
```

Summary

Now we see how far we can get when we have documents with a narrow set of language. These assumptions would not work if we tried to apply them to tweets, patents, or movie scripts. When we build applications like this, we must iterate on problems by reviewing the data, training our models, and looking at the product.

These topics have been heavy in linguistics. This is natural, since we are trying to extract information encoded in language. Linguistics is the study of language, so we can get a lot of advantage by using its knowledge. But what if we don't want to extract the information for human consumption, but for use in modeling? We'll need something better than TF.IDF. The next two chapters talk about *distributional semantics*. Chapter 10 is about topic modeling, in which we treat documents as a combination of different *topics*. Chapter 11 is about word embeddings, in which we try to represent words as vectors.

Exercises

In this exercise, you will be traversing the parse trees looking for SVO triplets.

```
from nltk.tree import Tree

def get_svo(sentence):
    parse = next(parser.raw_parse(sentence))
    svos = []
    # svos.append((subject, verb, object))
    return svos
```

Here are some test cases to use.

```
# [("The cows", "eat", "grass")]
get_svo('The cows eat grass.')

# [("the cows", "ate", "grass")]
get_svo('Yesterday, the cows ate the grass.')

# [("The cows", "ate", "grass")]
get_svo('The cows quickly ate the grass.')

# [("the cows", "eat", "grass")]
get_svo('When did, the cows eat the grass.')

# [("The cows", "eat", "grass"), ("The cows", "came", "home")]
get_svo('The cows that ate the grass came home.')
```

## CHAPTER 10

Topic Modeling

In the previous chapter we covered some of the techniques used to extract information from text. These techniques can be complicated to implement and may also be slow. If the application requires the information extracted to be readable by the users, these techniques are great. If we are looking to extract information as part of an intermediate processing step—for instance, building features for a classifier—then we don't need to extract readable information. As we saw in Chapters 5 and 7, simply using our vocabulary will create an unwieldy number of features. Therefore, we want to reduce the dimensionality of our data. This is where distributional semantics comes in.

Distributional semantics is the study, using statistical distributions, of elements of language to characterize similarities between documents (e.g., email), speech acts (e.g., spoken or written sentences), or elements thereof (e.g., phrases, words). The idea for this field comes from John R. Firth, a linguist in the first half of the 20th century. He noted how semantics was dependent on context and coined the oft-repeated quote, "You shall know a word by the company it keeps."

The idea is that you can represent a word as a probabilistic distribution over the contexts it appears in. The words will exist in a vector space where the dimensions are associated with these contexts. For example, "doctor" will have a larger value on the medical dimension than in the financial dimension. However, "bank" will have larger values on the financial dimension and the geological dimension. We can't simply use hand-chosen contexts, though. These too must be learned from the data. Commonly, we learn the contexts by looking at what words occur with each other. This back-and-forth means that most such algorithms iterate until they find the model that best fits the data. These approaches are a kind of clustering. Indeed, we can use more generic clustering algorithms on text data, though they may not work well.

In the following examples, we have a document-term matrix in which the rows are documents, and columns are terms. The values can be binary, representing word presence, or the number of times a term occurs, or they can be TF.IDF values. We will be using TF.IDF values in this chapter. Once we have such a matrix, we will want to map our documents to a space with fewer dimensions. This clusters the documents into topics.

We will be using the Python library scikit-learn to introduce the techniques. This library will allow us to more easily examine the internal data of these models than would Spark's implementation.

K-Means

As a first attempt at topic modeling, let's try a classic clustering technique—K-Means, as shown in Figure 10-1. Let's say we have a number of data points in a vector space. We can pick K points in the vector space, called centroids, and assign each data point to the closest centroid. We want to find the K points that minimize the distance between the data points and their centroid.

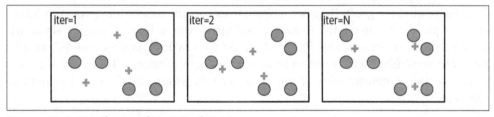

Figure 10-1. Simple visualization of K-Means

In our situation, we have documents in a vector space defined by the TF.IDF values. When we find our K points, we can say that each K represents a topic. Let's look at an example.

First, let's build our data set. We will be using the Brown corpus, which is a collection of articles, periodicals, and reports from newspapers, journals, and academic institutions. It is a classic data set that has been used in NLP since the 1960s.

```
from collections import defaultdict, Counter, OrderedDict

import numpy as np
import pandas as pd
import scipy.sparse as sparse

from wordcloud import WordCloud
import matplotlib.pyplot as plt
%matplotlib inline

from nltk.corpus import stopwords
```

```
from nltk.corpus import brown
en_stopwords = set(stopwords.words('english'))

def detokenize(sentence):
    text = ''
    for token in sentence:
        if text and any(c.isalnum() for c in token):
            text += ' '
        text += token
    return text
```

We will want to remove the punctuation and the stop words so our algorithms use only the "useful" words.

```
def process(sentence):
    terms = []
    for term in sentence:
        term = term.lower()
        if term not in en_stopwords and term.isalnum():
            terms.append(term)
    return terms
```

Let's gather our docs. Our documents will be lists of lists of terms.

```
docs = OrderedDict()

for fid in brown.fileids():
    docs[fid] = brown.sents(fid)
```

Now we will construct indices. This is similar to what we did when we were exploring information retrieval.

```
ix2doc = list(docs)
doc2ix = {fid: i for i, fid in enumerate(ix2doc)}
vocabulary = set()

term_counts = defaultdict(Counter)
document_counts = Counter()

for fid, doc in docs.items():
    unique_terms = set()
    for sentence in doc:
        sentence = process(sentence)
        term_counts[fid].update(sentence)
        unique_terms.update(sentence)
    document_counts.update(unique_terms)
    vocabulary.update(unique_terms)

ix2term = sorted(list(vocabulary))
term2ix = OrderedDict()
for i, term in enumerate(ix2term):
    term2ix[term] = i
```

Now that we have our indices, let's construct a matrix for TF and IDF.

```
term_count_mat = sparse.dok_matrix((len(doc2ix), len(term2ix)))

for fid, i in doc2ix.items():
    for term, count in term_counts[fid].items():
        j = term2ix[term]
        term_count_mat[i, j] = count
term_count_mat = term_count_mat.todense()

doc_count_vec = np.array(
    [document_counts[term] for term in term2ix.keys()])

tf = np.log(term_count_mat + 1)
idf = len(doc2ix) / (1 + doc_count_vec)

tfidf = np.multiply(tf, idf)

tfidf.shape

(500, 40881)
```

This is a rather large matrix for such a small data set. Apart from space efficiency concerns, having this many dimensions can worsen performance for some algorithms. This is when distributional semantics can help.

Now, we can build our model.

```
from sklearn.cluster import KMeans

K = 6
clusters = ['cluster#{}'.format(k) for k in range(K)]
model = KMeans(n_clusters=K, random_state=314)

clustered = model.fit_transform(tfidf)

clustered.shape

(500, 6)
```

We can see that we have now clustered our documents using our six centroids. Each of these centroids is a vector over our vocabulary. We can look at which words are most influential on our centroids. We will use word clouds for this, as shown in Figure 10-2.

```
model.cluster_centers_.shape

(6, 40881)

cluster_term = pd.DataFrame(
    model.cluster_centers_.T, index=ix2term, columns=clusters)
cluster_term = np.round(cluster_term, decimals=4)

font = {'weight' : 'bold', 'size'   : 22}
fig, axs = plt.subplots(K // 2, 2, figsize=(10, 8))

k = 0
for i in range(len(axs)):
    for j in range(len(axs[i])):
```

```
wc = WordCloud(colormap='Greys', background_color='white')
im = wc.generate_from_frequencies(cluster_term[clusters[k]])
axs[i][j].imshow(im, interpolation='bilinear')
axs[i][j].axis("off")
axs[i][j].set_title(clusters[k], **font)
k += 1

plt.tight_layout()
plt.show()
```

Figure 10-2. Word clouds built from the centroids

We can see some recognizable topics here. Cluster #5 seems to be about mathematical topics. Cluster #3 seems to be about food preparation, specifically pasteurization.

K-Means does not make many assumptions about our data—it just tries to find the K. One drawback to K-Means is that it tends to create equally sized clusters. This is an unrealistic expectation for a natural corpus. Additionally, we don't get much in the way if characterizing the similarity between documents. Let's try an algorithm that makes some more assumptions but that will give us a way to see the similarities between these documents.

Latent Semantic Indexing

Latent semantic indexing (LSI) is a technique for decomposing the document-term matrix using *singular value decomposition (SVD)*. In SVD we decompose a matrix into three matrices.

$$M \to U \Sigma V^T$$

Σ is a diagonal matrix of the singular values in descending order. We can take the top K, and this serves as an approximation of the original matrix. The first K columns of U are the representation of the documents in the K dimensional space. The first K columns of V are the representation of the terms in the K dimensional space. This allows us to compare the similarity of documents and terms. It is common to choose a larger number for the components because the more dimensions Σ has, the more dimensions we can use to approximate the original matrix. So we will set K to be the higher number here.

```
from sklearn.decomposition import TruncatedSVD

K = 100
clusters = ['cluster#{}'.format(k) for k in range(K)]
model = TruncatedSVD(n_components=K)

clustered = model.fit_transform(tfidf)
```

Let's look at the K singular values we are keeping.

```
model.singular_values_
```

```
array([3529.39905473, 3244.51395305, 3096.10335704, 3004.8882987 ,
       2814.77858204, 2778.96902533, 2754.2942512 , 2714.32865945,
       2652.4119094 , 2631.64362227, 2578.41230573, 2496.86392987,
       2478.31563312, 2466.82942537, 2465.83674175, 2450.22361278,
       2426.99364435, 2417.13989816, 2407.40572992, 2394.21460258,
       2379.89976747, 2369.78970648, 2344.36252585, 2337.77090924,
       2324.76055049, 2319.07434771, 2308.81232676, 2304.85707171,
       2300.6888689 , 2299.08592131, 2292.18931562, 2281.59638332,
       2280.80535179, 2276.55977269, 2265.29827699, 2264.49999278,
       2259.19162875, 2253.20088136, 2249.34547946, 2239.31921392,
       2232.24240145, 2221.95468155, 2217.95110287, 2208.94458997,
       2199.75216312, 2195.85509817, 2189.76213831, 2186.64540094,
       2178.92705724, 2170.98276352, 2164.19734464, 2159.85021389,
       2154.82652164, 2145.5169884 , 2142.3070779 , 2138.06410065,
       2132.8723198 , 2125.68060737, 2123.13051755, 2121.25651627,
       2119.0925646 , 2113.46585963, 2102.77888039, 2101.07116001,
       2094.0766712 , 2090.41516403, 2086.00515811, 2080.55424737,
       2075.54071367, 2070.03500007, 2066.78292077, 2064.93112208,
       2056.24857815, 2052.96995192, 2048.62550688, 2045.18447518,
       2038.27607405, 2032.74196113, 2026.9687453 , 2022.61629887,
       2018.05274649, 2011.24594096, 2009.64212589, 2004.15307518,
```

```
2000.17006712, 1995.76552783, 1985.15438092, 1981.71380603,
1977.60898352, 1973.78806955, 1966.68359784, 1962.29604116,
1956.62028269, 1951.54510897, 1951.25219946, 1943.75611963,
1939.85749385, 1933.30524488, 1928.57205628, 1919.57447254])
```

The components_ of the model are the highest K diagonal values of Σ. So now, let's look at the terms distributed over the components, as shown in Table 10-1.

```
cluster_term = pd.DataFrame(model.components_.T, index=ix2term, columns=clus-
ters)
cluster_term = np.round(cluster_term, decimals=4)

cluster_term.loc[['polynomial', 'cat', 'frankfurter']]
```

Table 10-1. Term distributions for "polynomial," "cat," and "frankfurter"

term	cluster#0	cluster#1	...	cluster#98	cluster#99
polynomial	0.0003	0.0012	...	0.0077	-0.0182
cat	0.0002	0.0018	...	0.0056	-0.0026
frankfurter	0.0004	0.0010	...	-0.0025	-0.0025

This table represents the distribution that the words have over each cluster.

Since we did not stem our words, let's see if we can find "polynomials," from the vector for "polynomial." We will use *cosine similarity* for this. Cosine similarity is a technique for looking at the similarity between two vectors. The idea is that we want to look at the angle between two vectors. If they are parallel, the similarity should be 1; if they are orthogonal, the similarity should be 0; and if they are going in opposite directions, the similarity should be –1. So we want to look at the cosine of the angle between them. The dot product of two vectors is equal to the product of the magnitudes of the two vectors times the cosine of the angle between them. So, we can take the dot product divided by the product of the magnitudes.

SciPy has a function for cosine *distance*, which is one minus the cosine similarity we just defined. We want the similarity, so we have to undo this.

```
from scipy.spatial.distance import cosine

def cossim(u, v):
    return 1 - cosine(u, v)

polynomial_vec = cluster_term.iloc[term2ix['polynomial']]

similarities = cluster_term.apply(
    lambda r: cossim(polynomial_vec, r), axis=1)

similarities.sort_values(ascending=False)[:20]

polynomial        1.000000
nilpotent         0.999999
diagonalizable    0.999999
```

```
commute              0.999999
polynomials          0.999999
subspace             0.999999
divisible            0.999998
satisfies            0.999998
differentiable       0.999998
monic                0.999998
algebraically        0.999998
primes               0.999996
spanned              0.999996
decomposes           0.999996
scalar               0.999996
commutes             0.999996
algebra              0.999996
integers             0.999991
subspaces            0.999991
exponential          0.999991
dtype: float64
```

We see that "polynomials" is very close, as are a number of other mathematically themed words. This is the "semantics" that people often use when referring to distributional semantics capturing. We can use these representations as features. The larger and more diverse the corpus, the more generally applicable these representations will be.

Let's build the word clouds for our LSI model now, as shown in Figure 10-3. We will look only at the first and last three because we have so many more clusters than our K-Means model.

```python
chosen_ix = [0, 97, 1, 98, 2, 99]

fig, axs = plt.subplots(3, 2, figsize=(10, 8))

k = 0
for i in range(len(axs)):
    for j in range(len(axs[i])):
        wc = WordCloud(colormap='Greys', background_color='white')
        im = wc.generate_from_frequencies(cluster_term[clusters[chosen_ix[k]]])
        axs[i][j].imshow(im, interpolation='bilinear')
        axs[i][j].axis("off")
        axs[i][j].set_title(clusters[chosen_ix[k]], **font)
        k += 1

plt.tight_layout()
plt.show()
```

Cluster #2 seems to be related to medical topics. The others don't appear very informative. This makes sense because this is an approximation of the original matrix, not a clustering of the matrix. This does reduce the dimensions, though, so we could still use this for downstream processing.

The idea that our data is composed of some features relating terms to documents can be directly addressed.

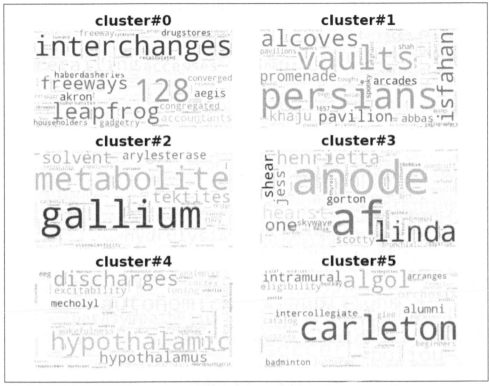

Figure 10-3. Word clouds built from the term distributions

Nonnegative Matrix Factorization

In *nonnegative matrix factorization (NMF)*, we assume that the document-term matrix is the product of two other matrices. The dimension along which these matrices are multiplied will have our clusters. This will give us a document matrix and a term matrix, each with distribution across clusters.

$$X = D \cdot T$$

If we have M documents and N terms, and we want K clusters, X is a MxN matrix, D is a MxK matrix, and T is an KxM matrix. In scikit-learn, these matrices are approximated, since there is no closed-form way to calculate these matrices. Let's try an example on some toy data.

```
from sklearn.decomposition import NMF
```

We will create our random matrix and then split into two clusters.

```
np.random.seed(314)
X = np.array(np.random.randint(1, 20, size=21).reshape(7, 3))

m = NMF(n_components=2, init='random', random_state=314)
D = m.fit_transform(X)
T = m.components_
X
```

```
array([[ 9, 14, 10],
       [11, 15, 17],
       [ 8,  3,  8],
       [17,  4, 13],
       [ 8,  5,  1],
       [ 5, 14,  9],
       [17, 16, 10]])
```

Now, the product of the two matrices should approximate the original matrix.

```
X_hat = np.dot(D, T)
X_hat
```

```
array([[ 8.82168512, 13.8817222 , 10.31193979],
       [12.94642621, 16.30109226, 13.58360985],
       [ 8.89151218,  3.59533529,  6.43588552],
       [17.69416104,  4.46299878, 11.78275144],
       [ 5.8818731 ,  3.5849985 ,  4.71678044],
       [ 5.32011204, 14.21139378,  8.44192057],
       [14.75882004, 14.50332786, 13.93210152]])
```

This looks close, but let's look at the absolute percentage error.

```
100 * np.abs(X - X_hat) / X
```

```
array([[  1.98127639,   0.84484142,   3.11939786],
       [ 17.69478376,   8.67394839,  20.09641264],
       [ 11.14390221,  19.8445095 ,  19.55143095],
       [  4.08330023,  11.57496939,   9.3634505 ],
       [ 26.47658629,  28.30002998, 371.67804413],
       [  6.40224086,   1.50995555,   6.20088253],
       [ 13.1834115 ,   9.35420086,  39.32101525]])
```

Most of the errors are less than 15%. There are some especially egregious errors, though. As with all these methods, you will need to tune to your needs. There is no one-size-fits-all.

Let's run this on a TF.IDF matrix.

```
model = NMF(n_components=100, init='nndsvdar', random_state=314)

# This will take a few minutes
D = model.fit_transform(tfidf)
T = model.components_
```

Now let's get our approximation of the tfidf.

```
tfidf_hat = np.dot(D, T)
```

Now we can calculate our absolute percentage error. Since our matrix has zeros, we need to add a fudge factor to avoid division by zero.

```
abs_pct_error = 100 * np.abs(tfidf - tfidf_hat + 1) / (tfidf + 1)

np.median(np.array(abs_pct_error))

76.86063392886243
```

This error seems high, but let's see how it clustered the terms together.

```
cluster_term = pd.DataFrame(
    model.components_.T,
    index=ix2term,
    columns=clusters)
cluster_term = np.round(cluster_term, decimals=4)

polynomial_vec = cluster_term.iloc[term2ix['polynomial']]
similarities = cluster_term.apply(
    lambda r: 1-cosine(polynomial_vec, r), axis=1)

similarities.sort_values(ascending=False)[:20]
```

```
satisfies        1.0
polynomial       1.0
polynomials      1.0
spanned          1.0
divisible        1.0
differentiable   1.0
subspace         1.0
scalar           1.0
monic            1.0
commutes         1.0
commute          1.0
nilpotent        1.0
decomposes       1.0
algebraically    1.0
algebra          1.0
primes           1.0
integers         1.0
exponential      1.0
expressible      1.0
subspaces        1.0
dtype: float64
```

It seems that it has successfully grouped similar words together. Now let's look at the word clouds, as shown in Figure 10-4.

```
chosen_ix = [0, 97, 1, 98, 2, 99]

fig, axs = plt.subplots(3, 2, figsize=(10, 8))

k = 0
for i in range(len(axs)):
    for j in range(len(axs[i])):
```

```
wc = WordCloud(colormap='Greys', background_color='white')
im = wc.generate_from_frequencies(
    cluster_term[clusters[chosen_ix[k]]])
axs[i][j].imshow(im, interpolation='bilinear')
axs[i][j].axis("off")
axs[i][j].set_title(clusters[chosen_ix[k]], **font)
k += 1

plt.tight_layout()
plt.show()
```

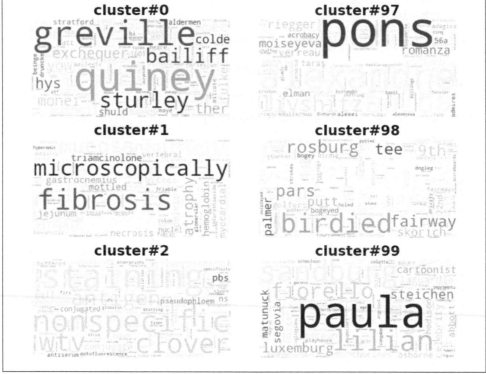

Figure 10-4. Word clouds built from the NMF clusters

It looks like Cluster #1 is related to medical terms and Cluster #97 is related to dance.

All of these techniques ultimately rely on finding transformations related to the space defined by the vocabulary. Let's look at a technique that tries to model the generation of the text.

Latent Dirichlet Allocation

The idea behind *latent Dirichlet allocation (LDA)* is that documents are generated based on a set of topics. In this process, we assume that each document is distributed over the topics, and each topic is distributed over the terms. Each document, and each word, are generated from sampling these distributions. The LDA learner works backward and tries to identify the distributions where the observed is most probable.

This is a much more complicated set of assumptions than that of our previous technique. This is because it is trying to model the term-generation process instead of just reducing the dimensions in the vector model.

Let's look at an example.

```
from sklearn.decomposition import LatentDirichletAllocation

model = LatentDirichletAllocation(
    n_components=K,
    random_state=314,
    max_iter=100)

# this can take a few minutes
clustered = model.fit_transform(tfidf)

cluster_term = pd.DataFrame(
    model.components_.T,
    index=ix2term,
    columns=clusters)
cluster_term = np.round(cluster_term, decimals=4)
```

Let's see what words are closest to "polynomial," as we've done for other techniques.

```
polynomial_vec = cluster_term.iloc[term2ix['polynomial']]

similarities = cluster_term.apply(
    lambda r: 1-cosine(polynomial_vec, r),
    axis=1)

similarities.sort_values(ascending=False)[:20]

polynomial       1.0
secants          1.0
diagonalizable   1.0
hino             1.0
secant           1.0
nilpotent        1.0
invariant        1.0
congruence       1.0
jastrow          1.0
szold            1.0
commute          1.0
polynomials      1.0
involution       1.0
kayabashi        1.0
```

```
subspace        1.0
galaxies        1.0
quadric         1.0
jo              1.0
beckett         1.0
tangents        1.0
dtype: float64
```

This seems less focused than the results from the other techniques. Let's look at the word clouds, as shown in Figure 10-5.

```
chosen_ix = [0, 97, 1, 98, 2, 99]

fig, axs = plt.subplots(3, 2, figsize=(10, 8))

k = 0
for i in range(len(axs)):
    for j in range(len(axs[i])):
        wc = WordCloud(colormap='Greys', background_color='white')
        im = wc.generate_from_frequencies(
            cluster_term[clusters[chosen_ix[k]]])
        axs[i][j].imshow(im, interpolation='bilinear')
        axs[i][j].axis("off")
        axs[i][j].set_title(clusters[chosen_ix[k]], **font)
        k += 1

plt.tight_layout()
plt.show()
```

These techniques give us ways to cluster documents, reduce the dimensionality of our document vector data, and even group words together. Recently, there has been great progress in distributional semantics using neural networks. In the next chapter, we will cover some of these newer techniques.

Figure 10-5. Word clouds built from topic-term distributions

Exercises

Let's see how these techniques work on our classification problem from Chapter 9. We will be using Spark's implementation of LDA for this.

First, let's load the data.

```
import os
import re

import numpy as np
import pandas as pd

from pyspark.sql.types import *
from pyspark.sql.functions import expr
from pyspark.sql import Row
from pyspark.ml import Pipeline
from pyspark.ml.feature import *
from pyspark.ml.clustering import LDA
from pyspark.ml.classification import LogisticRegression
from pyspark.ml.tuning import CrossValidator, ParamGridBuilder
from pyspark.ml.evaluation import MulticlassClassificationEvaluator
```

```
import sparknlp
from sparknlp import DocumentAssembler, Finisher
from sparknlp.annotator import *

%matplotlib inline

spark = sparknlp.start()

HEADER_PTN = re.compile(r'^[a-zA-Z-]+:.*')

def remove_header(path_text_pair):
    path, text = path_text_pair
    lines = text.split('\n')
    line_iterator = iter(lines)
    while HEADER_PTN.match(next(line_iterator)) is not None:
        pass
    return path, '\n'.join(line_iterator)

path = os.path.join('data', 'mini_newsgroups', '*')
texts = spark.sparkContext.wholeTextFiles(path).map(remove_header)

schema = StructType([
    StructField('path', StringType()),
    StructField('text', StringType()),
])

texts = spark.createDataFrame(texts, schema=schema) \
    .withColumn('newsgroup', expr('split(path, "/")[7]')) \
    .persist()

train, test = texts.randomSplit([0.8, 0.2], seed=123)
```

Now, let's build our NLP pipeline.

```
assembler = DocumentAssembler()\
    .setInputCol('text')\
    .setOutputCol('document')
sentence = SentenceDetector() \
    .setInputCols(["document"]) \
    .setOutputCol("sentences")
tokenizer = Tokenizer()\
    .setInputCols(['sentences'])\
    .setOutputCol('token')
lemmatizer = LemmatizerModel.pretrained()\
    .setInputCols(['token'])\
    .setOutputCol('lemma')
normalizer = Normalizer()\
    .setCleanupPatterns([
        '[^a-zA-Z.-]+',
        '^[^a-zA-Z]+',
        '[^a-zA-Z]+$',
    ])\
    .setInputCols(['lemma'])\
```

```
        .setOutputCol('normalized')\
        .setLowercase(True)
    finisher = Finisher()\
        .setInputCols(['normalized'])\
        .setOutputCols(['normalized'])\
        .setOutputAsArray(True)
```

Let's remove stop words and use TF.IDF vectors.

```
    stopwords = set(StopWordsRemover.loadDefaultStopWords("english"))

    sw_remover = StopWordsRemover() \
        .setInputCol("normalized") \
        .setOutputCol("filtered") \
        .setStopWords(list(stopwords))

    count_vectorizer = CountVectorizer(
        inputCol='filtered', outputCol='tf', minDF=10)
    idf = IDF(inputCol='tf', outputCol='tfidf')
```

Spark has an implementation of LDA. Let's use that in combination with logistic regression as our classifier. We will be combining the output of the LDA model with the TF.IDF vectors using the VectorAssembler.

```
    lda = LDA(
        featuresCol='tfidf',
        seed=123,
        maxIter=20,
        k=100,
        topicDistributionCol='topicDistribution',
    )

    vec_assembler = VectorAssembler(
        inputCols=['tfidf', 'topicDistribution'])

    logreg = LogisticRegression(
        featuresCol='topicDistribution',
        maxIter=100,
        regParam=0.0,
        elasticNetParam=0.0,
    )
```

Finally, we assemble our pipeline.

```
    label_indexer = StringIndexer(
        inputCol='newsgroup', outputCol='label')

    pipeline = Pipeline().setStages([
        assembler, sentence, tokenizer,
        lemmatizer, normalizer, finisher,
        sw_remover, count_vectorizer, idf,
        lda, vec_assembler,
        label_indexer, logreg
    ])
```

```
evaluator = MulticlassClassificationEvaluator(metricName='f1')

model = pipeline.fit(train)

train_predicted = model.transform(train)
test_predicted = model.transform(test)

print('f1', evaluator.evaluate(train_predicted))

f1 0.9956621119176594

print('f1', evaluator.evaluate(test_predicted))

f1 0.5957199376998746
```

This seems to overfit more than before. Try regularization, and try using only the topics.

Good luck!

## CHAPTER 11

Word Embeddings

Word embeddings are part of distributional semantics, similar to the topic models we discussed in the previous chapter. Unlike topic models, word embeddings do not work on term-document relationships. Instead, word embeddings work with smaller contexts like sentences or subsequences of tokens in a sentence.

The field of word embeddings is a rapidly evolving set of techniques. The most popular technique, *Word2vec*, was developed in 2013 by Tomas Mikolov et al. at Google. Since then, there has been much research (and hype). The idea is that you use a neural network to build a language model. Once this model is learned, you can take some of the intermediate values in the network as representations of the input term.

In this chapter, we will look at the implementation of Word2vec in code. This will help give us a clear understanding of the fundamentals of this family of techniques. We will discuss the more recent approaches at a higher level because they can be quite resource intensive.

Word2vec

One of the ideas behind deep learning is that the hidden layers are "higher level" representations of the data. This comes from analysis of the visual cortex. As the information travels from the eye through the brain, neurons appear to be associated with more complex shapes. The early layers of neurons recognize only points of light and dark, later neurons recognize lines and curves, and so on. Using this assumption, if we train a language model using a neural network, the hidden layers will be a "higher level" representation of the words.

There are two ways that Word2vec is commonly implemented: *continuous bag-of-words* (*CBOW*) and *continuous skip grams* (often just *skip grams*). In CBOW, we build a model that tries to predict a word based on the nearby words. In the skip-gram approach, a word is used to predict the context.

In either approach, the model is trained using a neural network with one hidden layer. Let's say we want to represent words as K dimensional vectors, and let's say we have N words in our vocabulary. The weights we learn will become the vectors. The intuition behind this is based on how neural networks function. A neural network learns higher-level representations of input features. These higher-level representations are the intermediate values produced in evaluating a neural-network model. In classic CBOW, the vectors that are fed into the hidden layer are these higher-level features. This means that we can simply take the rows of the first weight matrix as our word vectors. Let's implement CBOW, so we can get a clearer understanding.

First, let's define our imports and load our data.

```
import sparknlp
from nltk.corpus import brown

spark = sparknlp.start()

def detokenize(sentence):
    text = ''
    for token in sentence:
        if text and any(c.isalnum() for c in token):
            text += ' '
        text += token
    return text

texts = []

for fid in brown.fileids():
    text = [detokenize(s) for s in brown.sents(fid)]
    text = ' '.join(text)
    texts.append((text,))

texts = spark.createDataFrame(texts, ['text'])
```

Now that we have our data, let's process and prepare it for building our model.

```
from pyspark.ml import Pipeline

from sparknlp import DocumentAssembler, Finisher
from sparknlp.annotator import *

assembler = DocumentAssembler()\
    .setInputCol('text')\
    .setOutputCol('document')
sentence = SentenceDetector() \
    .setInputCols(["document"]) \
    .setOutputCol("sentences") \
    .setExplodeSentences(True)
tokenizer = Tokenizer()\
```

```
        .setInputCols(['sentences'])\
        .setOutputCol('token')
normalizer = Normalizer()\
    .setCleanupPatterns([
        '[^a-zA-Z.-]+',
        '^[^a-zA-Z]+',
        '[^a-zA-Z]+$',
    ])\
    .setInputCols(['token'])\
    .setOutputCol('normalized')\
    .setLowercase(True)
finisher = Finisher()\
    .setInputCols(['normalized'])\
    .setOutputCols(['normalized'])\
    .setOutputAsArray(True)

pipeline = Pipeline().setStages([
    assembler, sentence, tokenizer,
    normalizer, finisher
]).fit(texts)

sentences = pipeline.transform(texts)
sentences = sentences.select('normalized').collect()
sentences = [r['normalized'] for r in sentences]

print(len(sentences)) # number of sentences

59091
```

Now we have performed the text processing, so let's build our encoding. There are tools to do this in most deep learning libraries, but let's do it ourselves.

```
from collections import Counter
import numpy as np
import pandas as pd

UNK = '???'
PAD = '###'
w2i = {PAD: 0, UNK: 1}
df = Counter()

for s in sentences:
    df.update(s)

df = pd.Series(df)
df = df[df > 10].sort_values(ascending=False)

for word in df.index:
    w2i[word] = len(w2i)


i2w = {ix: w for w, ix in w2i.items()}
vocab_size = len(i2w)
```

```
print(vocab_size)
```

```
7814
```

We include a marker for padding and a marker for unknown words. We will be tiling over our sentences, creating windows of tokens. The middle token is what we are trying to predict, and the surrounding tokens are our context. We need to pad our sentences, otherwise we will lose words at the beginning and ending of the sentences.

Let's also make some utility functions that will convert a sequence of tokens to a sequence of indices, and one that does the inverse.

```
def texts_to_sequences(texts):
    return [[w2i.get(w, w2i[UNK]) for w in s] for s in texts]

def sequences_to_texts(seqs):
    return [' '.join([i2w.get(ix, UNK) for ix in s]) for s in seqs]

seqs = texts_to_sequences(sentences)
```

Now let's build our context windows. We will go over each sentence and create a window for each token in the sentence.

```
w = 4
windows = []
Y = []

for k, seq in enumerate(seqs):
    for i in range(len(seq)):
        if seq[i] == w2i[UNK] or len(seq) < 2*w:
            continue
        window = []
        for j in range(-w, w+1):
            if i+j < 0:
                window.append(w2i[PAD])
            elif i+j >= len(seq):
                window.append(w2i[PAD])
            else:
                window.append(seq[i+j])
        windows.append(window)

windows = np.array(windows)
```

We can't just turn all of our data into vectors because that would take up too much memory. So we will need to implement a generator. First, let's write the function that will turn a collection of windows into numpy arrays. This will take the windows and produce a matrix containing the one-hot–encoded words and a matrix containing the one-hot–encoded target words.

```
def windows_to_batch(batch_windows):
    w = batch_windows.shape[1] // 2
    X = []
    Y = []
```

```
    for window in batch_windows:
        X.append(np.concatenate((window[:w], window[w+1:])))
        Y.append(window[w])

    X = np.array(X)
    Y = ku.to_categorical(Y, vocab_size)
    return X, Y
```

Now we write the function that actually produces the generator. The training method takes a Python generator, so we need a utility function that creates a generator of batches.

```
def generate_batch(windows, batch_size=100):
    while True:
        indices = np.arange(windows.shape[0])
        indices = np.random.choice(indices, batch_size)
        batch_windows = windows[indices, :]
        yield windows_to_batch(batch_windows)
```

Now we can implement our model. Let's define our model. We will be creating 50-dimension word vectors. The number of dimensions should be based on the size of your corpus. However, there is no hard-and-fast rule.

```
from keras.models import Sequential
from keras.layers import *
import keras.backend as K
import keras.utils as ku

dim = 50

model = Sequential()
model.add(Embedding(vocab_size, dim, input_length=w*2))
model.add(Lambda(lambda x: K.mean(x, axis=1), (dim,)))
model.add(Dense(vocab_size, activation='softmax'))
```

The first layer is the actual embeddings we will be learning. The second layer collapses the context into a single vector. The last layer makes the prediction of what the word in the middle of the window should be.

```
print(model.summary())
```

Model: "sequential_2"

Layer (type)	Output Shape	Param #
embedding_2 (Embedding)	(None, 8, 50)	390700
lambda_2 (Lambda)	(None, 50)	0
dense_2 (Dense)	(None, 7814)	398514

```
Total params: 789,214
Trainable params: 789,214
Non-trainable params: 0
```

```
                                                          None
model.compile(loss='categorical_crossentropy', optimizer='adam')
```

This is a relatively simple Word2vec model, yet we still need to learn more than 700,000 parameters. Word embeddings models get complicated quickly.

Let's store the weights for every 50 epochs. We make 50 calls to the generator for each epoch.

```
batch_size = 1000
steps = 100
generator = generate_batch(windows, batch_size)

mc = ModelCheckpoint('weights{epoch:05d}.h5',
                     save_weights_only=True,
                     period=50)

model.fit_generator(generator, steps_per_epoch=steps,
                    epochs=500, callbacks=[mc])
```

Now let's look at the data. First, let's implement a class to represent the embeddings data. We will be using cosine similarity to compare vectors.

```
class Word2VecData(object):
    def __init__(self, word_vectors, w2i, i2w):
        self.word_vectors = word_vectors
        self.w2i = w2i
        self.i2w = i2w
        ## the implementation of cosine similarity uses the
        ## normalized vectors. This means that we can precalculate
        ## the vectors of our vocabulary
        self.normed_wv = np.divide(
            word_vectors.T,
            np.linalg.norm(word_vectors, axis=1)
        ).T
        self.all_sims = np.dot(self.normed_wv, self.normed_wv.T)
        self.all_sims = np.triu(self.all_sims)
        self.all_sims = self.all_sims[self.all_sims > 0]

    ## this transforms a word into a vector
    def w2v(self, word):
        return self.word_vectors[self.w2i[word],:]

    ## this calculates cosine similarity of the input word to all words
    def _get_sims(self, word):
        if isinstance(word, str):
            v = self.w2v(word)
        else:
            v = word
        v = np.divide(v, np.linalg.norm(v))
        return np.dot(self.normed_wv, v)
```

```
def nearest_words(self, word, k=10):
    sims = self._get_sims(word)
    nearest = sims.argsort()[-k:][::-1]
    ret = []
    for ix in nearest:
        ret.append((self.i2w[ix], sims[ix]))
    return ret

def compare_words(self, u, v):
    if isinstance(u, str):
        u = self.w2v(u)
    if isinstance(v, str):
        v = self.w2v(v)
    u = np.divide(u, np.linalg.norm(u))
    v = np.divide(v, np.linalg.norm(v))
    return np.dot(u, v)
```

Let's also implement something to output the results. We want to look at a couple things when looking at Word2vec. We want to find what words are similar to other words. If the model has learned information about the words, you should see related words.

There are also word analogies. One of the interesting uses of Word2vec was a word "algebra." The common example is king - man + woman ~ queen. This means that you subtract the man vector from the king vector, then add the woman vector. The result is approximately the queen vector. This generally works well only with a large diverse vocabulary. Our vocabulary is more limited because our data set is small.

Let's plot the histogram of all word-to-word similarities.

```
import matplotlib.pyplot as plt
%matplotlib inline

def display_Word2vec(model, weight_path, words, analogies):
    model.load_weights(weight_path)
    word_vectors = model.layers[0].get_weights()[0]
    W2V = Word2VecData(word_vectors, w2i, i2w)

    for word in words:
        for w, sim in W2V.nearest_words(word):
            print(w, sim)
        print()

    for w1, w2, w3, w4 in analogies:
        v1 = W2V.w2v(w1)
        v2 = W2V.w2v(w2)
        v3 = W2V.w2v(w3)
        v4 = W2V.w2v(w4)
        x = v1 - v2 + v3
        for w, sim in W2V.nearest_words(x):
            print(w, sim)
```

```
    print()
    print(w4, W2V.compare_words(x, v4))
    print()
    print('{}-{}+{}~{} quantile'.format(w1, w2, w3, w4),
        (W2V.all_sims < W2V.compare_words(x, v4)).mean())
    print()

plt.hist(W2V.all_sims)
plt.title('Word-to-Word similarity histogram')

plt.show()
```

Let's look at the results from the 50th epoch. First, let's look at the words similar to "space." This is a list of the nearest 10 words to "space" by cosine similarity.

```
space 0.9999999
shear 0.96719706
section 0.9615698
chapter 0.9592927
output 0.958699
phase 0.9580841
corporate 0.95798546
points 0.9575049
density 0.9573466
institute 0.9545017
```

Now let's look at the words similar to "polynomial."

```
polynomial 1.0000001
formula 0.9805055
factor 0.9684353
positive 0.96643007
produces 0.9631797
remarkably 0.96068406
equation 0.9601216
assumption 0.95971704
moral 0.9586859
unique 0.95754766
```

Now let's look at the king - man + woman ~ queen analogy. We will print out the words closest to the result vector, king - man + woman. Then we can look at the similarity of the result to the queen vector. Finally, let's look at what the quantile is for queen. The higher it is, the better the analogy works.

```
mountains 0.96987706
emperor 0.96913254
crowds 0.9688335
generals 0.9669207
masters 0.9664976
kings 0.9663711
roof 0.9653381
ceiling 0.96467453
ridge 0.96467185
```

```
woods 0.96466273

queen 0.9404894

king-man+woman~queen quantile 0.942
```

That the queen vector is closer than 94% of other words is a good sign, but that some of the other top results, like "ceiling," are so close is a sign that our data set may be too small and perhaps too specialized to learn such general relationships.

Finally, let's look at the histogram, as shown in Figure 11-1.

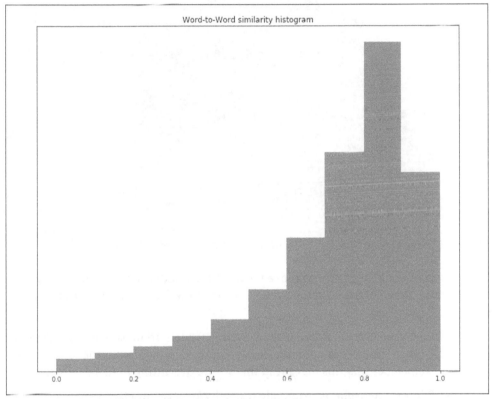

Figure 11-1. Histogram of word-to-word similarities at epoch 50

Most of the similarities are on the high side. This means that at epoch 50 the words are quite similar. Let's look at the histogram at epoch 100, as shown in Figure 11-2.

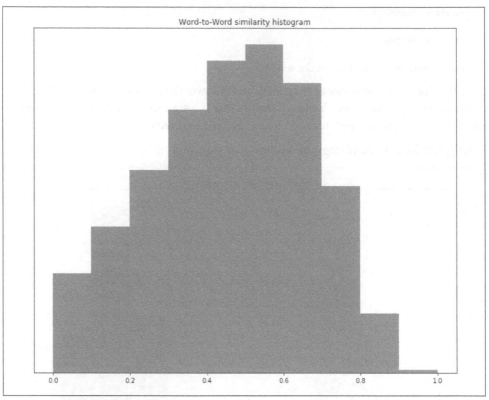

Figure 11-2. Histogram of word-to-word similarities at epoch 100

The weight of the histogram has moved toward the middle. This means that we are seeing more differentiation between our words. Now let's look at 500 epochs, as shown in Figure 11-3.

Note how the mass of the histogram has moved to the left, so most words are dissimilar to each other. This means that the words are more separated in the word-vector space. But remember that this may mean that we are overfitting to this data set.

Spark NLP lets us incorporate externally trained Word2vec models. Let's see how we can use these word embeddings in Spark NLP. First, let's write the embeddings to a file in a format that Spark NLP is familiar with.

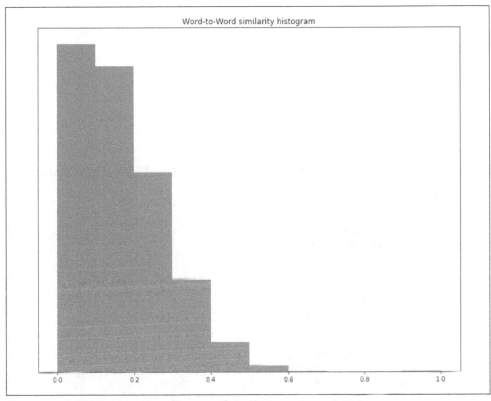

Figure 11-3. Histogram of word-to-word similarities at epoch 500

```python
model.load_weights('weights00500.h5')
word_vectors = model.layers[0].get_weights()[0]

with open('cbow.csv', 'w') as out:
    for ix in range(vocab_size):
        word = i2w[ix]
        vec = list(word_vectors[ix, :])
        line = ['{}'] + ['{:.18e}'] * dim
        line = ' '.join(line) + '\n'
        line = line.format(word, *vec)
        out.write(line)
```

Now we can create an embeddings annotator.

```python
Word2vec = WordEmbeddings() \
    .setInputCols(['document', 'normalized']) \
    .setOutputCol('embeddings') \
    .setDimension(dim) \
    .setStoragePath('cbow.csv', 'TEXT')

pipeline = Pipeline().setStages([
    assembler, sentence, tokenizer,
```

```
    normalizer, Word2vec
]).fit(texts)
```

Let's get out the embeddings generated by our model.

```
pipeline.transform(texts).select('embeddings.embeddings') \
    .first()['embeddings']
```

```
[[0.6336007118225098,
  0.7607026696205139,
  1.1777857542037964,
  ...]]
```

Spark has an implementation of the skip-gram approach. Let's look at how to use that.

```
from pyspark.ml.feature import Word2Vec

Word2vec = Word2Vec() \
    .setInputCol('normalized') \
    .setOutputCol('word_vectors') \
    .setVectorSize(dim) \
    .setMinCount(5)
finisher = Finisher()\
    .setInputCols(['normalized'])\
    .setOutputCols(['normalized'])\
    .setOutputAsArray(True)

pipeline = Pipeline().setStages([
    assembler, sentence, tokenizer,
    normalizer, finisher, Word2vec
]).fit(texts)

pipeline.transform(texts).select('word_vectors') \
    .first()['word_vectors']

DenseVector([0.0433, -0.0003, 0.0281, 0.0791, ...])
```

GloVe

GloVe (*Global Vectors*), created by Jeffrey Pennington, Richard Socher, and Christopher Manning from Stanford, is actually more similar to the techniques we covered in the previous chapter, like LSI. Instead of using a neural network to build a language model, GloVe attempts to learn the co-occurrence statistics of words. It outperformed many common Word2vec models on the word analogy task.

One benefit of GloVe is that it is the result of directly modeling relationships, instead of getting them as a side effect of training a language model.

Let's see how to use GloVe in Spark NLP:

```
glove = WordEmbeddingsModel.pretrained(name='glove_100d') \
    .setInputCols(['document', 'normalized']) \
    .setOutputCol('embeddings') \
```

```
pipeline = Pipeline().setStages([
    assembler, sentence, tokenizer,
    normalizer, glove
]).fit(texts)

pipeline.transform(texts).select('embeddings.embeddings') \
    .first()['embeddings']

[[-0.03819400072097778,
  -0.24487000703811646,
  0.7281200289726257,
  ...]]
```

fastText

In 2015, Facebook research developed an extension to Word2vec called *fastText*. One common problem with Word2vec is the way it treats words that are not in the vocabulary of the training corpus. For some problems, it may make sense to simply drop these words, under the assumption that they are too rare to have a significant effect on the outcome of downstream processes. In corpora with specialized vocabulary, like a clinical corpus, it is not uncommon to find a word that is important to the document that may not be found in training data. This *out-of-vocabulary* problem also makes it difficult to do transfer learning. *Transfer learning* is where you take a part or the whole model trained on one data set and task and use it on a different data set and even a different task. In fact, Word2vec itself is transfer learning. You build a model to solve a language-modeling problem, often contrived, and use part of this model in some other NLP-related task.

fastText makes transfer learning with word embeddings easier by learning character-level information. So, instead of learning higher-level representation of tokens, it learns a higher-level representation of character sequences. Once these character sequences are learned, we take the sum of the character-sequence vectors that make up a word for the word's vector.

Transformers

In 2017, researchers at Google created a new approach for modeling *attention*. Attention is a concept from sequence modeling. A sequence model that does not have a fixed context must learn how long to retain information from earlier in the sequence. Being able to better capture long-distance relationships is very important to automatic machine translation. Most words have multiple senses or meanings, and clarifying requires broader context. In linguistics, the property of having multiple senses is known as *polysemy* or *homonymy*.

Polysemy is when the senses are different but related, and homonymy is when the senses are not related in meaning. For example, let's look at the word "rock." When used as a noun, "rock" means a piece of stone. This is completely unrelated to the other meaning, the verb "to rock." The verb "to rock" refers to a back-and-forth motion, and it can also mean to perform or enjoy rock-and-roll music. So "rock" (a stone) is a homonym of "rock" (to move back and forth), which is polyseme that also has the meaning to perform or enjoy rock-and-roll music.

Cues to disambiguate homonyms and polysemes generally come from other words in the context. The example given in the paper defines the Transformer (Vaswani et al.) as a "bank," which has two meanings. The first is a financial institution, and the second is the edge of a river. This homonymous relationship does not translate. For example, in Spanish, the institution is "banco," and the edge of a river is "orilla." So if you are translating, using a neural network, it would be advantageous to represent the two words differently. To do this, you must encode your words with their context.

The word vectors of previous methods represent aggregations of these different senses. This allows a much richer representation of the text. However, it comes at a severe cost. These models are computationally much more intense to train and use. In fact, most of the current methods, at the time of writing in 2019, are not feasible without using GPUs or even more specialized hardware.

ELMo, BERT, and XLNet

Newer embedding techniques are based on the idea of representing words in a context-dependent way. This means that a full neural-network model is needed to use the embeddings, unlike in static embeddings where there is simply a lookup.

Embeddings from language models (ELMo) is a model that was developed at the Allen Institute in 2018. The language model that is being learned is bidirectional. This means that the model is learning to predict a word based on the words that come both before it and after it. The model learns at the character level, but the embeddings themselves are actually word based.

Bidirectional Encoder Representations from Transformers (BERT), published in 2018, is doing something very similar to ELMo, but it is using Google's Transformers—hence the name. The intent is that this model can be fine-tuned. This is done by building a generic pretrained model on a data set. There are other approaches that allow fine-tuning, but the authors of the BERT paper note that those are either unidirectional approaches, or more specialized bidirectional approaches. BERT is intended to solve the problem of needing to choose by building a model that tries to identify randomly masked words.

BERT became very popular by achieving high scores on a number of benchmarks. Roughly a year later, XLNet was published. *XLNet* was built to learn a model without the masking needed by BERT. The idea is that the masking is creating discrepancies between what the BERT model sees at training time and what it sees at time of use. XLNet then went on to achieve yet higher benchmarks.

Let's look at how to use BERT embeddings in Spark NLP.

```
bert = BertEmbeddings.pretrained() \
    .setInputCols(["sentences", "normalized"]) \
    .setOutputCol("bert")

pipeline = Pipeline().setStages([
    assembler, sentence, tokenizer,
    normalizer, bert
]).fit(texts)

pipeline.transform(texts).select('bert.embeddings') \
    .first()['embeddings']

[[-0.43669646978378296,
  0.5360171794891357,
  -0.051413312554359436,
  ...]]
```

A caveat to those interested in these techniques: one must always return to first principles when evaluating such new and complicated approaches. First, always consider what your product actually needs. Is your product similar to one of the tasks for which the BERT and XLNet achieved high scores? What is the level of accuracy you need versus the amount you are willing to spend on developer time, training time, and hardware? Just because these techniques are very popular with people in the field of NLP does not mean they are the best for every application.

In fact, there is the possibility that these techniques can overfit in difficult-to-detect ways. Researchers at the National Cheng Kung University in Taiwan created an adversarial data set for a question-and-answer task called Argument Reasoning Comprehension Task. Here, a model must take in a piece of text that makes some arguments and draw a conclusion. BERT was able to achieve scores higher than human scores on this task. The researchers modified the data set with examples that were contradictory. The BERT model was evaluated on this new adversarial data set, and it performed worse than humans and little better than models built with older, simpler techniques. A model should be able to make a conclusion based solely on the input text; that is, it should not be using statements in other examples.

doc2vec

Doc2vec is the set of techniques that lets us turn a document into a vector. Often, we want to use embeddings as sparser features for other tasks, like classification. How can we combine these word-level features into document-level features? One common way is to simply average the word-level vectors. This makes intuitive sense because we are hoping that the vector space represents a vague idea of meaning. So if we average all the vectors in a document, we should get the "average" meaning of the document.

The problem with this approach comes in when we consider rarity of words. Recalling our conversation on TF.IDF, it is often the case that unimportant words have a high frequency. For example, consider a clinical note. We may find a large number of generic words that are common to all notes. This can present a problem because these words will pull all of our documents toward a small number of places in our vector space. A model could still separate them, but it will converge more slowly. Worse yet, if there are natural clusters within the corpus, in other words, clinical notes from different departments, we may have a number of tightly packed clusters of documents. What we want is to be able to characterize a document by the words that are most important to that unique document. There are a few approaches for doing this.

You can perform weighted averaging on the word vectors by using IDF values as weights. This will help reduce the effect that more common words have on the document vector. This approach has the benefit of being simple to implement. Indeed, if you are using a static embedding technique, you can simply scale the vectors by the IDF values. There will be no need to compute this at evaluation time. The downside is that this is a bag-of-words approach and does not take into account the relationships between words.

Another approach is called *distributed memory paragraph vectors*. This is essentially CBOW, but with an additional set of weights that needs to be learned. In CBOW, we are predicting a word from its context, so we have vectors representing the context as input. For distributed memory paragraph vectors, we concatenate a one-hot encoding of our document IDs to input. This allows us to represent the document with the same dimension as the words.

A third approach to doc2vec parallels the skip-gram approach, *distributed bag-of-words paragraph vectors*. Recall that skip grams predict the context from a word. In distributed bag-of-words paragraph vectors, you learn to predict *a context* of the document from its document ID.

These last two approaches have the benefit of learning the relationships between co-occurring words. They are also relatively straightforward to implement if you can implement Word2vec. Their downside is that they learn only documents you have on hand. If you get a new document, you will not be able to produce a vector for it. So these approaches can be used only on offline processes.

When talking about doc2vec, also sometimes known as paragraph2vec, it's important to keep in mind that it can be applied to different sizes of text, from phrases to whole documents. However, if you are interested in converting phrases to vectors, you may also want to consider incorporating this into your tokenization. You can produce phrases as tokens and then learn one of the word-level embeddings discussed previously.

Exercises

Let's see how these techniques work on our classification problem from Chapter 9.

This time, writing code is up to you. Try Spark's skip-gram implementation, Spark NLP's pretrained GloVe model, and Spark NLP's BERT model.

PART III

Applications

In this part of the book we will build NLP applications. The goal of each chapter is to establish how we can build real applications using Spark NLP. This will also let us cover some topics from earlier chapters in a more practical manner.

As we mentioned earlier, when building NLP applications we need to keep three perspectives in mind: software engineering, data science, and linguistics. We will go through the design, development, experimentation, and deployment process.

A caveat for these chapters: we will try to use more realistically sized data sets in this part of the book. This means that the code may take a while to run.

## CHAPTER 12

Sentiment Analysis and Emotion Detection

Sentiment analysis is a set of techniques used for quantifying some sentiment based on text content. There are many community sites and e-commerce sites that allow users to comment and rate products and services. However, this is not the only place where people discuss products and services— there is also social media. We can leverage the data from the sites with comments and ratings to learn the relationship between the language used and positive or negative sentiment. These approaches can be extended to predicting the emotions of the author of a piece of text. Sentiment analysis is one of the most popular uses of NLP.

For this application, we are trying to build a program that we can use to quantify movie reviews. Although many, but not all, movie reviewers use some quantifiable metrics—for example, thumbs up/down, stars, or letter grades, these are not normalized. Two reviewers who use a 10-point scale may have different distributions. One reviewer may give most movies a 4–6 range, where another gives a 6–8 range. We could normalize them, but what about the other reviewers who use different metrics or no metrics at all? It might be better if we build a model that looks at the reviews and produces a score. This way, we know that the scores from a given reviewer are based on the text of the review, instead of on an ad-hoc score.

Problem Statement and Constraints

1. What is the problem we are trying to solve?

    We want to build an application that takes the text of a movie review and produces a score. We will use this to aggregate reviews, so this application will run as a batch process. We will surface this to the user using a display that shows how positively or negatively the movie was received. We will not worry about the other aspects of the presentation. We will assume that the display will be embedded in other content.

2. What constraints are there?

Here are our constraints:

- We are assuming that we are working with English-language reviews.

- We do not have much constraint on the speed of the program, since this is a batch offline process. We want to return the aggregate score for 95% of movies in less than 1 minute.

- We want to make sure that our model is performing well on this task, so we will use a well-known data set. We will use the Large Movie Review Dataset based on IMDb user reviews.

- We will assume that the input to this program is a *JavaScript Object Notation (JSON)* file of reviews. The output will be a score.

- The model must have an *F1 score of at least 0.7 on new data.*

It may seem unreasonable to set a desired metric threshold before we have even looked at the data, but this situation is common. Negotiating with stakeholders is important. If an arbitrary threshold has been set but experimentation reveals it is unrealistic, the data scientist should be able to explain to the stakeholders why the problem is more difficult than expected.

As you work on the project, this list may change. The earlier you catch missed constraints, the better. If you discover a constraint just before deployment, it can be very expensive to fix. This is why we want to iterate with stakeholders during development.

Now that we have listed our constraints, let's discuss how we can build our application.

3. How do we solve the problem with the constraints?

The first constraint, that the reviews are in English, actually makes our task easier. The second constraint, concerning how long it takes to calculate the aggregate score, controls how complex of a model we can build, but it is a light constraint. We have the IMDb data set. When we build our program, we will load from JSON. However, our modeling code does not need to follow such constraints.

Plan the Project

To plan the project, let's define what our acceptance criteria are. The product owner would normally define these by incorporating stakeholder requests. In this chapter, you are both product owner and developer.

We want a script that does the following:

- Takes a file with reviews in JSON objects, one per line
- Returns distribution information based on the output from the model
  — Mean
  — Standard deviation
  — Quartiles
  — Min
  — Max

We will use Spark NLP to process the data and a Spark MLlib model to predict the sentiment.

Now that we have these high-level acceptance criteria, let's look at the data. First, we will load the data into DataFrames and add the label columns.

```python
import sparknlp

from pyspark.ml import Pipeline
from pyspark.sql import SparkSession
from pyspark.sql.functions import lit

import sparknlp
from sparknlp import DocumentAssembler, Finisher
from sparknlp.annotator import *

spark = sparknlp.start()

pos_train = spark.sparkContext.wholeTextFiles(
    'aclImdb_v1/aclImdb/train/pos/')
neg_train = spark.sparkContext.wholeTextFiles(
    'aclImdb_v1/aclImdb/train/neg/')
pos_test = spark.sparkContext.wholeTextFiles(
    'aclImdb_v1/aclImdb/test/pos/')
neg_test = spark.sparkContext.wholeTextFiles(
    'aclImdb_v1/aclImdb/test/neg/')

pos_train = spark.createDataFrame(pos_train, ['path', 'text'])
pos_train = pos_train.repartition(100)
pos_train = pos_train.withColumn('label', lit(1)).persist()
neg_train = spark.createDataFrame(neg_train, ['path', 'text'])
neg_train = neg_train.repartition(100)
neg_train = neg_train.withColumn('label', lit(0)).persist()
pos_test = spark.createDataFrame(pos_test, ['path', 'text'])
pos_test = pos_test.repartition(100)
pos_test = pos_test.withColumn('label', lit(1)).persist()
neg_test = spark.createDataFrame(neg_test, ['path', 'text'])
neg_test = neg_test.repartition(100)
neg_test = neg_test.withColumn('label', lit(0)).persist()
```

Let's look at an example of a positive.

```
print(pos_train.first()['text'])
```

I laughed a lot while watching this. It's an amusing short with a
fun musical act and a lot of wackiness. The characters are simple,
but their simplicity adds to the humor stylization. The dialog is
funny and often unexpected, and from the first line to the last
everything just seems to flow wonderfully. There's Max, who has
apparently led a horrible life. And there's Edward, who isn't sure
what life he wants to lead. My favorite character was Tom, Edward's
insane boss. Tom has a short role but a memorable one. Highly
recommended for anyone who likes silly humor. And you can find it
online now, which is a bonus! I am a fan of all of Jason's cartoons
and can't wait to see what he comes out with next.

This seems like a clearly positive review. We can identify a few words that seem like a good signal, like "best."

Now, let's look an example of a negative.

```
print(neg_train.first()['text'])
```

I sat glued to the screen, riveted, yawning, yet keeping an
attentive eye. I waited for the next awful special effect, or the
next ridiculously clichéd plot item to show up full force, so I
could learn how not to make a movie.

It seems when they
set out to make this movie, the crew watched every single other
action/science-fiction/shoot-em-up/good vs. evil movie ever made,
and saw cool things and said: "Hey, we can do that." For example,
the only car parked within a mile on what seems like a one way road
with a shoulder not meant for parking, is the one car the
protagonist, an attractive brunette born of bile, is thrown on to.
The car blows to pieces before she even lands on it. The special
effects were quite obviously my biggest beef with this movie. But
what really put it in my bad books was the implausibility, and lack
of reason for so many elements! For example, the antagonist, a
flying demon with the ability to inflict harm in bizarre ways,
happens upon a lone army truck transporting an important VIP.
Nameless security guys with guns get out of the truck, you know
they are already dead. Then the guy protecting the VIP says "Under
no circumstances do you leave this truck, do you understand me?" He
gets out to find the beast that killed his 3 buddies, he gets
whacked in an almost comically cliché fashion. Then for no apparent
reason, defying logic, convention, and common sense, the dumb ass
VIP GETS OUT OF THE TRUCK!!! A lot of what happened along the
course of the movie didn't make sense. Transparent acting distanced
me from the movie, as well as bad camera-work, and things that just
make you go: "Wow, that's incredibly cheesy." Shiri Appleby saved
the movie from a 1, because she gave the movie the one element that
always makes viewers enjoy the experience, sex appeal.

This is a clear example of a negative review. We see many words here that seem like solid indicators of negative sentiment, like "awful" and "cheesy."

Notice that there are some HTML artifacts that we will want to remove.

Now, let's look at the corpus as a whole.

```
print('pos_train size', pos_train.count())
print('neg_train size', neg_train.count())
print('pos_test size', pos_test.count())
print('neg_test size', neg_test.count())

pos_train size 12500
neg_train size 12500
pos_test size 12500
neg_test size 12500
```

So we have 50,000 documents. Having such an even distribution between positive and negative is artificial in this case. Let's look at the length of the text, shown in Table 12-1.

```
pos_train.selectExpr('length(text) AS text_len')\
    .toPandas().describe()
```

Table 12-1. Summary of text lengths

	text_len
count	12500.000000
mean	1347.160240
std	1046.747365
min	70.000000
25%	695.000000
50%	982.000000
75%	1651.000000
max	13704.000000

There appears to be a lot of variation in character lengths. This may be a useful feature. Text length may seem very low level, but it can often be useful information about a text. We may find that longer comments may be more likely to be negative due to rants. In this situation, it would be more useful if we had reviewer IDs, so we could get a sense of what is normal for a reviewer; alas, that is not in the data.

Now that we have taken a brief look at the data, let's begin to design our solution.

Design the Solution

First, let's separate our project into two phases.

1. Training and measuring the model

    The quality of modeling code is often overlooked. This is an important piece of a project. You will want to be able to hand off your experiment, so the code should be reusable. You also need the model to be reproducible, not just for academic reasons but also in case the model needs to be rebuilt for business purposes. You may also want to return to the project at some point to improve the model.

    One common way of making a modeling project reusable is to build a notebook, or a collection of notebooks. We won't cover that in this chapter, since the modeling project is straightforward.

2. Building the script

    The script will take one argument, the path to the reviews in JSON format—one JSON-formatted review per line. It will output a JSON-formatted report on the distribution of reviews.

    The following are the acceptance criteria for the script:

    *   It should have a helpful usage output
    *   It should run in less than 1 minute (for 95% of movies)
    *   It should output a file in the following format

        ```
        {
            "count": ###,
            "mean": 0.###,
            "std": 0.###,
            "median": 0.###,
            "min": 0.###,
            "max": 0.###,
        }
        ```

    The scores, which we will take the mean of, should be floating-point numbers between 0 and 1. Many classifiers output predicted probabilities, but this does an assumption on the output of this script.

Now that we have a plan, let's implement it.

Implement the Solution

Recall the steps to a modeling project we discussed in Chapter 7. Let's go through them here.

1. Get data.
2. Look at the data.
3. Process data.

We already have the data, and we have looked at it. Let's do some basic processing and store it so we can more quickly iterate on our model.

First, let's combine positives and negatives into two data sets, train, and test.

```
train = pos_train.unionAll(neg_train)
test = pos_test.unionAll(neg_test)
```

Now, let's use Spark NLP to process the data. We will save both the lemmatized and normalized tokens, as well as GloVe embeddings. This way, we can experiment with different features.

Let's create our pipeline.

```
assembler = DocumentAssembler()\
    .setInputCol('text')\
    .setOutputCol('document')
sentence = SentenceDetector() \
    .setInputCols(["document"]) \
    .setOutputCol("sentences")
tokenizer = Tokenizer()\
    .setInputCols(['sentences'])\
    .setOutputCol('tokens')
lemmatizer = LemmatizerModel.pretrained()\
    .setInputCols(['tokens'])\
    .setOutputCol('lemmas')
normalizer = Normalizer()\
    .setCleanupPatterns([
        '[^a-zA-Z.-]+',
        '^[^a-zA-Z]+',
        '[^a-zA-Z]+$',
    ])\
    .setInputCols(['lemmas'])\
    .setOutputCol('normalized')\
    .setLowercase(True)
glove = WordEmbeddingsModel.pretrained(name='glove_100d') \
    .setInputCols(['document', 'normalized']) \
    .setOutputCol('embeddings') \

nlp_pipeline = Pipeline().setStages([
    assembler, sentence, tokenizer,
```

```
    lemmatizer, normalizer, glove
]).fit(train)
```

Let's select just the values we are interested in—namely, the original data plus the normalized tokens and embeddings.

```
train = nlp_pipeline.transform(train) \
    .selectExpr(
        'path', 'text', 'label',
        'normalized.result AS normalized',
        'embeddings.embeddings'
    )

test = nlp_pipeline.transform(test) \
    .selectExpr(
        'path', 'text', 'label',
        'normalized.result AS normalized',
        'embeddings.embeddings'
    )

nlp_pipeline.write().overwrite().save('nlp_pipeline.3.12')
```

Recall the simplest version of doc2vec that we covered in Chapter 11, in which we average the word vectors in a document to create a document vector. We will use this technique here.

```
import numpy as np
from pyspark.sql.types import *
from pyspark.ml.linalg import DenseVector, VectorUDT

def avg_wordvecs_fun(wordvecs):
    return DenseVector(np.mean(wordvecs, axis=0))

avg_wordvecs = spark.udf.register(
    'avg_wordvecs',
    avg_wordvecs_fun,
    returnType=VectorUDT())

train = train.withColumn('avg_wordvec', avg_wordvecs('embeddings'))
test = test.withColumn('avg_wordvec', avg_wordvecs('embeddings'))
train.drop('embeddings')
test.drop('embeddings')
```

Now, we will save it as parquet files. This will let us free up some memory.

```
train.write.mode('overwrite').parquet('imdb.train')
test.write.mode('overwrite').parquet('imdb.test')
```

Let's clean up the data we persisted before so can have more memory to work with.

```
pos_train.unpersist()
neg_train.unpersist()
```

```
pos_test.unpersist()
neg_test.unpersist()
```

Now we load our data and persist.

```
train = spark.read.parquet('imdb.train').persist()
test = spark.read.parquet('imdb.test').persist()
```

4. Featurize

Let's see how well our model does with just TF.IDF features.

```
from pyspark.ml.feature import CountVectorizer, IDF

tf = CountVectorizer()\
    .setInputCol('normalized')\
    .setOutputCol('tf')
idf = IDF()\
    .setInputCol('tf')\
    .setOutputCol('tfidf')

featurizer = Pipeline().setStages([tf, idf])
```

5. Model

Now that we have our features, we can build our first model. Let's start with logistic regression, which is often a good baseline.

```
from pyspark.ml.feature import VectorAssembler
from pyspark.ml.classification import import LogisticRegression

vec_assembler = VectorAssembler()\
    .setInputCols(['avg_wordvec'])\
    .setOutputCol('features')
logreg = LogisticRegression()\
    .setFeaturesCol('features')\
    .setLabelCol('label')

model_pipeline = Pipeline()\
    .setStages([featurizer, vec_assembler, logreg])

model = model_pipeline.fit(train)
```

Now let's save the model.

```
model.write().overwrite().save('model.3.12')
```

Now that we have fit a model, let's get our predictions.

```
train_preds = model.transform(train)

test_preds = model.transform(test)
```

6. Evaluate

Let's calculate our F1 score on train and test.

```
from pyspark.ml.evaluation import MulticlassClassificationEvaluator
```

```
evaluator = MulticlassClassificationEvaluator()\
    .setMetricName('f1')

evaluator.evaluate(train_preds)

0.8029598474121058

evaluator.evaluate(test_preds)

0.8010723532212578
```

This is above the minimal acceptance criteria, so we are ready to ship this model.

7. Review

   We can, of course, identify ways to improve the model. But it is important to get a first version out. After we have deployed an initial version, we can begin to look at ways to improve the model.

8. Deploy

   For this application, deployment is merely making the script available. Realistically, offline "deployments" often involve creating a workflow that can be run on demand or periodically. For this application, having the script in a place that can be run for new reviews is all that is needed.

```
%%writefile movie_review_analysis.py


"""
This script takes file containing reviews of the same.
It will output the results of the analysis to std.out.
"""


import argparse as ap
import json
from pyspark.sql import SparkSession
from pyspark.ml import PipelineModel


if __name__ == '__main__':
    print('beginning...')
    parser = ap.ArgumentParser(description='Movie Review Analysis')
    parser.add_argument('-file', metavar='DATA', type=str,
                        required=True,
                        help='The file containing the reviews '\
                             'in JSON format, one JSON review '\
                             'per line')

    options = vars(parser.parse_args())

    spark = SparkSession.builder \
        .master("local[*]") \
```

```
        .appName("Movie Analysis") \
        .config("spark.driver.memory", "12g") \
        .config("spark.executor.memory", "12g") \
        .config("spark.jars.packages",
                "JohnSnowLabs:spark-nlp:2.2.2") \
        .getOrCreate()

nlp_pipeline = PipelineModel.load('nlp_pipeline.3.12')
model = PipelineModel.load('model.3.12')

data = spark.read.json(options['file'])

nlp_procd = nlp_pipeline.transform(data)
preds = model.transform(nlp_procd)

results = preds.selectExpr(
    'count(*)',
    'mean(rawPrediction[1])',
    'std(rawPrediction[1])',
    'median(rawPrediction[1])',
    'min(rawPrediction[1])',
    'max(rawPrediction[1])',
).first().asDict()

print(json.dump(results))
```

This script can be used for taking a set of reviews and aggregating into a single
score plus some additional statistics.

Test and Measure the Solution

Now that we have a first implementation of the application, let's talk about metrics. In
a more realistic scenario, you would define your metrics in the planning stage. However, it is easier to explain some of these topics once we have something concrete to
refer to.

Business Metrics

Normally, an NLP project ties into a new or existing product or service. In this case,
let's say that the output of this script will be used in a film blog. Likely, you will
already be tracking views. When first introducing this feature to the blog, you may
want to do some A/B testing. Ideally, you would do the testing by randomly showing
or not showing the score on blog entries. If that isn't technically feasible, you could
show the scores in some entries and not in others during the initial deployment.

Aggregated scores, like those produced by this tool, can be added to blog entries but
may not necessarily affect views much. This feature may make your review more

attractive for mentions by other outlets. This can be an additional metric. You can possibly capture this by logging where visitors are coming from.

You might want to consider including the aggregate in the messages and notifications you send out. For example, if you notify people of new entries via email, you can include the aggregate in the subject. Also, consider adding the aggregate in the title of the entry.

Once you have decided on your business metrics, you can start working on the technical metrics.

Model-Centric Metrics

For sentiment analysis, you will generally be using classification metrics, like we are here. Sometimes, sentiment labels have grades—for example, very bad, bad, neutral, good, very good. In these situations you can potentially build a regression model instead of a classifier.

There are traditional metrics used with classifiers like precision and recall. In order to make sense, you need to decide which label is the "positive." With precision and recall, "positive" is in the sense of "testing positive." This can make discussing these metrics a little confusing. Let's say that for this application, the good sentiment has the positive label. Assuming this, precision is the proportion of reviews that are predicted to be good that are actually good. Recall is the proportion of actually good reviews that are predicted to be good. Another common classification metric used with precision and recall is *f-score*. This is the harmonic mean of precision and recall. This is a convenient way of summarizing these metrics. We can calculate precision, recall, and the f-score with `MulticlassClassificationEvaluator` in Spark.

Another way of measuring classifier models is with a metric called *log-loss*. This is also called cross-entropy. The idea behind log-loss is measuring how different the observed distribution of labels is from the predicted distribution. This has the benefit of not relying on a mapping of the meaning of good and bad labels to positive and negative. On the downside, this is less interpretable than precision and recall.

When deciding on your model metrics, you should decide on which ones will be useful for experimentation and what singular metric is best for reporting out to share with stakeholders. The metric you select for stakeholders should be one that can be easily explained to an audience that may not be familiar with data-science concepts.

An important part of every machine learning project is deployment. You want to make sure that you have metrics for this stage as well.

Infrastructure Metrics

The infrastructure metrics you choose depend on how your application is deployed. In this case, because the application is a script you likely want to measure the time it takes to run the script. We could put this in the script, but if we are deploying this in some sort of a workflow system, it will likely measure this.

We will talk about more common infrastructure metrics when we get to other applications. Now that we have talked about the metrics for monitoring the technology behind our application, let's talk about metrics we can use to make sure that we are properly supporting the application.

Process Metrics

There are many software development metrics out there, and most of them depend on how you track work—for example, number of tickets per unit of time or average time from opening a ticket to closing a ticket.

In an application like this, you are not developing new features, so ticket-based metrics won't make sense. You can measure responsiveness to bugs with this. The process around this application is that of evaluating reviews for a movie. Measure how long it takes to gather the aggregate score for a new movie. As you automate the process of submitting a set of reviews for aggregation, this will improve.

Another valuable metric for machine-learning-based applications is how long it takes to develop a new model. A simple model like this should not require more than a week, including gathering data, data validation, iterating on model training, documenting results, and deployment. If you find that making a new model takes prohibitively long, try and determine what part of the development process is slowing you down. The following are some common problems:

Data problems are discovered when iterating on the model
- Do improve the data validation so these problems are caught earlier
- Don't just remove the problems in an ad-hoc way without knowing the scope of the data problem—this can lead to invalid models

Every time a new model is needed there is too much data-cleaning work required
- Do improve the ETL pipeline to handle some of this cleaning in an automated manner, or, if possible, find a better data source
- Don't pad the time necessary to build the model and accept that each new developer cleans the data—this can lead to inconsistent models over time

The score of a new model is very different than the previous model
- Do review the evaluation code used in the current and previous models; the difference may be valid, or the measurement code could have a bug

- Don't ignore these changes—this can lead to deploying a worse model that was improperly measured

Now that we have ways to measure the technology and processes of our application, let's talk about monitoring. This is essential in data-science–based applications because we make assumptions about the data when doing modeling. These assumptions may not hold in production.

Offline Versus Online Model Measurement

The difficulty in monitoring a model is that we generally do not have labels in production. So we can't measure our model with things like precision or *root mean square error (RMSE)*. What we should do is measure that the distributions of features and predictions in production are similar to what we saw during experimentation. We can measure this in offline applications—in other words, applications that are run at request like the application in this chapter and online applications like a model that is available as a web service.

For an application like this, we have only offline measurement. We should track the aggregates over time. Naïvely, we can assume that the mean average score for movies should be stable. This may very well not be the case, but if there is a trend, we should review the data to make sure that reviews are indeed changing overall and it's not that our model may have been overfit.

When we look at applications that are deployed as real-time applications, we will discuss online metrics. In spirit, they are similar—they monitor the features and the scores.

There is one more step we need to discuss for this application—that is the review. Data-science–based applications are more complicated to review than most other software because you must review the actual software just as thoroughly as any other application, but you must also review the methodology. NLP applications are even more complicated. The theory behind linguistics and natural language data is not as cleanly modeled as other simpler kinds of data.

Review

The review process is another vital part of writing any application. It is easy for a developer to have blind spots in their own projects. This is why we must bring in others to review our work. This process can be difficult for technical and human reasons. The most important part of any review process is that it not be personal. Both the reviewer and the developer should approach the process with the goal of collaboration. If a problem is found, that is an opportunity. The developer has avoided a later problem, and the reviewer can learning something that may help them avoid problems in future work.

Let's talk about the steps of the review.

1. Architecture review: this is where other engineers, product owners, and stakeholders review how the application will be deployed. This should be done at the end of the planning stage of development

2. Model review: this is done when the developer or data scientist has a model that they believe will meet the expectations of the stakeholder. The model should be reviewed with other data scientists or those familiar with machine learning concepts, and another review should be conducted with stakeholders. The technical review should cover the data, processing, modeling, and measurement aspects of the project. The nontechnical review should explain the assumptions and limitations of the model to verify that it will meet the expectations of the stakeholders.

3. Code reviews: this is necessary for any software application. The code should be reviewed by someone who has some knowledge of the project. If the reviewer has no context on the application, it will be difficult or impossible for them to catch logical bugs in the code.

In our situation, this application is very simple. We are not developing anything but a script, so there is no actual architecture to review. However, the plan to deploy this as a script must be reviewed by the stakeholders. The model review would also be straightforward, since we have a clean data set and simple model. This will generally not be the case. Similarly, our script is very simple. A code review might suggest that we develop a small test data set to make sure that a model will run the data we expect.

These reviews take place during the development of the model. Once we are ready to deploy, we should have some more reviews to make sure that we have prepared for deployment.

Initial Deployment

Work with your product owner and DevOps (if you have DevOps) to discuss how your project will be deployed. In this situation, our project is merely a script, so there is not an actual deployment.

Fallback Plans

When deploying your application, you should also have a fallback plan. If there is a major problem, can you bring down your application until it is fixed, or must there be something there no matter what? If it is the latter, consider having a "dummy" stand-in that you can deploy. You should work out the specifics with the stakeholders. Ideally, this should be discussed early in the project because this can help guide development and testing.

In our situation, this script is not mission critical. If the script doesn't run, it will cause a delay only in the use of the aggregate score. Perhaps a backup script that uses a much simpler model could be devised if there absolutely must be a score added.

Next Steps

Finally, once you are ready to deploy, you should decide what will be the next steps. In our situation, we would likely want to talk about how the model can be improved. The model's performance is not terrible, but it is well below state-of-the-art. Perhaps we can consider building a more complex model.

Additionally, we may eventually want to put this model behind a service. This will allow reviews to be scored immediately.

Conclusion

Now we have built our first application. This is a simple application, but it has allowed us to learn many things about how we will deploy more complex applications. In the next chapter we will again be looking at an offline application, but this will not be based on just the output of a model. We will be building an ontology that we can query.

Many Spark-based applications are offline tools like this. If we want to serve a live model behind a service, we would need to look elsewhere. There are several options for this, which we will discuss in Chapter 19.

Sentiment analysis is a fascinating task, and it uses the tools and techniques we have already covered. There are more complex examples, but by using good development processes we can always grow a simple application.

## CHAPTER 13

Building Knowledge Bases

This application is about organizing information and making it easy to access by humans and computers alike. This is known as a *knowledge base*. The popularity of knowledge bases in the field of NLP has waned in recent decades as the focus has moved away from "expert systems" to statistical machine learning approaches.

An *expert system* is a system that attempts to use *knowledge* to make decisions. This knowledge is about entities, relationships between entities, and rules. Generally, expert systems had *inference engines* that allowed the software to utilize the knowledge base to make a decision. These are sometimes described as collections of if-then rules. However, these systems were much more complicated than this. The knowledge bases and rule sets could be quite large for the technology of the time, so the inference engines needed to be able to efficiently evaluate many logical statements.

Generally, an expert system has a number of actions it can take. There are rules for which action it should take. When the time to take an action comes, the system has a collection of statements and must use these to identify the best action. For example, let's say we have an expert system for controlling the temperature in a house. We need to be able to make decisions based on temperature and time. Whenever the system makes a decision to toggle the heater, or air conditioner, or to do nothing it must take the current temperature (or perhaps a collection of temperature measurements) and the current time, combined with the rule set to determine what action to take. This system has a small number of entities—the temperatures and the time. Imagine if a system had thousands of entities, with multiple kinds of relationships, and a growing ruleset. Resolving the statements available at decision time in a knowledge base this large can be expensive.

In this chapter we will be building a knowledge base. We want a tool for building a knowledge base from a wiki and a tool for querying the knowledge base. This system should fit on a single machine now. We also want to be able to update the knowledge base with new kinds of entities and relationships. Such a system could be used by a domain expert in exploring a topic, or it could be integrated with an expert system. This means that it should have a human usable interface and a responsive API.

Our fictional scenario is a company that is building a machine learning platform. This company primarily sells to other businesses. The sales engineers sometimes fall out of sync with the current state of the system. The engineers are good and update the wiki where appropriate, but the sales engineers are having a hard time keeping up to date. The sales engineers create help tickets for engineers to help them update sales demos. The engineers do not like this. So this application will be used to create a knowledge base that will make it easier for the sales engineers to check out what may have changed.

Problem Statement and Constraints

1. What is the problem we are trying to solve?

   We want to take a wiki and produce a knowledge base. There should also be ways for humans and other software to query the knowledge base. We can assume that the knowledge base will fit on a single machine.

2. What constraints are there?

   - The knowledge-base builder should be easily updatable. It should be easy to configure new types of relationships.

   - The storage solution should allow us to easily add new entities and relationships.

   - Answering queries will require less than 50GB disk space and less than 16 GB memory.

   - There should be a query for getting related entities. For example, at the end of a wiki article there are often links to related pages. The "get related" query should get these entities.

   - The "get related" query should take less than 500ms.

3. How do we solve the problem with the constraints?

   - The knowledge-base builder can be a script that takes a wiki dump and processes the XML and the text. This is where we can use Spark NLP in a larger Spark pipeline.

   - Our building script should monitor resources, to warn if we are nearing the prescribed limits.

   - We will need a database to store our knowledge base. There are many options. We will use Neo4j, a graph database. Neo4j is also relatively well known. There are other solutions possible, but graph databases inherently structure data in the way that facilitates knowledge bases.

- Another benefit to Neo4j is that it comes with a GUI for humans to query and a REST API for programmatic queries.

Plan the Project

Let's define the acceptance criteria. We want a script that does the following:

- Takes a wiki dump, generally a compressed XML file
- Extracts entities, such as article titles
- Extracts relationships, such as links between articles
- Stores the entities and relationships in Neo4J
- Warns if we are producing too much data

We want a service that does the following:

- Allows a "get related" query for a given entity—results must be at least the articles linked in the entity's article
- Performs a "get related" query in under 500ms
- Has a human-usable frontend
- Has a REST API
- Requires less than 16GB memory to run

This is somewhat similar to the application in Chapter 12. However, unlike in that chapter, the model is not a machine learning model—it is instead a data model. We have a script that will build a model, but now we also want a way to serve the model. An additional, and important, difference is that the knowledge base does not come with a simple score (e.g., an F1-score). This means that we will have to put more thought into metrics.

Design the Solution

So we will need to start up Neo4J (*https://neo4j.com*). Once you have it installed, you should be able to go to localhost:7474 for the UI.

Since we are using an off-the-shelf solution, we will not be going very much into graph databases. Here are the important facts.

Graph databases are built to store data as nodes and edges between nodes. The meaning of *node* in this case is usually some kind of entity, and the meaning of an *edge* is some kind of relationship. There can be different types of nodes and different types of relationships. Outside of a database, graph data can be easily stored in CSVs. There will be CSVs for the nodes. This CSV will have an ID column, some sort of name, and properties—depending on the type. Edges are similar, except that the row for an edge will also have the IDs of the two nodes the edge connects. We will not be storing properties.

Let's consider a simple scenario in which we want to store information about books. In this scenario we have three kinds of entities: authors, books, and genres. There are three kinds of relationships: an author *writes* a book, an author *is* a genre author, a book *is in* a genre. For Neo4j, this data could be stored in six CSVs. The entities are the nodes of the graph, and the relationships are the edges, as shown in Figure 13-1.

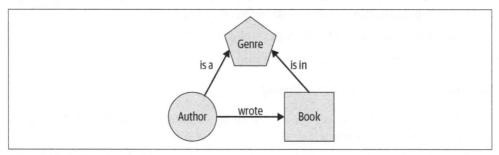

Figure 13-1. Simple graph example

Since we don't have access to a company's internal wiki, we will be using an actual Wikipedia dump. But rather than getting the full English language dump, which would be enormous, we will use the Simple English wikidump.

Simple English is a subset of the English language. It uses about 1,500 words, not counting proper nouns and some technical terms. This is useful for us because this will help us simplify the code we need to write. If this were a real company wiki, there would likely need to be a few iterations of data cleaning. Take a look at a dump of the Simple English Wikipedia (*https://oreil.ly/xMiTA*).

Here is our plan:

1. Get the data
2. Explore the data
3. Parse the wiki for entities and relationships
4. Save the entities and relationships in CSVs
5. Load the CSVs into Neo4J

Implement the Solution

First, let's load the data. Most wikidumps are available as bzip2 compressed XML files. Fortunately, Spark has the ability to deal with this kind of data. Let's load it.

```python
import json
import re
import pandas as pd
import sparknlp

from pyspark.ml import Pipeline
from pyspark.sql import SparkSession, Row
from pyspark.sql.functions import lit, col

import sparknlp
from sparknlp import DocumentAssembler, Finisher
from sparknlp.annotator import *

packages = [
    'JohnSnowLabs:spark-nlp:2.2.2',
    'com.databricks:spark-xml_2.11:0.6.0'
]

spark = SparkSession.builder \
    .master("local[*]") \
    .appName("Knowledge Graph") \
    .config("spark.driver.memory", "12g") \
    .config("spark.jars.packages", ','.join(packages)) \
    .getOrCreate()
```

To give Spark a hint for parsing the XML, we need to configure what the `rootTag` is—the name of the element that contains all of our "rows." We also need to configure the `rowTag`—the name of the elements that represent our rows.

```python
df = spark.read\
    .format('xml')\
    .option("rootTag", "mediawiki")\
    .option("rowTag", "page")\
    .load("simplewiki-20191020-pages-articles-multistream.xml.bz2")\
    .persist()
```

Now, let's see what the schema looks like.

```python
df.printSchema()
```

```
root
 |-- id: long (nullable = true)
 |-- ns: long (nullable = true)
 |-- redirect: struct (nullable = true)
 |    |-- _VALUE: string (nullable = true)
 |    |-- _title: string (nullable = true)
 |-- restrictions: string (nullable = true)
 |-- revision: struct (nullable = true)
```

```
|    |   |-- comment: struct (nullable = true)
|    |   |   |-- _VALUE: string (nullable = true)
|    |   |   |-- _deleted: string (nullable = true)
|    |   |-- contributor: struct (nullable = true)
|    |   |   |-- _VALUE: string (nullable = true)
|    |   |   |-- _deleted: string (nullable = true)
|    |   |   |-- id: long (nullable = true)
|    |   |   |-- ip: string (nullable = true)
|    |   |   |-- username: string (nullable = true)
|    |   |-- format: string (nullable = true)
|    |   |-- id: long (nullable = true)
|    |   |-- minor: string (nullable = true)
|    |   |-- model: string (nullable = true)
|    |   |-- parentid: long (nullable = true)
|    |   |-- sha1: string (nullable = true)
|    |   |-- text: struct (nullable = true)
|    |   |   |-- _VALUE: string (nullable = true)
|    |   |   |-- _space: string (nullable = true)
|    |   |-- timestamp: string (nullable = true)
|-- title: string (nullable = true)
```

That is somewhat complicated, so we should try and simplify. Let's see how many documents we have.

```
df.count()
```

```
284812
```

Let's look at the page for "Paper," so we can get a handle on how to simplify the data.

```
row = df.filter('title = "Paper"').first()

print('ID', row['id'])
print('Title', row['title'])
print()
print('redirect', row['redirect'])
print()
print('text')
print(row['revision']['text']['_VALUE'])
```

```
ID 3319
Title Paper

redirect None

text
[[File:...
[[File:...
[[File:...
[[File:...
[[File:...
[[File:...

Modern '''paper''' is a thin [[material]] of (mostly)
```

```
[[wood fibre]]s pressed together. People write on paper, and
[[book]]s are made of paper. Paper can absorb [[liquid]]s such as
[[water]], so people can clean things with paper.

The '''pulp and paper industry''' comprises companies that use wood as
raw material and produce [[Pulp (paper)|pulp]], paper, board and other
cellulose-based products.

== Paper making ==
Modern paper is normally ...

==Related pages==
* [[Paper size]]
* [[Cardboard]]

== References ==
{{Reflist}}

[[Category:Basic English 850 words]]
[[Category:Paper| ]]
[[Category:Writing tools]]
```

It looks like the text is stored in `revision.text._VALUE`. There seem to be a few special entries, namely *categories* and *redirects*. In most wikis, pages are organized into different categories. Pages are often in multiple categories. These categories have their own pages that link back to the articles. Redirects are pointers from an alternate name for an article to the actual entry.

Let's look at some categories.

```
df.filter('title RLIKE "Category.*"').select('title')\
    .show(10, False, True)

-RECORD 0------------------------
 title | Category:Computer science
-RECORD 1------------------------
 title | Category:Sports
-RECORD 2------------------------
 title | Category:Athletics
-RECORD 3------------------------
 title | Category:Body parts
-RECORD 4------------------------
 title | Category:Tools
-RECORD 5------------------------
 title | Category:Movies
-RECORD 6------------------------
 title | Category:Grammar
-RECORD 7------------------------
 title | Category:Mathematics
-RECORD 8------------------------
 title | Category:Alphabet
-RECORD 9------------------------
```

```
title | Category:Countries
only showing top 10 rows
```

Now let's look at a redirect. It looks like the redirect *target*, where the redirect points, is stored under `redirect._title`.

```
df.filter('redirect IS NOT NULL')\
    .select('redirect._title', 'title')\
    .show(1, False, True)

-RECORD 0------------
 _title | Catharism
 title  | Albigensian
only showing top 1 row
```

This essentially gives us a synonymy relationship. So, our entities will be titles of articles. Our relationships will be redirects, and links will be in the related section of the page. First let's get our entities.

```
entities = df.select('title').collect()
entities = [r['title'] for r in entities]
entities = set(entities)
print(len(entities))

284812
```

We may want to introduce a same-category relationship, so we extract the categories, too.

```
categories = [e for e in entities if e.startswith('Category:')]
entities = [e for e in entities if not e.startswith('Category:')]
```

Now, let's get the redirects.

```
redirects = df.filter('redirect IS NOT NULL')\
    .select('redirect._title', 'title').collect()
redirects = [(r['_title'], r['title']) for r in redirects]
print(len(redirects))

63941
```

Now we can get the articles from `revision.text._VALUE`.

```
data = df.filter('redirect IS NULL').selectExpr(
    'revision.text._VALUE AS text',
    'title'
).filter('text IS NOT NULL')
```

To get the related links, we need to know what section we are in. So let's split the texts into sections. We can then use the `RegexMatcher` annotator to identify links. Viewing the data, it looks like sections look like == `Paper making` == as we saw in the previous example. Let's define a regex for this, adding in the possibility for extra whitespace.

```
section_ptn = re.compile(r'^ *==[^=]+ *== *$')
```

Now, we will define a function that will take a partition of the data and generate new rows for the sections. We will need to keep track of the article title, the section, and the text of the section.

```
def sectionize(rows):
    for row in rows:
        title = row['title']
        text = row['text']
        lines = text.split('\n')
        buffer = []
        section = 'START'
        for line in lines:
            if section_ptn.match(line):
                yield (title, section, '\n'.join(buffer))
                section = line.strip('=').strip().upper()
                buffer = []
                continue
            buffer.append(line)
```

Now we will call `mapPartitions` to create a new RDD and convert that to a DataFrame.

```
sections = data.rdd.mapPartitions(sectionize)
sections = spark.createDataFrame(sections, \
    ['title', 'section', 'text'])
```

Let's look at the most common sections.

```
sections.select('section').groupBy('section')\
    .count().orderBy(col('count').desc()).take(10)

[Row(section='START', count=115586),
 Row(section='REFERENCES', count=32993),
 Row(section='RELATED PAGES', count=8603),
 Row(section='HISTORY', count=6227),
 Row(section='CLUB CAREER STATISTICS', count=3897),
 Row(section='INTERNATIONAL CAREER STATISTICS', count=2493),
 Row(section='GEOGRAPHY', count=2188),
 Row(section='EARLY LIFE', count=1935),
 Row(section='CAREER', count=1726),
 Row(section='NOTES', count=1724)]
```

Plainly, START is the most common because it captures the text between the start of the article and the first section, so almost all articles will have this. This is from Wikipedia, so REFERENCES is the next most common. It looks like RELATED PAGES occurs on only 8,603 articles. Now, we will use Spark-NLP to extract all the links from the texts.

```
%%writefile wiki_regexes.csv
\[\[[^\]]+\]\]~link
\{\{[^\}]+\}\}~anchor

Overwriting wiki_regexes.csv
```

```
assembler = DocumentAssembler()\
    .setInputCol('text')\
    .setOutputCol('document')
matcher = RegexMatcher()\
    .setInputCols(['document'])\
    .setOutputCol('matches')\
    .setStrategy("MATCH_ALL")\
    .setExternalRules('wiki_regexes.csv', '~')
finisher = Finisher()\
    .setInputCols(['matches'])\
    .setOutputCols(['links'])

pipeline = Pipeline()\
    .setStages([assembler, matcher, finisher])\
    .fit(sections)

extracted = pipeline.transform(sections)
```

Now, we could define a relationship based on just links occurring anywhere. For now, we will stick to the related links only.

```
links = extracted.select('title', 'section','links').collect()
links = [(r['title'], r['section'], link) for r in links for link in r['links']]
links = list(set(links))
print(len(links))
```

```
4012895
```

```
related = [(l[0], l[2]) for l in links if l[1] == 'RELATED PAGES']
related = [(e1, e2.strip('[').strip(']').split('|')[-1]) for e1, e2 in related]
related = list(set([(e1, e2) for e1, e2 in related]))
print(len(related))
```

```
20726
```

Now, we have extracted our entities, redirects, and related links. Let's create CSVs for them.

```
entities_df = pd.Series(entities, name='entity').to_frame()
entities_df.index.name = 'id'
entities_df.to_csv('wiki-entities.csv', index=True, header=True)

e2id = entities_df.reset_index().set_index('entity')['id'].to_dict()

redirect_df = []
for e1, e2 in redirects:
    if e1 in e2id and e2 in e2id:
        redirect_df.append((e2id[e1], e2id[e2]))
redirect_df = pd.DataFrame(redirect_df, columns=['id1', 'id2'])
redirect_df.to_csv('wiki-redirects.csv', index=False, header=True)

related_df = []
for e1, e2 in related:
    if e1 in e2id and e2 in e2id:
        related_df.append((e2id[e1], e2id[e2]))
```

```
related_df = pd.DataFrame(related_df, columns=['id1', 'id2'])
related_df.to_csv('wiki-related.csv', index=False, header=True)
```

Now that we have our CSVs, we can copy them to /var/lib/neo4j/import/ and import them using the following:

- Load entities

  ```
  LOAD CSV WITH HEADERS FROM "file:/wiki-entities.csv" AS csvLine
  CREATE (e:Entity {id: toInteger(csvLine.id), entity: csvLine.entity})
  ```

- Load "REDIRECTED" relationship

  ```
  USING PERIODIC COMMIT 500
  LOAD CSV WITH HEADERS FROM "file:///wiki-redirected.csv" AS csvLine
  MATCH (entity1:Entity {id: toInteger(csvLine.id1)}),(entity2:Entity
  {id: toInteger(csvLine.id2)})
  CREATE (entity1)-[:REDIRECTED {conxn: "redirected"}]->(entity2)
  ```

- Load "RELATED" relationship

  ```
  USING PERIODIC COMMIT 500
  LOAD CSV WITH HEADERS FROM "file:///wiki-related.csv" AS csvLine
  MATCH (entity1:Entity {id: toInteger(csvLine.id1)}),(entity2:Entity
  {id: toInteger(csvLine.id2)})
  CREATE (entity1)-[:RELATED {conxn: "related"}]->(entity2)Let's go see
  what we can query. We will get all entities related to "Language" and
  related to entities that are related to Language (i.e., second-order
  relations).
  ```

Let's go see what we can query. We will get all entities related to "Language", and related to entities that are related to "Language" (i.e., second-order relations).

```
import requests

query = '''
MATCH (e:Entity {entity: 'Language'})
RETURN e
UNION ALL
MATCH (:Entity {entity: 'Language'})--(e:Entity)
RETURN e
UNION ALL
MATCH (:Entity {entity: 'Language'})--(e1:Entity)--(e:Entity)
RETURN e
'''
payload = {'query': query, 'params': {}}
endpoint = 'http://localhost:7474/db/data/cypher'

response = requests.post(endpoint, json=payload)

response.status_code

200
```

```
related = json.loads(response.content)
related = [entity[0]['data']['entity']
           for entity in related['data']]
related = sorted(related)
related

1989 in movies
Alphabet
Alphabet (computer science)
Alphabet (computer science)
American English
...
Template:Jctint/core
Testing English as a foreign language
Vowel
Wikipedia:How to write Simple English pages
Writing
```

We have processed a wikidump and have created a basic graph in Neo4j. The next steps in this project would be to extract some more node types and relationships. It would also be good to find a way to attach a weight to the edges. This would allow us to return better results from our query.

Test and Measure the Solution

We now have an initial implementation, so let's go through metrics.

Business Metrics

This will depend on the specific use case of this application. If this knowledge base is used for organizing a company's internal information, then we can look at usage rates. This is not a great metric, since it does not tell us that the system is actually helping the business—only that it is getting used. Let's consider a hypothetical scenario.

Using our example, the sales engineer can query for a feature they want to demo and get related features. Hopefully, this will decrease the help tickets. This is a business-level metric we can monitor.

If we implement this system and do not see sufficient change in the business metrics, we still need metrics to help us understand if the problem is with the basic idea of the application or if it is with the quality of the knowledge base.

Model-Centric Metrics

Measuring the quality of a collection is not as straightforward as measuring a classifier. Let's consider what intuitions we have about what should be in the knowledge base and turn these intuitions into metrics.

- Sparsity versus density: if too many entities have no relationship to any other entity, they decrease the usefulness of the knowledge base; similarly, relationships that are ubiquitous cost resources and provide little benefit. Following are some simple metrics that can be used to measure connectivity.
  — Average number of relationships per entity
  — Proportion of entities with no relationships
  — Ratio of occurrences of a relationship to a fully connected graph
- The entities and relationships that people query are ones we must focus on. Similarly, relationships that are almost never used may be superfluous. Once the system is deployed and queries are logged, we can monitor the following to learn about usage.
  — Number of queries where an entity was not found
  — Number of relationships that are not queried in a time period (day, week, month)

The benefit of having an intermediate step of outputting CSVs is that we don't need to do a large extraction from the database—we can calculate these graph metrics using the CSV data.

Now that we have some idea of how to measure the quality of the knowledge base, let's talk about measuring the infrastructure.

Infrastructure Metrics

We will want to make sure that our single-server approach is sufficient. For a company that is small- to medium-sized, this should be fine. If the company were large, or if the application were intended for much broader use, we would want to consider replication. That is, we would have multiple servers with database, and the users would be redirected through a load balancer.

With Neo4j you can look at system info by querying `:sysinfo`. This will give you information about the amount of data being used.

For an application like this, you would want to monitor response time when queried and update time when adding new entities or relationships.

Process Metrics

On top of the generic process metrics, for this project you want to monitor how long it takes for someone to be able to update the graph. There are a few ways that this graph is likely to be updated.

- Periodic updates to capture wiki updates

- Adding a new type of relationship
- Adding properties to entities or relationships

The first of these is the most important to monitor. The whole point of this application is to keep sales engineers up to date, so this data has to keep up to date. Ideally, this process should be monitored. The next two are important to monitor because the hope of this project is to decrease the workload on developers and data scientists. We don't want to replace the work needed to support sales efforts with effort maintaining this application.

Review

Many of the review steps from Chapter 12 will apply to this application too. You will still want to do the architecture review and the code review. The model review will look different in this situation. Instead of reviewing a machine learning model, you will be reviewing the data model. In building a knowledge graph, you need to balance the needs of performance while structuring the data in a way that makes sense for the domain. This is not a new problem; in fact, traditional relational databases have many ways of balancing these needs.

There are some common structural problems that you can watch out for. First, there is a node type that has only one or two properties; you may want to consider making it a property of the nodes it connects to. For example, we could define a name-type node and have it connect to entities, but this would needlessly complicate the graph.

Deployment will be easier with this kind of application, unless it is customer facing. Your backup plan should be more concerned with communicating with users than with substituting a "simpler" version.

Conclusion

In this chapter, we explored creating an application that is not machine learning based. One of the most valuable things we can do with NLP is make it easier for people to access the information inside. This can, of course, be done by building models, but it can also be done by organizing the information. In Chapter 14, we will look into building an application that uses search to help people organize and access information in text.

Search Engine

In Chapter 13 we discussed how to organize the knowledge we extract from text so that humans and expert systems can utilize it. Most people do not interact with data via graphs, though—especially text data. People generally want to search and retrieve the text. In Chapter 6, we introduced the basic concepts of information retrieval. We learned how to process text as well as how to calculate TF.IDF. In this chapter, we will build an actual search application.

The first thing we need to think about is what problem we are trying to solve. Rather than contrive a specific use case, let's try and build an application that others can use to solve specific tasks. We want to build a tool that users can use to create a customized search.

We will need our application to do a few different things:

1. Process text data
2. Index the processed text
3. Query the index
4. Label search results to measure and improve the search experience

We used fictional scenarios in Chapters 12 and 13. Let's see if we can make a tool that will actually be useful to us. We are the users here. This exercise will be useful because it is not uncommon that you will need to build tools for your own use.

Problem Statement and Constraints

1. What is the problem we are trying to solve?

   We want to be able to build custom search engines that we can improve over time. We want this to be as reusable as possible. So we will want to build some abstractions into our application.

2. What constraints are there?

   We will start with documents that have a title and text. Optionally, they can also contain other attributes—for example, categories, authors, and keywords. We want to be able to improve our search results without needing to re-index all the data. Also, we need to be able to label document-query pairs in order to improve our search engine.

3. How do we solve the problem with the constraints?

   We need to consider multiple parts. First, we will process the text with Spark NLP and index it into Elasticsearch directly with Spark. We will build a special query that will utilize the fields of our documents. We will log the queries and the selection for each query.

Plan the Project

We will break this into chunks like in our previous project. This project will rely on organizing multiple open source technologies.

1. Build processing and indexing script (Spark NLP, Elasticsearch)
2. Customize query function
3. Label document-query pairs (doccano)

For the first three steps, we will be using the Simple English Wikipedia data set. This is a good data set to use because it is not too large to work with on a personal machine, as the English Wikipedia would be. The benefit of using a wiki for this is that we will not require special knowledge to evaluate search results.

Design the Solution

In any real-world scenario, the code for the first two parts would need to be customized. What we can do is separate out the specialized code. This will allow us to reutilize the tools more easily in the future.

We will build an indexing script. First, this will parse and prepare the data for indexing. These are specialized steps that will need to be reimplemented for different data sources. The script will index the data. This is a more general piece of code. We will then build a query function that will allow the user to use different fields of the indexed documents in their query. Finally, we will look at labeling search results. The output of this can be used to improve the indexing script or to potentially implement a machine-learning–based ranker.

Implement the Solution

Before beginning the implementation, follow the appropriate instructions for installing Elasticsearch (*https://oreil.ly/_tf4r*). You could also consider using the Elasticsearch Docker (*https://oreil.ly/TB1nT*).

Once Elasticsearch is running, we can start to load and process the text.

```
import json
import re
import pandas as pd
import requests
import sparknlp

from pyspark.ml import Pipeline
from pyspark.sql import SparkSession, Row
from pyspark.sql.functions import lit, col

import sparknlp
from sparknlp import DocumentAssembler, Finisher
from sparknlp.annotator import *

packages = [
    'JohnSnowLabs:spark-nlp:2.2.2',
    'com.databricks:spark-xml_2.11:0.6.0',
    'org.elasticsearch:elasticsearch-spark-20_2.11:7.4.2'

]

spark = SparkSession.builder \
    .master("local[*]") \
    .appName("Indexing") \
    .config("spark.driver.memory", "12g") \
    .config("spark.jars.packages", ','.join(packages)) \
    .getOrCreate()
```

Loading and parsing the data will need to be specialized for different data sets. We should make sure that the output contains at least a text field, and a title field. You can include other fields that can be used to augment the search. For example, you could add the categories to the data. This allows for faceted searching, which is another way to say that you are filtering your results based on them having some property or facet.

```
# Loading the data - this will need to be specialized
df = spark.read\
```

```
        .format('xml')\
        .option("rootTag", "mediawiki")\
        .option("rowTag", "page")\
        .load("simplewiki-20191020-pages-articles-multistream.xml.bz2")\
        .repartition(200)\
        .persist()

# Selecting the data - this will need to be specialized
df = df.filter('redirect IS NULL').selectExpr(
        'revision.text._VALUE AS text',
        'title'
).filter('text IS NOT NULL')
# you must output a DataFrame that has a text field and a
# title field
```

Now that we have our data, let's use Spark NLP to process it. This is similar to how we've processed data previously.

```
assembler = DocumentAssembler()\
    .setInputCol('text')\
    .setOutputCol('document')
tokenizer = Tokenizer()\
    .setInputCols(['document'])\
    .setOutputCol('tokens')
lemmatizer = LemmatizerModel.pretrained()\
    .setInputCols(['tokens'])\
    .setOutputCol('lemmas')
normalizer = Normalizer()\
    .setCleanupPatterns([
        '[^a-zA-Z.-]+',
        '^[^a-zA-Z]+',
        '[^a-zA-Z]+$',
    ])\
    .setInputCols(['lemmas'])\
    .setOutputCol('normalized')\
    .setLowercase(True)
finisher = Finisher()\
    .setInputCols(['normalized'])\
    .setOutputCols(['normalized'])

nlp_pipeline = Pipeline().setStages([
    assembler, tokenizer,
    lemmatizer, normalizer, finisher
]).fit(df)

processed = nlp_pipeline.transform(df)
```

Now, let's select the fields we are interested in. We will be indexing the text, the title, and the normalized data. We want to store the actual text so that we can show it to the user. This may not always be the case, however. In *federated search*, you are combining data stored in different indices, and perhaps in other kinds of data stores, and searching it all at once. In federated search, you do not want to copy the data you will serve. Depending on how you are combining the search across data stores, you may need to copy some processed form of data. In this case, everything will be in Elastic-search. We will search the title text and the normalized text. Think of these fields as helping with two different metrics. If a query matches a title, it is very likely a relevant document, but there are many queries for which the document is relevant that will not match with the title. Searching the normalized text will improve recall, but we still want title matches to affect the ranking more.

```
processed = processed.selectExpr(
    'text',
    'title',
    'array_join(normalized, " ") AS normalized'
)
```

Now we can index the `DataFrame` as is. We will pass the data directly to Elasticsearch. There are many options when creating an Elasticsearch index, so you should check out the API for Elasticsearch (*https://oreil.ly/YGT1p*).

```
processed.write.format('org.elasticsearch.spark.sql')\
    .save('simpleenglish')
```

We can check what indices are available with the following cURL command.

```
! curl "http://localhost:9200/_cat/indices?v"

health status index          uuid                     pri rep docs.count
docs.deleted store.size pri.store.size
yellow open    simpleenglish jVeJPRyATKKzPPEnuUp3ZQ    1   1
220858          0      1.6gb          1.6gb
```

It looks like everything is there. We can now query the index using the REST API. In order to query our index, we need to choose which fields we'll query. Notice the fields that we list. The initial weights of the fields are guessed. As we learn how our users query the data, we can tune the weights.

```
headers = {
    'Content-Type': 'application/json',
}

params = (
    ('pretty', ''),
)

data = {
    "_source": ['title'],
    "query": {
        "multi_match": {
            "query": "data",
            "fields": ["normalized^1", "title^10"]
        },
    }
}
```

```
response = requests.post(
    'http://localhost:9200/simpleenglish/_search',
    headers=headers, params=params, data=json.dumps(data))

response.json()

{'took': 32,
 'timed_out': False,
 '_shards': {'total': 1, 'successful': 1, 'skipped': 0, 'failed': 0},
 'hits': {'total': {'value': 9774, 'relation': 'eq'},
  'max_score': 54.93799,
  'hits': [{'_index': 'simpleenglish',
    '_type': '_doc',
    '_id': '13iVYG4BfVJ3yetiTdZJ',
    '_score': 54.93799,
    '_source': {'title': 'Data'}},
   {'_index': 'simpleenglish',
    '_type': '_doc',
    '_id': '13iUYG4BfVJ3yeti720D',
    '_score': 45.704754,
    '_source': {'title': 'Repository (data)'}},
   ...
   {'_index': 'simpleenglish',
    '_type': '_doc',
    '_id': 'eHmWYG4BfVJ3yetiIs2m',
    '_score': 45.704754,
    '_source': {'title': 'Data collection'}}]}}
```

Now, let's build our query function. The `fields` argument is expected to be a list of tuples of field names and boosts. *Boosts* are essentially weights that are applied to the scores returned from the index for different fields.

```python
def query_index(query, fields=None, size=10):
    data = spark.createDataFrame([(text,)], ('text',))
    row = nlp_pipeline.transform(data).first()
    query = row['normalized'][0]

    if fields is None:
        fields = [('normalized', 1), ('title', 10)]

    headers = {
    'Content-Type': 'application/json',
    }
    params = (
        ('pretty', ''), ('size', size)
    )
    data = {
        "_source": ['title'],
        "query": {
            "multi_match": {
                "query": query,
                "fields": ['{}^{}'.format(f, b) for f, b in fields]
            },
```

```
        }
    }
    response = requests.post(
        'http://localhost:9200/simpleenglish/_search',
        headers=headers, params=params,
        data=json.dumps(data)).json()

    return [(r['_source']['title'], r['_score'])
            for r in response['hits']['hits']]
```

Now let's build our set, which we will label. Let's query the index for "Language."

```
language_query_results = query_index('Language', size=13)
language_query_results
```

```
[('Language', 72.923416),
 ('Baure language', 60.667435),
 ('Luwian language', 60.667435),
 ('Faroese language', 60.667435),
 ('Aramaic language', 60.667435),
 ('Gun language', 60.667435),
 ('Beary language', 60.667435),
 ('Tigrinya language', 60.667435),
 ('Estonian language', 60.667435),
 ('Korean language', 60.667435),
 ('Kashmiri language', 60.667435),
 ('Okinawan language', 60.667435),
 ('Rohingya language', 60.667435)]
```

Returning articles about actual languages is a very reasonable result for the query "Language."

We will need to make sure that we export the information necessary for our labeling, namely title and text. If your data has extra fields that you think will be relevant to judgments, you should modify the exported fields to include them. We will be creating documents for labeling. These documents will contain the query, the title, the score, and the text.

```
language_query_df = spark.createDataFrame(
    language_query_results, ['title', 'score'])

docs = df.join(language_query_df, ['title'])

docs = docs.collect()
docs = [r.asDict() for r in docs]

with open('lang_query_results.json', 'w') as out:
    for doc in docs:
        text = 'Query: Language\n'
        text += '=' * 50 + '\n'
        text += 'Title: {}'.format(doc['title']) + '\n'
        text += '=' * 50 + '\n'
        text += 'Score: {}'.format(doc['score']) + '\n'
```

```
text += '=' * 50 + '\n'
text += doc['text']
line = json.dumps({'text': text})
out.write(line + '\n')
```

Now that we have created the data we will need to label, let's start using *doccano*. Doccano is a tool built to help in NLP labeling. It allows for document classification labeling (for tasks like sentiment analysis), segment labeling (for tasks like NER), and sequence-to-sequence labeling (for tasks like machine translation). You can set up this service locally or launch it in a docker. Let's look at launching it in a docker.

First, we will pull the image.

```
docker pull chakkiworks/doccano
```

Next, we will run a container.

```
docker run -d --rm --name doccano \
    -e "ADMIN_USERNAME=admin" \
    -e "ADMIN_EMAIL=admin@example.com" \
    -e "ADMIN_PASSWORD=password" \
    -p 8000:8000 chakkiworks/doccano
```

If you plan on using doccano to have other people label, you should consider changing the admin credentials.

Once you have started the container, go to `localhost:8000` (or whichever port you chose if you modified the `-p` argument). You should see the page in Figure 14-1.

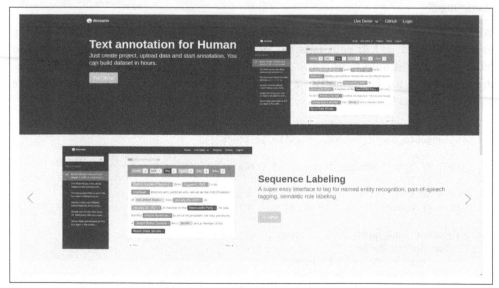

Figure 14-1. Doccano landing page

Click on the login and use the credentials from the docker run command. Then click "Create Project." Here, in Figure 14-2, the project fields are filled out.

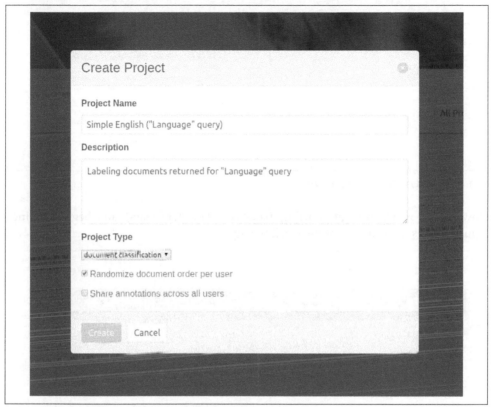

Figure 14-2. Creating a project in doccano

Next, click on "Select a file", and navigate to the location lang_query_results.json created previously. This will add the documents for labeling to the project.

After this, click on "Labels," and click "New label." I added three, "relevant," "partially relevant," and "not relevant." In the underlying data, these labels will be represented by the order in which you created them. For example, if you created "relevant," "partially relevant," and "not relevant" their representation will be 1, 2, 3, respectively.

I think it is a good idea to write guidelines for labeling tasks, even if you are the one doing the labeling. This will help you think about how you want your data labeled. Figuring it out as you go can lead to inconsistencies.

Figure 14-3 is an example of the guidelines I created for this example task.

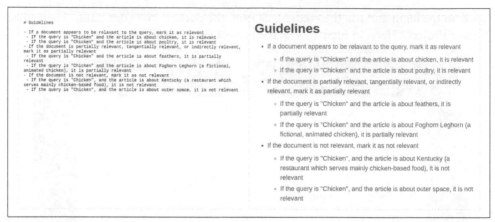

Figure 14-3. Guidelines in doccano

Now we are ready to begin labeling. Click on "Annotate Data," and begin labeling. Figure 14-4 is a screenshot of the labeling page.

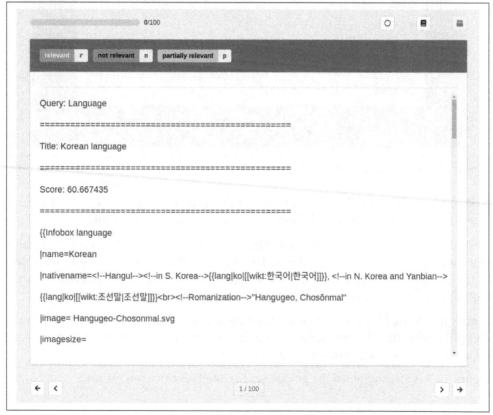

Figure 14-4. Doccano labeling

Once you are finished, you can click on "Edit Data," which will take you back to the project page. From here, you can export the data by clicking "Export Data." You can export as JSON lines or as CSV. We won't be using this data, however, because labeling enough query-document pairs to improve the ranking would take some time.

Test and Measure the Solution

Now that we have created an index and have looked at how we can use doccano to label, we can talk about how we can measure our solution. This is a different scenario than most applications, since this tool will be used for organizing and retrieving documents for us—we are the customers.

Business Metrics

When you are building applications for yourself, the notion of "business" metrics is pointless. What you want is to be happy with your own product. So let's go straight to measuring our model of the data.

Model-Centric Metrics

When measuring an index, there are many possible metrics. Primarily, we want the best ranking. One way to measure ranking is through recall and precision, which is similar to binary classification problems. The problem is that if we return a hundred documents, recall and precision will not tell us about the order they are in. For that, we need ranking metrics. One of the most popular kinds of metrics is *Normalized Discounted Cumulative Gain (NDCG)*. To explain this, we need to build to it. First, let's define *gain*. In this context, the gain is the information in the text. We use the relevancy of the document as gain. Cumulative gain is the sum of the gain up to a chosen cutoff. Up until this point there is nothing about rank, so we discount the gain the more we descend the list. We will need to reduce the gain using the rank. We use the logarithm of the rank so that the discount more strongly separates the items early in the list than those later in the list. The last part is the normalization. It is much easier to report a metric if it is between 0 and 1. So we need to determine the ideal discounted cumulative gain. If you cannot calculate it directly, you can estimate it assuming that all documents above the cutoff are relevant. Now let's look at the actual metric.

K = the chosen cutoff; usual cutoffs are $5, 10, 50$

r_i = the relevance of the ith document

$$CG_K = \sum_{i=1}^{K} r_i$$

$$DCG_K = \sum_{i=1}^{K} \frac{r_i}{log_2(i+1)}$$

$$IDCG_K = \sum_{i=1}^{K} \frac{max(r)}{log_2(i+1)}$$

$$NDCG_K = \frac{DCG}{IDCG}$$

Now, we can quantify how well our index works. Even if you are building a tool for yourself, it is important to quantify the quality of data-driven applications. Humans are the ultimate source of truth, but we are also fickle and moody. Using metrics can help make our evaluations dependable.

Review

When you are working on your own, reviewing is more difficult. If you have someone who is willing to help you review the work, they can provide a vital outside perspective. You want to value the time of your volunteer, so you should prepare a demo. More in-depth reviews are a more onerous request, so you can't depend on being able to get a code review from a volunteer.

So how can we check for quality without assistance? We must put more effort into testing and documentation. This creates another problem—the increased effort in pursuit of quality can cause you to lose steam. This means that you should use such projects as an opportunity to set reasonable goals and milestones.

Conclusion

Information retrieval is a rich field of study. This chapter can serve as a starting point for you to delve into that field. The other important thing emphasized in this chapter is the value of projects built for yourself. In data science, it is often hard to find a professional opportunity to learn a new technique. Building a project for your own purpose can be a great opportunity to expand your collection of skills.

In Chapter 15, we will learn about building a model that works interactively with the user.

Chatbot

When we discussed language models, we showed how we can generate text. Building a chatbot is similar, except that we are modeling an exchange. This can make our requirements more complex or, actually, more simple depending on how we want to approach the problem.

In this chapter we will discuss some of the ways this can be modeled, and then we will build a program that will use a generative model to take and then generate responses. First, let's talk about what discourse is.

Morphology and syntax tell us how morphemes are combined into words, and words into phrases and sentences. The combination of sentences into larger language acts is not as easily modeled. There is an idea of an inappropriate combination of sentences. Let's look at some examples:

> I went to the doctor, yesterday. It is just a sprained ankle.
> I went to the doctor, yesterday. Mosquitoes have 47 teeth.

In the first example, the second sentence is obviously related to the first. From these two sentences, combined with common knowledge, we can infer that the speaker went to the doctor for an ankle problem that turned out to be a sprain. The second example makes no sense. From a linguistics point of view, sentences are generated from concepts and then encoded into words and phrases. The concepts that are expressed by sentences are connected, so a sequence of sentences should be connected by similar concepts. This will be true whether there is only one speaker or more in a conversation.

The pragmatics of a discourse is important to understanding how to model it. If we are modeling a customer-service exchange, the range of responses can be limited. These limited types of responses are often called *intents*. When building a customer-service chatbot, this greatly reduces the potential complexity. If we are modeling general conversation, this can become much more difficult. Language models learn what is likely to occur in a sequence, but they cannot learn to generate concepts. So our choice is to either build something that models the probable sequences or find a way to cheat.

We can cheat by building canned responses to unrecognized intents. For example, if the user makes a statement that our simple model is not expecting, we can have it respond with, "Sorry, I don't understand." If we are logging the conversations, we can use exchanges that use the canned responses to expand the intents we cover.

In the example we are covering, we will be building a program that purely models the full text of the discourse. Essentially, it is a language model. The difference will be in how we use it.

This chapter is different than previous ones in that it doesn't make use of Spark. Spark is great for processing large amounts of data in batches. It's not great in interactive applications. Also, recurrent neural networks can take a long time to train with large amounts of data. So, in this chapter we are working a small piece of data. If you have the right hardware, you change the NLTK processing to use Spark NLP.

Problem Statement and Constraints

We will build a story-building tool. The idea is to help someone write an original story similar to one of the Grimm fairy tales. This model will be much more complex, in the sense of containing many more parameters, than the previous language model was. The program will be a script that asks for an input sentence and generates a new sentence. The user then takes that sentence, modifies and corrects it, and enters it.

1. What is the problem we are trying to solve?

   We want a system that will recommend the next sentence in a story. We also must recognize the limitations of text generation techniques. We will need to have the user in the loop. So we need a model that can generate related text and a system that lets us review the output.

2. What constraints are there?

   First, we need a model that has two notions of context—the previous sentence and the current sentence. We don't need to worry about performance as much, since this will be interacting with a person. This might seem counterintuitive because most interactive systems require quite low latency. However, if you consider what this program is producing, it is not unreasonable to wait one to three seconds for a response.

3. How do we solve the problem with the constraints?

We will be building a neural network for generating text, specifically an RNN, as discussed in Chapters 4 and 8. We could learn the word *embeddings* in this model, but we can instead use a prebuilt embedding. This will help us train a model more quickly.

Plan the Project

Most of the work on this project will be developing a model. Once we have a model, we will build a simple script that we can use to write our own Grimm-style fairy tale. Once we've developed this script, this model could potentially be used to power a Twitter bot or Slackbot.

In a real production setting for text generation, we would want to monitor the quality of generated text. This would allow us to improve the generated text over time by developing more targeted training data.

Design the Solution

If you recall our language model, we used three layers.

1. Input
2. Embedding
3. LSTM
4. Dense output

We input windows of characters of a fixed size and predicted the following character. Now we need to find a way to take into account larger portions of text. There are a couple of options.

Many RNN architectures include a layer for learning an embedding for the words. This would merely require us to learn more parameters, so we will use a pretrained GloVe model instead. Also, we will be building our model on the token level, and not on the character level as before.

We could make the window size much larger than the average sentence. This has the benefit of keeping the same model architecture. The downside is that our LSTM layer will have to maintain information over quite long distances. We can use one of the architectures used for machine translations.

Let's consider the concatenating approach.

1. Context input
2. Context LSTM

3. Current input

4. Current LSTM

5. Concatenate 2 and 4

6. Dense output

The current inputs will be windows over sentences, so for each window of a given sentence we will use the same context vector. This approach has the benefit of being able to be extended to multiple sentences. The downside is that the model has to learn to balance the information from far away and from nearby.

Let's consider the stateful approach.

1. Context input

2. Context LSTM

3. Current input

4. Current LSTM, initialized with state of 2

5. Dense output

This helps make training easier by reducing the influence of the previous sentence. This is a double-edged sword, however, because the context gives us less information. We will be using this approach.

Implement the Solution

Let's start out by doing our imports. This chapter will rely on Keras.

```
from collections import Counter
import pickle as pkl

import nltk
import numpy as np
import pandas as pd

from keras.models import Model
from keras.layers import Input, Embedding, LSTM, Dense, CuDNNLSTM
from keras.layers.merge import Concatenate
import keras.utils as ku
import keras.preprocessing as kp
import tensorflow as tf

np.random.seed(1)
tf.set_random_seed(2)
```

Let's also define some special tokens for the beginning and ending of sentences, as well as for unknown tokens.

```
START = '>'
END = '###'
UNK = '???'
```

Now, we can load the data. We will need to replace some of the special characters.

```
with open('grimms_fairytales.txt', encoding='UTF-8') as fp:
    text = fp.read()

text = text\
    .replace('\t', ' ')\
    .replace('"', '"')\
    .replace('"', '"')\
    .replace('"', '"')\
    .replace(''', "'")\
    .replace(''', "'")
```

Now, we can process our text into tokenized sentences.

```
sentences = nltk.tokenize.sent_tokenize(text)
sentences = [s.strip()for s in sentences]
sentences = [[t.lower() for t in nltk.tokenize.wordpunct_tokenize(s)] for s in
sentences]
word_counts = Counter([t for s in sentences for t in s])
word_counts = pd.Series(word_counts)
vocab = [START, END, UNK] + list(sorted(word_counts.index))
```

We need to define some hyperparameters for our model.

- dim is the size of the token embeddings

- w is the size of the windows we'll use

- max_len is the sentence length that we use

- units is the size of the state vectors we'll use for our LSTMs

```
dim = 50
w = 10
max_len = int(np.quantile([len(s) for s in sentences], 0.95))
units = 200
```

Now, let's load the GloVe embeddings.

```
glove = {}
with open('glove.6B/glove.6B.50d.txt', encoding='utf-8') as fp:
    for line in fp:
        token, embedding = line.split(maxsplit=1)
        if token in vocab:
            embedding = np.fromstring(embedding, 'f', sep=' ')
            glove[token] = embedding

vocab = list(sorted(glove.keys()))
vocab_size = len(vocab)
```

We will also need to have a lookup for the one-hot–encoded output.

```
i2t = dict(enumerate(vocab))
t2i = {t: i for i, t in i2t.items()}

token_oh = ku.to_categorical(np.arange(vocab_size))
token_oh = {t: token_oh[i,:] for t, i in t2i.items()}
```

Now, we can define some utility functions.

We will need to pad the end of the sentences; otherwise, we will not learn from the last words in the sentences.

```
def pad_sentence(sentence, length):
    sentence = sentence[:length]
    if len(sentence) < length:
        sentence += [END] * (length - len(sentence))
    return sentence
```

We also need to convert sentences to matrices.

```
def sent2mat(sentence, embedding):
    mat = [embedding.get(t, embedding[UNK]) for t in sentence]
    return np.array(mat)
```

We need a function for converting sequences to a sequence of sliding windows.

```
def slide_seq(seq, w):
    window = []
    target = []
    for i in range(len(seq)-w-1):
        window.append(seq[i:i+w])
        target.append(seq[i+w])
    return window, target
```

Now we can build our input matrices. We will have two input matrices. One is from the context, and one is from the current sentence.

```
Xc = []
Xi = []
Y = []

for i in range(len(sentences)-1):

    context_sentence = pad_sentence(sentences[i], max_len)
    xc = sent2mat(context_sentence, glove)

    input_sentence = [START]*(w-1) + sentences[i+1] + [END]*(w-1)
    for window, target in zip(*slide_seq(input_sentence, w)):
        xi = sent2mat(window, glove)
        y = token_oh.get(target, token_oh[UNK])

        Xc.append(np.copy(xc))
        Xi.append(xi)
        Y.append(y)
```

```
Xc = np.array(Xc)
Xi = np.array(Xi)
Y = np.array(Y)

print('context sentence: ', xc.shape)
print('input sentence: ', xi.shape)
print('target sentence: ', y.shape)

context sentence:  (42, 50)
input sentence:  (10, 50)
target sentence:  (4407,)
```

Let's build our model.

```
input_c = Input(shape=(max_len,dim,), dtype='float32')
lstm_c, h, c = LSTM(units, return_state=True)(input_c)

input_i = Input(shape=(w,dim,), dtype='float32')
lstm_i = LSTM(units)(input_i, initial_state=[h, c])

out = Dense(vocab_size, activation='softmax')(lstm_i)
model = Model(input=[input_c, input_i], output=[out])

print(model.summary())

Model: "model_1"
```

Layer (type)	Output Shape	Param #	Connected to
input_1 (InputLayer)	(None, 42, 50)	0	
input_2 (InputLayer)	(None, 10, 50)	0	
lstm_1 (LSTM)	[(None, 200), (None,	200800	input_1[0][0]
lstm_2 (LSTM)	(None, 200)	200800	input_2[0][0]
			lstm_1[0][1]
			lstm_1[0][2]
dense_1 (Dense)	(None, 4407)	885807	lstm_2[0][0]

```
Total params: 1,287,407
Trainable params: 1,287,407
Non-trainable params: 0
```

```
None

model.compile(
    loss='categorical_crossentropy', optimizer='adam',
    metrics=['accuracy'])
```

Now we can train our model. Depending on your hardware, this can potentially take four minutes per epoch on CPU. This is our most complex model yet with almost 1.3 million parameters.

```
Epoch 1/10
145061/145061 [==============================] - 241s 2ms/step
- loss: 3.7840 - accuracy: 0.3894
...
Epoch 10/10
145061/145061 [==============================] - 244s 2ms/step
- loss: 1.8933 - accuracy: 0.5645
```

Once we have this model trained, we can try to generate some sentences. This func-tion will need a context sentence and an input sentence—we can simply supply one word to begin. The function will append tokens to the input sentence until the END token is generated or we have hit the maximum allowed length.

```
def generate_sentence(context_sentence, input_sentence, max_len=100):
    context_sentence = [t.lower() for t in nltk.tokenize.wordpunct_tokenize(con-
text_sentence)]
    context_sentence = pad_sentence(context_sentence, max_len)
    context_vector = sent2mat(context_sentence, glove)
    input_sentence = [t.lower() for t in nltk.tokenize.wordpunct_token-
ize(input_sentence)]
    input_sentence = [START] * (w-1) + input_sentence
    input_sentence = input_sentence[:w]
    output_sentence = input_sentence

    input_vector = sent2mat(input_sentence, glove)
    predicted_vector = model.predict([[context_vector], [input_vector]])
    predicted_token = i2t[np.argmax(predicted_vector)]
    output_sentence.append(predicted_token)
    i = 0
    while predicted_token != END and i < max_len:
        input_sentence = input_sentence[1:w] + [predicted_token]
        input_vector = sent2mat(input_sentence, glove)
        predicted_vector = model.predict([[context_vector], [input_vector]])
        predicted_token = i2t[np.argmax(predicted_vector)]
        output_sentence.append(predicted_token)
        i += 1
    return output_sentence
```

Because we need to supply the first word of the new sentence, we can simply sample from the beginning tokens found in our corpus. Let's save the distribution of first words that we will need as JSON.

```
first_words = Counter([s[0] for s in sentences])
first_words = pd.Series(first_words)
first_words = first_words.sum()

first_words.to_json('grimm-first-words.json')

with open('glove-dict.pkl', 'wb') as out:
    pkl.dump(glove, out)

with open('vocab.pkl', 'wb') as out:
    pkl.dump(i2t, out)
```

Let's see what is generated without human intervention.

```python
context_sentence = '''
In old times, when wishing was having, there lived a King whose
daughters were all beautiful, but the youngest was so beautiful that
the sun itself, which has seen so much, was astonished whenever it
shone in her face.
'''.strip().replace('\n', ' ')

input_sentence = np.random.choice(first_words.index, p=first_words)

for _ in range(10):
    print(context_sentence, END)
    output_sentence = generate_sentence(context_sentence, input_sentence,
max_len)
    output_sentence = ' '.join(output_sentence[w-1:-1])
    context_sentence = output_sentence
    input_sentence = np.random.choice(first_words.index, p=first_words)
print(output_sentence, END)
```

```
In old times, when wishing was having, there lived a King whose daughters
were all beautiful, but the youngest was so beautiful that the sun
itself, which has seen so much, was astonished whenever it shone in her
face. ###
" what do you desire ??? ###
the king ' s son , however , was still beautiful , and a little chair
there ' s blood and so that she is alive ??? ###
the king ' s son , however , was still beautiful , and the king ' s
daughter was only of silver , and the king ' s son came to the forest ,
and the king ' s son seated himself on the leg , and said , " i will go
to church , and you shall be have lost my life ??? ###
" what are you saying ??? ###
cannon - maiden , and the king ' s daughter was only a looker - boy . ###
but the king ' s daughter was humble , and said , " you are not afraid
??? ###
then the king said , " i will go with you ??? ###
" i will go with you ??? ###
he was now to go with a long time , and the bird threw in the path , and
the strong of them were on their of candles and bale - plants . ###
then the king said , " i will go with you ??? ###
```

This model won't be passing the Turing test any time soon. This is why we need to have a human in the loop. Let's build our script. First, let's save our model.

```python
model.save('grimm-model')
```

Our script will need to have access to some of our utility functions, as well as to the hyperparameters—for example, dim, w.

```python
%%writefile fairywriter.py
"""
This script helps you generate a fairytale.
"""
```

```python
import pickle as pkl

import nltk
import numpy as np
import pandas as pd

from keras.models import load_model
import keras.utils as ku
import keras.preprocessing as kp
import tensorflow as tf


START = '>'
END = '###'
UNK = '???'


FINISH_CMDS = ['finish', 'f']
BACK_CMDS = ['back', 'b']
QUIT_CMDS = ['quit', 'q']
CMD_PROMPT = ' | '.join(','.join(c) for c in [FINISH_CMDS, BACK_CMDS,
QUIT_CMDS])
QUIT_PROMPT = '"{}" to quit'.format('" or "'.join(QUIT_CMDS))
ENDING = ['THE END']


def pad_sentence(sentence, length):
    sentence = sentence[:length]
    if len(sentence) < length:
        sentence += [END] * (length - len(sentence))
    return sentence


def sent2mat(sentence, embedding):
    mat = [embedding.get(t, embedding[UNK]) for t in sentence]
    return np.array(mat)


def generate_sentence(context_sentence, input_sentence, vocab, max_len=100,
hparams=(42, 50, 10)):
    max_len, dim, w = hparams
    context_sentence = [t.lower() for t in nltk.tokenize.wordpunct_tokenize(con-
text_sentence)]
    context_sentence = pad_sentence(context_sentence, max_len)
    context_vector = sent2mat(context_sentence, glove)
    input_sentence = [t.lower() for t in nltk.tokenize.wordpunct_token-
ize(input_sentence)]
    input_sentence = [START] * (w-1) + input_sentence
    input_sentence = input_sentence[:w]
    output_sentence = input_sentence

    input_vector = sent2mat(input_sentence, glove)
```

```python
        predicted_vector = model.predict([[context_vector], [input_vector]])
        predicted_token = vocab[np.argmax(predicted_vector)]
        output_sentence.append(predicted_token)
        i = 0
        while predicted_token != END and i < max_len:
            input_sentence = input_sentence[1:w] + [predicted_token]
            input_vector = sent2mat(input_sentence, glove)
            predicted_vector = model.predict([[context_vector], [input_vector]])
            predicted_token = vocab[np.argmax(predicted_vector)]
            output_sentence.append(predicted_token)
            i += 1
        return output_sentence


if __name__ == '__main__':
    model = load_model('grimm-model')
    (_, max_len, dim), (_, w, _) = model.get_input_shape_at(0)
    hparams = (max_len, dim, w)
    first_words = pd.read_json('grimm-first-words.json', typ='series')
    with open('glove-dict.pkl', 'rb') as fp:
        glove = pkl.load(fp)
    with open('vocab.pkl', 'rb') as fp:
        vocab = pkl.load(fp)

    print("Let's write a story!")
    title = input('Give me a title ({}) '.format(QUIT_PROMPT))
    story = [title]
    context_sentence = title
    input_sentence = np.random.choice(first_words.index, p=first_words)
    if title.lower() in QUIT_CMDS:
        exit()

    print(CMD_PROMPT)
    while True:
        input_sentence = np.random.choice(first_words.index, p=first_words)
        generated = generate_sentence(context_sentence, input_sentence, vocab,
hparams=hparams)
        generated = ' '.join(generated)
        ### the model creates a suggested sentence
        print('Suggestion:', generated)
        ### the user responds with the sentence they want add
        ### the user can fix up the suggested sentence or write their own
        ### this is the sentence that will be used to make the next suggestion
        sentence = input('Sentence: ')
        if sentence.lower() in QUIT_CMDS:
            story = []
            break
        elif sentence.lower() in FINISH_CMDS:
            story.append(np.random.choice(ENDING))
            break
        elif sentence.lower() in BACK_CMDS:
            if len(story) == 1:
```

```
        print('You are at the beginning')
        story = story[:-1]
        context_sentence = story[-1]
        continue
    else:
        story.append(sentence)
        context_sentence = sentence

print('\n'.join(story))
print('exiting...')
```

Let's give our script a run. I'll use it to read the suggestion and take elements of it to add the next line. A more complex model might be able to produce sentences that can be edited and added, but this model isn't quite there.

```
%run fairywriter.py

Let's write a story!
Give me a title ("quit" or "q" to quit) The Wolf Goes Home
finish,f | back,b | quit,q
Suggestion: > > > > > > > > > and when they had walked for the time , and
the king ' s son seated himself on the leg , and said , " i will go to
church , and you shall be have lost my life ??? ###
Sentence: There was once a prince who got lost in the woods on the way
to a church.
Suggestion: > > > > > > > > > she was called hans , and as the king ' s
daughter , who was so beautiful than the children , who was called clever
elsie . ###
Sentence: The prince was called Hans, and he was more handsome than the
boys.
Suggestion: > > > > > > > > > no one will do not know what to say , but i
have been compelled to you ??? ###
Sentence: The Wolf came along and asked, "does no one know where are?"
Suggestion: > > > > > > > > > there was once a man who had a daughter who
had three daughters , and he had a child and went , the king ' s daughter
, and said , " you are growing and thou now , i will go and fetch
Sentence: The Wolf had three daughters, and he said to the prince, "I
will help you return home if you take one of my daughters as your
betrothed."
Suggestion: > > > > > > > > > but the king ' s daughter was humble , and
said , " you are not afraid ??? ###
Sentence: The prince asked, "are you not afraid that she will be killed
as soon as we return home?"
Suggestion: > > > > > > > > > i will go and fetch the golden horse ???
###
Sentence: The Wolf said, "I will go and fetch a golden horse as dowry."
Suggestion: > > > > > > > > > one day , the king ' s daughter , who was
a witch , and lived in a great forest , and the clouds of earth , and in
the evening , came to the glass mountain , and the king ' s son
Sentence: The Wolf went to find the forest witch that she might conjure
a golden horse.
Suggestion: > > > > > > > > > when the king ' s daughter , however , was
sitting on a chair , and sang and reproached , and said , " you are not
```

```
to be my wife , and i will take you to take care of your ??? ###
Sentence: The witch reproached the wolf saying, "you come and ask me such
a favor with no gift yourself?"
Suggestion: > > > > > > > > > then the king said , " i will go with you
??? ###
Sentence: So the wolf said, "if you grant me this favor, I will be your
servant."
Suggestion: > > > > > > > > > he was now to go with a long time , and
the other will be polluted , and we will leave you ??? ###
Sentence: f
The Wolf Goes Home
There was once a prince who got lost in the woods on the way to a church.
The prince was called Hans, and he was more handsome than the boys.
The Wolf came along and asked, "does no one know where are?"
The Wolf had three daughters, and he said to the prince, "I will help
you return home if you take one of my daughters as your betrothed."
The prince asked, "are you not afraid that she will be killed as soon as
we return home?"
The Wolf said, "I will go and fetch a golden horse as dowry."
The Wolf went to find the forest witch that she might conjure a golden
horse.
The witch reproached the wolf saying, "you come and ask me such a favor
with no gift yourself?"
So the wolf said, "if you grant me this favor, I will be your servant."
THE END
exiting..
```

You can do additional epochs to get better suggestions, but beware of overfitting. If you overfit this model, then it will generate worse results if you provide it with contexts and inputs that it doesn't recognize.

Now that we have a model that we can interact with, the next step would be to integrate it with a chatbot system. Most systems require some server that will serve the model. The specifics will depend on your chatbot platform.

Test and Measure the Solution

Measuring a chatbot depends more on the end purpose of the product than it does for most applications. Let's consider the different kinds of metrics we will use for measuring.

Business Metrics

If you are building a chatbot to support customer service, then the business metrics will be centered around the customer experience. If you are building a chatbot for entertainment purposes, as is the case here, there are no obvious business metrics. However, if the entertaining chatbot is being used for marketing, you can use marketing metrics.

Model-Centric Metrics

It's difficult to measure live interactions in the same way that the model measures in training. In training, we know the "correct" response, but due to the interactive nature of the model we don't have a definite correct answer. To measure a live model, you will need to manually label conversations.

Now let's talk about the infrastructure.

Review

When reviewing a chatbot, you will need to do the normal reviews needed for any project. The additional requirement will be to get the chatbot in front of a proxy for the actual user. As with any application that requires user interaction, user testing is central.

Conclusion

In this chapter, we learned how to build a model for an interactive application. There are many different kinds of chatbots. The example we see here is based on a language model, but we can also build a recommendation model. It all depends on what kind of interaction you are expecting. In our situation, we are entering and receiving full sentences. If your application has a constrained set of responses, then your task becomes easier.

## CHAPTER 16

Object Character Recognition

So far, we've dealt with writing stored as text data. However, a large portion of written data is stored as images. To use this data we need to convert it to text. This is different than our other NLP problems. In this problem, our knowledge of linguistics won't be as useful. This isn't the same as reading; it's merely character recognition. It is a much less intentional activity than speaking or listening to speech. Fortunately, writing systems tend to be easily distinguishable characters, especially in print. This means that image recognition techniques should work well on images of print text.

Object character recognition (OCR) is the task of taking an image of written language (with characters) and converting it into text data. Modern solutions are neural-network based, and are essentially classifying sections of an image as containing a character. These classifications are then mapped into a character or string of characters in the text data.

Let's talk about some of the possible inputs.

Kinds of OCR Tasks

There are several kinds of OCR tasks. The tasks differ in what kind of image is the input, what kind of writing is in the image, and what is the target of the model.

Images of Printed Text and PDFs to Text

Unfortunately, there are many systems that export their documents as images. Some will export as PDFs, but since there is such a wide variety of ways in which a document can be coded into a PDF, PDFs may not be better than images. The good news is that in a PDF the characters are represented very consistently (except for font and size differences) with a high-contrast background. Converting documents like this to text data is the easiest OCR task.

This can be complicated if the images are actually scans of documents, which can introduce the following errors:

Print errors
> The printer had a dirty head and produced blotches, or left lines in the text.

Paper problems
> The paper is old, stained, or has creases. This can reduce the contrast and smudge or distort some parts of the image.

Scanning problems
> The paper is skewed, which means that text is not in lines.

Images of Handwritten Text to Text

This situation still has the high-contrast background, but the consistency of characters is much worse. Additionally, the issue of text not being in lines can be much harder if a document has marginal notes. The well-worn data set of handwritten digits from the MNIST database is an example of this task.

You will need some way to constrain this problem. For example, the MNIST data set is restricted to just 10 characters. Some electronic pen software constrains the problem by learning one person's handwriting. Trying to solve this problem for everyone's handwriting would be significantly more difficult. There is so much variety in writing styles that it is not uncommon for humans to be unable to read a stranger's handwriting. What the model learns in recognizing writing in letters from the American Civil War will be useless in recognizing doctors' notes or parsing signatures.

Images of Text in Environment to Text

An example of images of text in an environment would be identifying what a sign says in a picture of a street. Generally, such text is printed, but the font and size can vary widely. There can also be distortions similar to the problems in our scanning example. The problem of skewed text in this type of image is more difficult than when scanned. When scanning, one dimension is fixed, so the paper can be assumed to be flat on the scanning bed. In the environment, text can be rotated in any way. For example, if you are building an OCR model for a self-driving car, some of the text will be to the right of the car, and some will be elevated above the car. There will also be text on the road. This means that the shapes of the letters will not be consistent.

This problem is also often constrained. In most jurisdictions, there are some regulations on signage. For example, important instructions are limited and are published. This means that instead of needing to convert images to text, you can recognize particular signs. This changes the problem from OCR to object recognition. Even if you want to recognize location signs—for example, addresses and town names—there are usually specific colors that the signs are printed in. This means that your model can learn in stages.

```
Is this part of an image...

- a sign
- if so, is it a) instructions, or b) a place of interest
- if a) classify it
- if b) convert to text
```

Images of Text to Target

In some situations, we may want to skip the text altogether. If we are classifying scanned documents, we can do this in two ways. First, we can convert to text and then use our text classification techniques. Second, we can simply do the classification directly on the images. There are couple of trade-offs.

- Image to text to target
  - Pro: we can examine the intermediate text to identify problems
  - Pro: we can reuse the image-to-text and text-to-target models separately (especially valuable if some inputs are text and some are images)
  - Cons: when converting to text, we may lose features in the image that could have helped us classify—for example, if there is an image in the letterhead that could give us a great signal
- Image to target
  - Pro: this is simpler—no need to develop and combine two separate models
  - Pro: additional features, as mentioned previously
  - Con: harder to debug problems, as mentioned previously
  - Con: can only be reused on similar image-to-target problems

It is better to start with the two-part approach because this will let you explore your data. Most image-to-text models today are neural nets, so adding some layers and retraining later in the project should not be too difficult.

Note on Different Writing Systems

The difficulty of the task is very much related to the writing system used. If you recall, in Chapter 2 we defined the different families of writing systems. Logographic systems are difficult because there are a much larger number of possible characters. This is difficult for two reasons. First, the obvious reason is that there are more classes to predict and therefore more parameters. Second, logographic systems will have many similar-looking characters, since all characters are dots, lines, and curves in a small box. There are also other complications that make a writing system difficult. In printed English, each character has a single form, but in cursive English, characters can have up to four forms—isolated, initial, medial, and final. Some writing systems have multiple forms even in printed text—for example, Arabic. Also, if a writing system makes much use of diacritics it can exacerbate problems like smudging and skewing (see Figure 16-1). You will want to be wary of this with most abugidas—for example, Devanagari and some alphabets, like Polish and Vietnamese.

Figure 16-1. "Maksannyo" [Tuesday] in Amharic written in Ge'ez

Problem Statement and Constraints

In our example, we will be implementing an ETL pipeline for converting images to text. This tools is quite general in its purpose. One common use for a tool like this is to convert images of text from legacy systems into text data. Our example will be using a (fake) electronic medical record. We will be using Tesseract from Google. We will use Spark to spread the workload out so we can parallelize the processing. We will also use a pretrained pipeline to process the text before storing it.

1. What is the problem we are trying to solve?

We will build a script that will convert the images to text, process the text, and finally store it. We will separate the functionality so that we can potentially augment or improve these steps in the future.

2. What constraints are there?

We will be working only with images of printed English text. The documents will have only one column of text. In our fictitious scenario, we also know the content will be medically related, but that will not affect this implementation

3. How do we solve the problem with the constraints?

We want a repeatable way to convert images to text, process the text, and store it.

Plan the Project

The solution is relatively straightforward. First, we will write a script that will allow us to pass data to Tesseract, instead of just to a file. Then we will write a Python script that will use the first script to get the text, and then use Spark NLP to process the text.

Implement the Solution

Let's start by looking at an example of using Tesseract. Let's look at the usage output for the program.

```
! tesseract -h

Usage:
  tesseract --help | --help-extra | --version
  tesseract --list-langs
  tesseract imagename outputbase [options...] [configfile...]

OCR options:
  -l LANG[+LANG]         Specify language(s) used for OCR.
NOTE: These options must occur before any configfile.

Single options:
  --help                 Show this help message.
  --help-extra           Show extra help for advanced users.
  --version              Show version information.
  --list-langs           List available languages for tesseract engine.
```

It looks like we simply need to pass it an image, imagename, and output name, output base. Let's look at the text that is in the image.

```
CHIEF COMPLAINT
Ankle pain

HISTORY OF PRESENT ILLNESS:

The patient is 28 y/o man who tripped when hiking. He struggled back to his
car, and immediately came in. Due to his severe ankle pain, he
thought the right ankle may be broken.

EXAMINATION:
An x-ray of right ankle ruled out fracture.

IMPRESSION:
The right ankle is sprained.

RECOMMENDATION:
- Take ibuprofen as needed
- Try to stay off right ankle for one week
```

Let's look at the image we will be experimenting with (see Figure 16-2).

Now, let's try and pass the image through Tesseract

```
! tesseract EHR\ example.PNG EHR_example
```

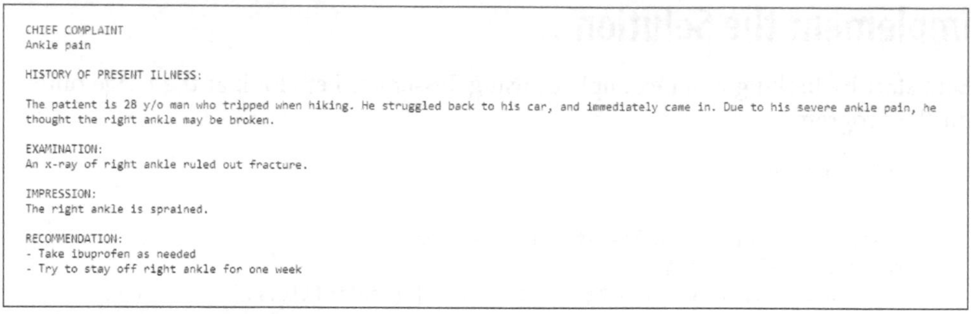

```
CHIEF COMPLAINT
Ankle pain

HISTORY OF PRESENT ILLNESS:

The patient is 28 y/o man who tripped when hiking. He struggled back to his car, and immediately came in. Due to his severe ankle pain, he
thought the right ankle may be broken.

EXAMINATION:
An x-ray of right ankle ruled out fracture.

IMPRESSION:
The right ankle is sprained.

RECOMMENDATION:
- Take ibuprofen as needed
- Try to stay off right ankle for one week
```

Figure 16-2. EHR image of text

Now let's see what Tesseract extracted.

```
! cat EHR_example.txt

CHIEF COMPLAINT
Ankle pain

HISTORY OF PRESENT ILLNESS:

The patient is 28 y/o man who tripped when hiking. He struggled back to his
car, and immediately came in. Due to his severe ankle pain, he
thought the right ankle may be broken.

EXAMINATION:
An x-ray of right ankle ruled out fracture.

IMPRESSION:
The right ankle is sprained.

RECOMMENDATION:
- Take ibuprofen as needed
- Try to stay off right ankle for one week
```

This worked perfectly. Now, let's put together our conversion script. The input to the script will be the type of image, and then the actual image will be encoded as a base64 string. We create a temporary image file and extract the text with Tesseract. This will also create a temporary text file, which we will stream into the stdout. We need to replace new lines with a special character, "~", so that we can know which lines are from which input.

```
%%writefile img2txt.sh
#!/bin/bash

set -e

# assumed input is lines of "image-type base64-encoded-image-data"

type=$1
```

```
data=$2
file="img.$type"
echo $data | base64 -d > $file
tesseract $file text
cat text.txt | tr '\n' '~'
```

Let's try our script out.

```
! ! ./img2txt.sh "png" $(base64 EHR\ example.PNG |\
    tr -d '\n') |\
    tr '~' '\n'

Tesseract Open Source OCR Engine v4.0.0-beta.1 with Leptonica
CHIEF COMPLAINT
Ankle pain

HISTORY OF PRESENT ILLNESS:

The patient is 28 y/o man who tripped when hiking. He struggled back to his
car, and immediately came in. Due to his severe ankle pain, he
thought the right ankle may be broken.

EXAMINATION:
An x-ray of right ankle ruled out fracture.

IMPRESSION:
The right ankle is sprained.

RECOMMENDATION:
- Take ibuprofen when needed
- Try to stay off right ankle for one week
```

Now let's work on the full processing code. First, we will get a pretrained pipeline.

```
import base64
import os

import sparknlp
from sparknlp.pretrained import PretrainedPipeline

spark = sparknlp.start()

pipeline = PretrainedPipeline('explain_document_ml')

explain_document_ml download started this may take some time.
Approx size to download 9.4 MB
[OK!]
```

Now let's create our test input data. We will copy our image a hundred times into the EHRs folder.

```
! mkdir EHRs
for i in range(100):
    ! cp EHR\ example.PNG EHRs/EHR{i}.PNG
```

Now, we will create a `DataFrame` that contains the filepath, image type, and image data as three string fields.

```
data = []
for file in os.listdir('EHRs') :
    file = os.path.join('EHRs', file)
    with open(file, 'rb') as image:
        f = image.read()
        b = bytearray(f)
    image_b64 = base64.b64encode(b).decode('utf-8')
    extension = os.path.splitext(file)[1][1:]
    record = (file, extension, image_b64)
    data.append(record)

data = spark.createDataFrame(data, ['file', 'type', 'image'])\
    .repartition(4)
```

Let's define a function that will take a partition of data, as an iterable, and return a generator of filepaths and text.

```
def process_partition(partition):
    for file, extension, image_b64 in partition:
        text = sub.check_output(['./img2txt.sh', extension, image_b64])\
            .decode('utf-8')
        text.replace('~', '\n')
        yield (file, text)

post_ocr = data.rdd.mapPartitions(process_partition)
post_ocr = spark.createDataFrame(post_ocr, ['file', 'text'])

processed = pipeline.transform(post_ocr)
processed.write.mode('overwrite').parquet('example_output.parquet/')
```

Now let's put this into a script.

```
%%writefile process_image_dir.py
#!/bin/python

import base64
import os
import subprocess as sub
import sys

import sparknlp
from sparknlp.pretrained import PretrainedPipeline

def process_partition(partition):
    for file, extension, image_b64 in partition:
        text = sub.check_output(['./img2txt.sh', extension, image_b64])\
            .decode('utf-8')
        text.replace('~', '\n')
        yield (file, text)

if __name__ == '__main__':
```

```
spark = sparknlp.start()

pipeline = PretrainedPipeline('explain_document_ml')

data_dir = sys.argv[1]
output_file = sys.argv[2]

data = []
for file in os.listdir(data_dir) :
    file = os.path.join(data_dir, file)
    with open(file, 'rb') as image:
        f = image.read()
        b = bytearray(f)
    image_b64 = base64.b64encode(b).decode('utf-8')
    extension = os.path.splitext(file)[1][1:]
    record = (file, extension, image_b64)
    data.append(record)

data = spark.createDataFrame(data, ['file', 'type', 'image'])\
    .repartition(4)
post_ocr = data.rdd.map(tuple).mapPartitions(process_partition)
post_ocr = spark.createDataFrame(post_ocr, ['file', 'text'])
processed = pipeline.transform(post_ocr)
processed.write.mode('overwrite').parquet(output_file)
```

Now we have a script that will take a directory of images, and it will produce a directory of text files extracted from the images.

```
! python process_image_dir.py EHRs ehr.parquet

Ivy Default Cache set to: /home/alex/.ivy2/cache
The jars for the packages stored in: /home/alex/.ivy2/jars
:: loading settings :: url = jar:file:/home/alex/anaconda3/envs/...
JohnSnowLabs#spark-nlp added as a dependency
:: resolving dependencies :: org.apache.spark#spark-submit-parent...
    confs: [default]
    found JohnSnowLabs#spark-nlp;2.2.2 in spark-packages
...
Tesseract Open Source OCR Engine v4.0.0-beta.1 with Leptonica
Tesseract Open Source OCR Engine v4.0.0-beta.1 with Leptonica
Tesseract Open Source OCR Engine v4.0.0-beta.1 with Leptonica
Tesseract Open Source OCR Engine v4.0.0-beta.1 with Leptonica
Tesseract Open Source OCR Engine v4.0.0-beta.1 with Leptonica
Tesseract Open Source OCR Engine v4.0.0-beta.1 with Leptonica
Tesseract Open Source OCR Engine v4.0.0-beta.1 with Leptonica
Tesseract Open Source OCR Engine v4.0.0-beta.1 with Leptonica
```

Test and Measure the Solution

For an application that is fully internal, there are no actual business metrics; instead, monitoring the quality is the sole focus. We must make sure that this internal application is not unnecessarily increasing the error of the application.

Model-Centric Metrics

We can measure the accuracy of an OCR model by character and word accuracy. You can measure this character error rate by calculating the Levenshtein distance between the expected and observed text then dividing by the size of the text.

In addition to monitoring the actual model error rates, you can capture statistics about output. For example, monitoring the distribution of words can potentially diagnose a problem.

Review

When you build an internal service, like an OCR tool may very well be, you will want to review the work with the teams that will need it. Ultimately, the success of your application requires that your users be satisfied with both the technical correctness and the support available. In some organizations, especially larger ones, there can be significant pressure to use in-house tools. If these tools are poorly engineered, under-documented, or unsupported, other teams will rightfully try and avoid them. This can potentially create hard feelings and lead to duplicated work and the siloing of teams. This is why it is a good idea to review the internal products and seek and accept feedback early and often.

Conclusion

In this chapter we looked at an NLP application that is not focused on extracting structured data from unstructured data but is instead focused on converting from one type of data to another. Although this is only tangentially related to linguistics, it is immensely important practically. If you are building an application that uses data from long-established industries, it is very likely you will have to convert images to text.

In this part of the book, we talked about building simple applications that apply some of the techniques we learned in Part II. We also discussed specific and general development practices that can help you succeed in building your NLP application. To revisit a point made previously about Spark NLP, a central philosophical tenet of this library is that there is no one-size-fits-all. You will need to know your data, and know how to build your NLP application. In the next part we will discuss some more general tips and strategies for deploying applications.

## PART IV

Building NLP Systems

In this part of the book, we will be going over topics relevant to putting an NLP system into production. Each chapter will cover a selection of topics and end with a checklist for you to consider when productionizing your application.

## CHAPTER 17

Supporting Multiple Languages

When building an NLP system, the first thing you should answer is what language or languages will you support. This can affect everything from data storage, to modeling, to the user interface. In this chapter, we will talk about what you want to consider if you are productionizing a multilingual NLP system.

At the end of the chapter, we will have a checklist of questions to ask yourself about your project.

Language Typology

When supporting multiple languages, one way you can manage complexity is by identifying commonalities between your expected languages. For example, if you are dealing with only Western European languages, you know that you need to consider only the Latin alphabet and its extensions. Also, you know that all the languages are fusional languages, so stemming or lemmatizing will work. They also have similar grammatical gender systems: masculine, feminine, and maybe an inanimate neuter.

Let's look at a hypothetical scenario.

Scenario: Academic Paper Classification

In this scenario, your inputs will be text documents, PDF documents, or scans of text documents. The output is expected to be JSON documents with text, title, and tags. The languages you will be accepting as input are English, French, German, and Russian. You have labeled data, but it is from only the last five years of articles. This is when the publisher started requiring that articles be tagged during submission. The initial classifications can be at the departmental level—for example, mathematics, biology, or physics. However, we need to have a plan to support subdisciplines.

First, we should consider the different input formats. We need to have OCR models for converting the images and PDF documents to text. We saw in Chapter 16 that we can use tools like Tesseract for this. We can use the text files to create a data set for training if we cannot find a satisfactory model. Some of the scanned documents will have issues. For example, the document may not have been well aligned with the scanning bed, and so the text is skewed. The document may have been aged and the text is eroded. Our model will need to accommodate for this. So, we will need to find some way of generating eroded and skewed text to support the scanned documents. We could transcribe some documents, but that is very labor intensive. You try and make the transcription process easier by breaking it into pieces. Another complication to transcription is that if you use transcribers that do not know the language, they will be much more error prone.

Second, we want to consider the classification task. For the initial model, we could potentially use lexical features and a simple linear classifier. Separating papers at the department level is very doable using just keywords. You can use experts to generate these keywords, or you can find them from vocabulary analysis. You will still want to review the keywords with domain experts who are fluent in these languages. In the future, simple lexical features will be useful at separating subdisciplines, especially niche subdisciplines that may not have many unique keywords. In this situation, we may want to move on to a more sophisticated model. First, we can start with a bag-of-words with a more complex model or go straight to an RNN. Either way, we must structure our code so that we can support different preprocessing and modeling frameworks.

Text Processing in Different Languages

Before we discuss model building in a project, we need to determine how we're going to process the text. We've already talked about some common considerations of tokenization in Chapters 2 and 5. Most writing systems use a space as a word separator; some use other symbols, and some don't separate words at all. Another consideration is word compounding.

Compound Words

Word compounding is when we combine two words into one. For example, "moonlight" is a combination of two words. In some languages, like German, this is more common. In fact, it is common enough in German that a word splitter is a common text-processing technique for German. Consider the word "Fixpunktgruppe" ("fixed point group"), which is a mathematical term for a special kind of algebraic structure. If we wanted to find all group structures mentioned in a document, we would need to have the "gruppe" separated. This could potentially be useful in languages that have more productive suffixes.

In English, it is as common to borrow a word as it is to add a prefix or suffix to create a new word. For example, we use the word "tractor" for a machine that is used for pulling—"tractor" is simply the Latin word for "puller." In some other languages, borrowing is less common, like in Greek, Icelandic, and Mandarin. In these languages, we may want to consider splitting these words into their component morphemes. This can be especially important for languages in which compound words might not be compounded in all contexts. These separable words are similar to some phrasal verbs in English. A phrasal verb is a verb like "wake up." The "up" particle can be separated from the verb, or not.

> I woke up the dog.
> I woke the dog up.

However, some objects require separation.

> *I woke up her.
> I woke her up.

The German translation, "aufstehen" loses the prefix when in a finite form.

> zu aufstehen den Hund ["to wake the dog up"]
> Ich stand den Hund auf ["I woke the dog up"]

Because these derived words often have very distinct meanings from their base, we may not need to deal with them. In document-level work—for example, document classification—it is unlikely that these words will affect the model. You are more likely to need to deal with this in search-based applications. I recommend not dealing with this in your first iteration and monitoring usage to see if compound words are commonly searched for.

Morphological Complexity

In Chapter 2, we talked about the different ways languages combine morphemes into words. Analytic languages, like Mandarin, tend to use particles to express things like the past tense. Meanwhile, synthetic (or agglutinative) languages, like Turkish, have systems of affixes for expressing a noun's role in a sentence, tense, prepositions, and so on. In between these two are fusional languages, like Spanish, that don't have as many possible word forms as synthetic languages do but have more than analytic languages. For these different types of morphologies there are trade-offs when considering stemming versus lemmatization.

The more possible word forms there are, the more memory will be required for lemmatization. Also, some fusional languages are more regular than others. The less regular the language, the more difficult the stemming algorithm will be. For example, Finnish nouns can have up to 30 different forms. This means that there will need to be 30 entries for each verb. Finnish verbs are much more complex. This means that if you have a one-million-word vocabulary, you will need well in excess of 30 million entries.

Analytic languages can use either stemming or lemmatization, or even neither. Mandarin likely does not need such processing. English, which is a language in transition from fusional to analytical, can use either. There are few enough forms that lemmatization is feasible, and stemming is not too difficult. Let's look at a regular verb in English (also called a weak verb). The verb "call" has the forms "call," "calling," "called," and "calls." Nouns are even simpler in English—there are only two forms (singular and plural). The rules for determining the forms of nouns and regular verbs are also straightforward enough to build a `lemmatizer` for.

Synthetic languages, like Finnish, are often quite regular, so stemming algorithms are straightforward. For fusional languages you can potentially use a combined approach. Irregular forms are more common in the most frequently used words. So you can use lemmatization for the most common words and use stemming as a fallback.

Transfer Learning and Multilingual Deep Learning

One of the ideas behind embeddings and transfer learning is that the neural network is learning *higher-level* features from the data. These features can be used to take a model, or part of a model, trained on one data set and use it on a different data set or different problem altogether. However, we must be mindful of how different the data is. If the differences between the English on Twitter and in medical records are enough to reduce transferability, imagine how much is lost in translation between English and another language. That being said, if you are looking to build a model with a better than random starting point, you should experiment with transferability. This makes more sense for some problems than for others. For example, in our scenario earlier, the classification of academic documents is going to be dependent on technical terms that may have similar distributions in all of our languages. This means that transferability might be helpful—it would certainly be worth experimenting with. On the other hand, if we are building a model that processes medical records from different countries, transferability across language will likely be less useful. Not only do the underlying phenomena differ (different common ailments in different places), but also the regulatory requirements on documentation differ. So the documents differ not only in language but also in content and purpose.

Word embeddings are a general enough technique that there is hope for transferability. This is still a topic of research. The idea is that although word frequencies may differ for equivalent words, the distribution of concepts is more universal. If this is so, perhaps we can learn a transformation from the vector space of one language to another that preserves relationships between the semantic content.

One way of doing this is to learn a transformation based on reference translations. Let's say we have two languages, L1 and L2. We take a list of words from L1, with their translations in L2. Each of these reference words will be mapped to a point in the vector space for L2. So let's say that L1 is Latin, and L2 is English. The word "nauta" has the vector w in the Latin vector space, and v in the English vector space after transformation. The English equivalent "sailor" has the vector u. We can define the error of the transformation for that word by looking at the Euclidean distance between u and v. The transformation that minimizes this difference should hopefully work well. The problem for this is that different cultures can use *equivalent* words very differently. Also, polysemy is different between languages, and this approach works only with static embeddings.

This is an active area of research, and there will be new developments. One of the hopes for these techniques is that it will let us use some of these advanced techniques for languages that do not have the huge corpora required to build deep learning models.

Search Across Languages

If you are building a search solution across languages, you generally separate the documents by language and have the user select a language when searching. It is possible to build a multilanguage index, but it can be difficult. There are multiple approaches, but ultimately you need some common way to represent the words or concepts in your corpus. Here are some possible approaches.

You can translate everything into a single language using machine translation. In our scenario, we could translate all the documents into English. The benefit of this is that you can review the quality of these translations. The drawback is that the search quality will suffer for the non-English documents.

On the other hand, if you can serve the translation model efficiently, you can translate at query time into all available languages. This has the benefit of not biasing toward one particular language. The drawback is that you need to find a way to make a common score from these indices. An additional complication is that automatic machine translation is built with complete texts and not queries. So a query may be mistranslated, especially if it is a word with multiple meanings.

If automatic machine translation is not an option, you can also consider using word embeddings. This will require the transformations talked about previously. This is essentially building a translation model without the sequence prediction.

Checklist

Consider these questions about your project:

- What languages do I need to support?
- What writing systems do I need to support?
- What Unicode blocks do I need to support?
- Do I have language experts with whom I can consult?
- Text processing
  - What are the language types I will need to support?
  - Do I have the necessary reference data (lemmas, stemming algorithm) to support my languages?
- Multilingual classification
  - Do I need a multilingual model, or do I need one model per language?
  - Are the labels the same across languages, or just similar?
  - Do I have labelers for labeling data?
- Multilingual deep learning
  - How different are the *languages* I'm working with?
  - How different are the *cultures* I'm working with?
- Search across languages
  - Will users need to search across language with a *single query*?
  - Do I have access to an automatic machine-translation model?

Conclusion

Dealing with multilanguage applications can be complicated, but it also offers great opportunities. There are not many NLP applications out there that are multilanguage. There are also not many people who have experience creating such applications.

One of the reasons that multilanguage applications are so difficult is that the availability of labeled multilanguage data is poor. This means that multilanguage NLP projects will often require you to gather labeled data. We will discuss human labeling in Chapter 18.

Human Labeling

We've mentioned human labeling in parts of this book. In this chapter we will consider how humans can actually do labeling for different kinds of NLP tasks. Some of the principles—for example, guidelines—are applicable to general labeling. Most special consideration required for NLP labeling tasks is around the technical aspects and the hidden caveats when dealing with language tasks. For example, asking someone to label parts of speech requires that they understand what parts of speech are. Let's first consider some basic issues.

It is probably worth some thought as to what your actual input is. For example, if you are labeling a document for a classification task, the input is obvious—the document. However, if you are marking named entities, humans do not need to see the whole document to find them, so you can break this up by paragraphs or even by sentences. On the other hand, coreference resolution, which we discussed in Chapter 9, may have long-distance coreferents, so you likely need to human the whole document.

Another thing to think about is whether your task requires domain expertise or just general knowledge. If you require expertise, gathering labels is likely to take more time and money. If you are unsure, you can run an experiment to find out. Have a group of nonexperts, as well as an expert (or a group of experts if possible), label a subset of the data. If the nonexperts and experts have a high enough level of agreement, then you can get by without expert labeling. We will go over inter-labeler agreement, measuring how often labelers agree, later in this chapter.

The first thing we need to think about when doing labeling is defining the task for our labelers. This is a sometimes controversial subject, as opinions differ on how much instruction you should give.

Note on Terminology

There are many terms for labeling and for the people who do the labeling: labeling/labelers, rating/raters, judging/judges, etc. There are also many terms for prelabeled examples that are used for evaluating labelers—ground truth set, golden set, and so on. In this chapter I will use "labeling/labelers" and "golden set."

Guidelines

Guidelines are instructions that tell your labelers how to do the task. The amount of details required for tasks is often debatable. Fortunately, there are some rules of thumb that you can keep in mind. First, make sure that your guidelines reflect what is expected for the product. For example, if you are gathering labels for a spam email classifier, you will need to be clear about what you mean by *spam*. People sometimes refer to newsletters and other automated emails as spam. Your model will be expected not only to approximate the process of the human labelers but also to serve as a product feature. This means that there are two sets of expectations that we can use to clearly define our task. I like to begin with a thought experiment. What if I forgot all time and budgetary constraints and hired an army of labelers to work on my product? What would I tell them is necessary for the customer? The answer is the basis for the guidelines.

Now that we have a good definition of the task, we still have some other considerations. The second rule is to avoid overconstraining what a correct label is. Some tasks are naturally ambiguous. If you attempt to constrain this natural ambiguity, you may introduce a number of problems. The first problem is that you will introduce bias into the model. The second problem is that if you unnaturally constrain the problem, you may cause labelers to give wrong results in situations you did not consider. Let's consider a scenario to make this idea more concrete.

Scenario: Academic Paper Classification

We will take our scenario from the previous chapter. We are building an application that takes research papers in multiple languages (English, French, German, and Russian) and classifies them by which academic department they belong to—for example, mathematics, biology, and physics. Our labeling pool consists of undergraduate and graduate students from various departments. We will be giving documents out randomly, except we will make sure that the labeler speaks the language of the research paper. This means that an undergraduate from the linguistics department who speaks English and French may get a physics paper that is in French but will never get a paper in German.

Let's apply our first rule of thumb. The users of our product will expect a correctly assigned department tag for each document. However, there are interdisciplinary papers, so perhaps there is not a single correct answer to each document. This creates a somewhat vague boundary between correct and incorrect. We can define some simple rules to constrain the problem reasonably. Physics papers will always include something mathematical, with possible exceptions being philosophical and pedagogical papers. However, this does not mean that every paper with a physics tag should have a mathematics tag. In fact, it would be much worse to proliferate false positives than false negatives. The user of an application like this is likely searching or browsing papers. If almost every physics paper has a mathematics tag, then people looking at mathematics papers will need to wade through all the physics papers. If we do not support multiple labels, it means that interdisciplinary papers will have less discoverability. We can address the latter problem with techniques related to inter-labeler agreement and iterative labeling techniques. For now, though, we should make clear in our guidelines that labelers are not allowed to specify multiple labels. We will instead instruct labelers to pick the department that is the best match for a given document

The second rule of thumb is about not unnaturally constraining the task. It seems like we have already done this by following the first rule. We start to reduce this problem by making sure that every paper is seen by more than one person. This does mean that the workload will double or more, depending on how many eyes we want on each paper.

So our guidelines will instruct our labelers to pick the best department tag for each document. It will warn them that ambiguity is possible. We also need to include examples in our guidelines. I usually like to show a couple of clear examples where the label is easy to discern and one ambiguous example. For example, include Einstein's paper on special relativity, "On the Electrodynamics of Moving Bodies," as a clear example of a physics paper. You want to prepare your labelers for ambiguity early, so that they are not derailed when they come across ambiguous examples.

Even when using external labelers (labelers who work for a different organization), it is good to test the guidelines in-house. I recommend getting a few people from your team and having them read the guidelines and judge a handful of examples. After this, review the examples with your product owner and, if possible, a stakeholder. Writing guidelines forces you to write down many of your assumptions. By having other people use your guidelines and evaluate the results, you get to check these assumptions.

Now that we have guidelines, let's talk about some of the techniques that can improve our use of labels.

Where to Find Labelers

Where you find labelers depends on what your task is. If you are looking to gather labels for a task using public data that requires general knowledge, you can use crowd-sourcing solutions like Amazon Mechanical Turk or Figure Eight. If you need specialized knowledge, you may be able to use crowd sourcing, although it will be more expensive. If the skill is rare enough, you will likely need to seek out labelers.

If your data can't be made public, then you may need to recruit within your own organization. Some organizations have their own full-time labelers for this purpose.

Inter-Labeler Agreement

Inter-labeler agreement is the agreement between labelers. This term is also used to refer to a metric for the proportion of examples labeled identically by different labelers. This concept has many uses in human labeling. First, we can use it to determine how well our models can realistically be expected to do. For example, if we find that in our scenario 85% of documents labeled by multiple labelers are identically labeled, then we know that, on this task model, performing at a human level can be expected to get 85% accuracy. This does not always have to be true. If the task requires only that labelers approve of the model-based recommendation, then you may very well see a much higher accuracy. This is due to the model-based recommendation biasing the human.

Another use for inter-labeler agreement is to find labelers who are having difficulty with the task, or who are not putting in the effort to actually label. If you find that there is a labeler who has a low rate of agreement with the other labelers, you may want to review their work. There can be many possible explanations for this. The following are some possible reasons:

- Your guidelines are vague
- They interpret the guidelines differently from the other labelers
- They have different expertise on the matter, leading them to come to different conclusions
- They did not read the guidelines and possibly are not putting effort into labeling

You should probably rule out other explanations before jumping to bad intent. If it is one of the first two explanations, you can tune your guidelines appropriately. If it is the third explanation, then you should consider whether their conclusions are valid for your product. If so, then the labels are fine, but the problem may be more difficult than you originally thought. If the conclusions are not valid, then you should put guidance about these kinds of examples in your guidelines. If you think it is due to bad intent, then you should discard these labels because they will add noise to your data.

You can also measure labeling quality using a golden set of validated-label examples that you mix into your unlabeled data. This golden set can be from a public data set that is similar to your data, or we can hand-curate it ourselves. This will let you find labelers who are producing potentially problematic labels, even if you do not show examples to multiple labelers. Remember that these *validated* labels may still be based on your assumptions, so if your assumptions are wrong it may falsely appear that labelers are producing incorrect labels.

Perhaps the most helpful use case for inter-labeler agreement is to find ambiguous examples. After you have reviewed the inter-labeler agreement and believe the labels are of good quality, we can consider differing labels for an example to indicate whether it is ambiguous. First, we should find the prevalence of this. If a quarter of the research papers have multiple labels, then you may want to consider this as a multilabel problem and not a multiclass problem. If only a small number of documents have multiple labels, then you can simply take the label with majority support, or random if tied. Alternatively, you can also keep the multiple labels in your validation and hold-out sets. This will keep your training data consistent, but it won't penalize you for recommending a valid alternative. Another technique we can use to deal with ambiguity in labels is iterative labeling. This lets us use labelers to anonymously check each other's work.

Iterative Labeling

Iterative labeling can be used to improve the quality of labels without increasing your workload much. The idea is that you break your labeling task into at least two steps. The first step is for the labelers to quickly assign an appropriate label, with the understanding that there may be errors due to ambiguity and perhaps to lack of domain expertise. Then you have another labeler with more expertise validate or invalidate the label. Let's see what this would look like in our scenario.

The first task is a research paper sent to an undergraduate labeler who knows the language of the paper. The paper is then sent to a graduate student, who also knows the language, in the department assigned by the first labeler. The second labeler, the graduate, will only validate the first labeler's work. This has some pros and cons. This means that the workload on graduates, who may be more expensive, is less, which saves us money. It also means that a research paper that is assigned to a department is reviewed by someone in the department. The con is that it requires each department-language pair to have a graduate student, which may not be possible. You ease this requirement by allowing graduate students to volunteer to represent departments they are familiar with. For example, the physics graduate who speaks Russian might volunteer to do mathematics in Russian as well.

Iterative labeling can also be used to simplify complex tasks into a sequence of simple tasks. This is especially useful in text-related labeling. Let's look at some of the special considerations of text-related labeling.

Labeling Text

Most of what we have covered so far applies to labeling in general. Let's look at some special considerations we should keep in mind when labeling text.

Classification

You should be mindful of the size of the documents you are classifying. If you are classifying tweets or similar small pieces of text, your labelers should be able to work through tasks quickly. If they are larger texts, like in our scenario, there is the danger of labeler fatigue. Labeler fatigue occurs when the individual task (classifying a document), is very time-consuming, and the labeler becomes less attentive after many tasks. It can be debated that humans are naturally lazy, and this is why we made computers to do things for us. This means that the labelers will, sometimes unintentionally, find shortcuts to the tasks—for example, searching for specific words in the document. These labels will be of poor quality. If you want to make this task smaller, you can do it in two ways. First, have the labelers classify the abstracts. This means that the labelers have less information for the task, but they will also get through tasks more quickly. The other possibility is to use the guidelines to advise labelers to not spend much time on an individual task. With the latter approach, you should definitely try to get the documents in front of multiple people.

Tagging

The second kind of text-labeling task is tagging. This is where you are asking labelers to identify pieces of the text. Finding the named entities in a document would be an example of this. In our scenario, we might use this to find technical words in the document. These could then be used to build a concept extraction annotator, which is fed downstream to the classification model. If your documents are longer than a few sentences, individual tasks can become extremely laborious. If you are doing something like named-entity recognition, you should consider breaking the documents into sentences and making your tasks to identify entities in sentences, instead of documents. Another caveat to consider with this kind of task is that it may require linguistics knowledge. For example, let's say that we will be accepting papers written in Polish. However, all the other languages are supported by a processing pipeline that includes a part-of-speech tagger, but we have no such model for Polish. Identifying parts of speech may not be general knowledge. You will need to find people who not only speak Polish but also know the technicalities of Polish grammar. Some Polish speakers will have this knowledge, but you should specify this requirement when you are looking for labelers.

Checklist

Consider these questions about your project:

- What is the input (document, sentence, metadata, etc.)?
- Can the input be broken up?
- Does this task require domain expertise or just general knowledge?
- Guidelines checklist
  - Can I explain how this task supports feature(s) of the product?
  - How ambiguous is this task? Could there be multiple correct answers?
  - What constraints am I putting on the task?
  - Who can test these guidelines with me?
- Inter-labeler agreement checklist
  - Can I afford to have multiple labelers for all examples? How about for a portion of examples?
  - Do I have a golden set to measure labeler correctness?
- Iterative labeling checklist
  - Can my task be broken into multiple stages?
  - Do I have the right labelers for each stage?
- Labeling text checklist
  - What kind of text labeling task am I doing?
  - Are my tasks large? Can they be made smaller?
  - Does my task require technical knowledge of the language?

Conclusion

Gathering labels is a valuable skill needed for any application that can be helped by measuring human judgment. Being able to create your own labeled data can make an otherwise impossible task possible.

Now that we have talked about gathering labels, let's look to what we should do to release our application.

## CHAPTER 19

Productionizing NLP Applications

In this book we have talked about many different possible approaches and techniques that we can use to build our NLP application. We've talked about how to plan and develop an NLP application. Now, let's talk about deploying NLP applications.

We will also talk about deploying models in production environments. Before we talk about how to deploy the models, we need to know the requirements on our product. If the model is being used in a batch process versus being used by a web service for individual evaluations, this changes how we want to deploy. We also need to know what kind of hardware will be required by the models. Some of the things we discuss here should be considered before modeling has begun—for example, the available hardware in production.

The easiest situation is where your application is running as a batch process on an internal cluster. This means that your performance requirements are based only on internal users (in your organization), and securing the data will also be simpler. But not everything is this simple.

Another important part of deploying a production-quality system is making sure that the application works fast enough for user needs without taking up too many resources. In this chapter we will discuss how to optimize the performance of your NLP system. First, we need to consider what we want to optimize.

When people talk about performance testing, they generally mean testing how long it takes for the program to run and how much memory it takes. Because of the possible variance in document size, this can make performance testing NLP-based applications more difficult. Additionally, annotation frameworks, like Spark NLP, can produce many times more data than is input, so optimizing disk usage is important as well. Spark NLP is a distributed framework, so you should also take into consideration performance as a distributed system.

Distributed systems need to take into account all the performance requirements of individual machines and make sure that the cluster is used efficiently. This means that you are not locking up resources unnecessarily and are using what is allocated to your process.

Even once the application is in production, there is still work to be done. We need to monitor the performance of the software and the model. In this chapter, we will talk about what we need to do when we want to take our application live.

The first step in taking any application live is making sure that the product owner and stakeholders are satisfied. For some applications this will be as simple as showing that we can demo the functionalities in the requirements. With NLP-based applications, this can more difficult. This is because intuitions about how NLP works are often wrong. This is why testing is so important.

The checklist for this chapter is much larger than for the others in this part of the book. This is because deployment of NLP applications can be very complicated. It may seem overwhelming, but we can also use the answers to these questions to get a clearer scope of our project.

Let's start with model deployment.

Spark NLP Model Cache

We've used pretrained models from Spark NLP in several chapters of this book. These models are stored in a local cache. Pretrained pipelines are stored here, as are models for individual steps in a pipeline, as well as TensorFlow models. We've used Keras in this book when exploring neural networks. Keras, however, is a high-level API for neural network libraries. TensorFlow is the framework that performs the actual computation. The TensorFlow models are a different animal, though, because they are required on the worker machines and not just the driver. Spark NLP will handle setting up this cache for you as long as those machines have internet access. If you do not have internet access, you can put the files in shared storage, like HDFS, and modify your code to load from that location.

This model cache requires access to persistent disk storage. Most deployment scenarios meet this requirement, but if you were to deploy on Amazon Lambda this is not a good idea.

Generally, Spark is not a good solution for real-time NLP applications. Although the cache improves performance, there is a minimum overhead for Spark. You can use the Spark NLP light pipelines, which are pretrained pipelines that run outside of Spark, where available, but you should test performance before deploying in any external scenario.

Another thing to consider is the availability of memory in your production environment. Spark NLP uses RocksDB as an in-memory key-value store for static embeddings. You should make sure that your environment can support this memory load. If you are using Spark, then it is almost certainly the case that you have enough memory for the embeddings.

We've talked about how Spark NLP accesses models; now let's talk about how it integrates with TensorFlow.

Spark NLP and TensorFlow Integration

TensorFlow is implemented in C++ and CUDA, although most data scientists use it from its Python interface. Since Spark NLP is implemented in Scala, it runs on the JVM, although we have also been using it from its Python interface. Spark NLP interfaces with TensorFlow through the Java interface. This requires that TensorFlow be installed on any machine that will use these models. Unfortunately, this means that we have a dependency outside our JAR file. It's less of an issue if you are using the Python Spark NLP package because it has TensorFlow as dependency. This dependency requires that you are able to install this software on all production machines running your application. You should also note whether you will be using a GPU since the dependency for TensorFlow on the GPU is different.

The reason GPUs can improve training time so much is that GPUs are built to do batches of parallel processing. This is great for doing matrix operations. However, not all machines have appropriate hardware for this. This means that enabling GPU support for your project may require an additional investment. If you are training on your development machine, there are common video cards that are good for some simple GPU training. Since training is much more computationally intensive than serving a model, it may be the case that you need only GPU support for training. Some models are complex enough that evaluating the model on a CPU is prohibitively slow. If you are planning to use such a complex model, you need to coordinate with the team handling hardware infrastructure. They will need to requisition the machines, and you will need to do performance testing to make sure that you can serve the model in an appropriate amount of time.

Now that we have talked about the deployment considerations specific to Spark NLP, let's discuss deployment of a composite system.

Spark Optimization Basics

An important aspect of optimizing Spark-based programs, and therefore Spark NLP-based programs, is persistence. To talk about persistence, let's review how Spark organizes work.

When you have a reference to a `DataFrame`, it does not necessarily refer to actual data on the cluster, since Spark is lazy. This means that if you load data and perform some simple transformations, like change strings to lowercase, no data will be loaded or transformed. Instead, Spark makes an execution plan. As you add more instructions to this execution plan it forms a *directed acyclic graph (DAG)*. When you request data from the `DataFrame`, it triggers Spark to create a job. The job is split into stages. Stages are sequences of processing steps necessary to produce the data for the object that you have a reference to. These stages are then split into tasks, one for each partition, that are distributed to the executors. The executors will run as many tasks as they have processors for.

When you persist a `DataFrame`, that will cause Spark to store the actual data once it is realized. This is useful when you will be reusing a particular set of data. For example, when you train a logistic regression model there will be iterations over the data. You don't want Spark to reload from disk for each iteration, so you should persist the `DataFrame` containing the training data. Fortunately, you don't need to do this yourself because it is implemented in the training code for logistic regression.

There are parameters that control how your data is persisted. The first is whether to use disk. If you persist to disk you will have more space, but reloading it will be much more time-consuming. The second parameter is whether to use memory. You must use disk or memory, or you can choose both. If you choose both, Spark will store what it can in memory and "spill" to disk if necessary. You can also choose to use off-heap memory. In Java, there are two parts to the memory. The heap, or on-heap memory, is where the Java objects are stored. The JVM garbage collector works on the heap. The other part is off-heap memory. Java stores classes, threads, and other data used by the JVM in off-heap memory. Persisting data in the off-heap memory space means that you are not restricted to the memory allocated to the JVM. This can be dangerous, since the JVM does not manage or limit this space. If you take up too much heap memory, your program will get an `OutOfMemoryError`; if you take up too much nonheap memory, you could potentially bring down the machine.

Apart from configuring where you store your persisted data, you can also decide whether to serialize it. Storing serialized data can be more space-efficient, but it will be more CPU-intensive. The last parameter is replication. This will cause the data to be replicated on different workers, which can be useful if a worker fails.

Persisting will help us avoid redoing work unnecessarily, but we also want to make sure that we do the work efficiently. If your partitions are too large, then executors will not be able to process them. You could add more memory to the executors, but this causes poor CPU utilization. If your workers have multiple cores but you take most of the memory to just process one partition on one core, then all the other cores are being wasted. Instead, you should try and reduce the size of your partitions. However, you do not want to go to the other extreme. There is an overhead to partitions, since Spark may need to shuffle the data. This will cause aggregations and group-by operations to be very inefficient. Ideally, each partition should be 200 MB in size.

The Spark developers are constantly working on new ways to improve performance, so you should check the programming guides in each version to see if there are new ways to optimize your application.

Now that we have talked about how to optimize Spark operations, let's talk about some design-level considerations to improve performance.

Design-Level Optimization

When you are designing your NLP application, you should consider how to divide your pipelines into manageable pieces. It may be tempting to have a single über-pipeline, but this causes several problems. First, it is harder to maintain the code by having everything in your job. Even if you organize the code into a maintainable structure, errors at runtime will be harder to diagnose. The second problem it can cause is inefficiencies in the design of your job. If your data extraction is memory intensive, but your batch model evaluation is not memory intensive, then you are taking up unnecessary resources during evaluation. Instead, you should have two jobs—data extraction and model evaluation. You should be using the job orchestrator of your cluster (Airflow, Databricks job scheduler, etc.). If your application loads data and runs the model as a batch job, here is a list of potential jobs you can create to break your code into more manageable chunks:

- Data preparation
- Feature creation
- Hyperparameter tuning
- Final training
- Metrics calculation
- Model evaluation

You could potentially combine these, but be considerate of the other inhabitants of the cluster, and be mindful of the resource needs of different parts of your workflow.

Another important aspect is monitoring your pipelines and the data that they consume and produce. There have been many "mysterious" failures that are due to a strange document, an empty document, or a document that is three hundred times larger than normal. You should log information from your pipelines. Sometimes, this creates big data of its own. Unless you are trying to debug a pipeline, you do not need to output information for each document or record what you are processing. Instead, you can at least track minima, means, and maxima. The basic values that should be tracked are document size and processing time. If you implement this, then you have a quick first step to triage problems.

Profiling Tools

There are a variety of profiling tools available for examining performance. These tools each have a context in which they should be used. Let's look first at the Java Microbenchmark Harness.

The *Java Microbenchmark Harness (JMH)* is a JVM framework that will allow you to test atomic (or nearly atomic) operations in your code. For example, if you are using a custom data structure, you can use the JMH to test inserts and retrievals. The JMH is more useful in testing library code than testing applications. This is because most application code relies on a number of library functions and so is not atomic. This is not something that you can use to monitor, though. It works by compiling a separate program that runs (and reruns) parts of your code.

VisualVM is free profiler for JVM applications. It allows you to track the number of instances of classes created, as well as time spent in methods. If you find a performance problem, this is a great tool for investigating. One downside is that it really requires that you can run your application on one machine. VisualVM runs an application that inspects your application's JVM, so it can negatively impact performance.

Monitoring

If you want to monitor NLP applications, Ganglia is an application I'm fond of. Ganglia allows you to view CPU and memory utilization in a cluster in essentially real time. Many modern resource managers, like Mesos and Kubernetes, have similar functionality baked in. Ganglia, or the resource monitoring available from resource managers, is a must-have if you need your application to run reliably.

Now that we know how we will examine the resources used by our application, we need to think about the data that our application consumes and produces.

Managing Data Resources

There are three kinds of data used in NLP applications. There is input data, which is the data that your application processes. Examples of input data include a corpus of documents, an individual document, or a search query. There is output data, which is the data your application produces. Examples of output data include a directory of serialized, annotated documents, a document object containing the annotations, or a list of documents and relevance scores. The third data is the data that your application uses as configuration. Examples of configuration data include trained models, lemma dictionaries, or stop-word lists.

Testing NLP-Based Applications

When you are building NLP applications, as with any software application, you want to develop your software tests first. Test-driven development is a great way to state your expected behaviors in code before you start writing the actual application code. However, in my experience, this is rarely done. Test-driven development can be difficult if you don't have a clear idea of how the product will work or you need to show results immediately. If you have to write tests as you are writing your code, you run the risk of writing tests that are built to pass—not test—the code. It is always better to have a test plan before you've built your application. Let's look at the different kinds of tests.

Unit Tests

The most well-known kind of test is the *unit test*. The unit test is to test a unit of functionality in your code. For example, if you have a phrase chunker that uses a helper function to extract the POS tags, you shouldn't write separate tests for the helper function. That helper function is not a separate functionality of your chunker, it is part of its chunking functionality. Unit tests should require only the code they are testing. They should not require network resources, production data, other services, and so on. If your code does assume these things, you will need to *mock* these. *Mocking* is a technique that creates a façade of the components you need. With data, you can either take the smallest necessary sample of data or create a small amount of fake data.

Integration Tests

Once you have built a component of a system, you will need to make sure that it works with other components. This is called *integration testing*. Often, integration tests are implemented in unit-testing frameworks, so they may be mistakenly referred to as "unit" tests. Let's look at our research paper classifier project for a hypothetical example of an integration test. If we will be integrating with an existing system that is used for submitting papers to the university's database, we will need to have two sets of integration tests. The first set will test how the classifier service integrates with the code that manages the database. The second set will test how the classifier integrates with UI of the paper submission system.

Smoke and Sanity Tests

You will also need tests that will help us test whether the system, overall, does what we expect. There are generally two kinds of test like this. The first is the *smoke test*. A smoke test tests as much of the code as possible to find out if there are any showstopper problems. The metaphor comes from testing plumbing. If you want to find a leak in a septic system, you can pump smoke into the pipes. If you see smoke rising, that tells you where the problem is. You generally want smoke tests that cover the major uses of your system. The other kind of overall system test is the *sanity test*. The sanity test is used to make sure that the system works with "routine" inputs. If the smoke tests or sanity tests fail, you should not deploy. If you find a bug in the system after it is deployed, you should use reproduction steps as a future smoke test. These are called regression tests. They help us from accidentally reintroducing bugs.

Performance Tests

Once you have the functional testing, you can look at testing other aspects of the system. Let's start with *performance testing*. Previously in this chapter, we discussed ways to optimize the performance of our application. To know whether a new version of the application will introduce performance problems you should have automated tests. This is something that you use in combination with performance monitoring. If performance is not an important requirement, then it is reasonable to skip this kind of test. Sometimes, performance tests are skipped because of the expense of creating a production-like environment. Instead of doing this, you should change the scale of your performance test. While it is true that you cannot test the application's performance without a production-like environment, you can still test the performance of components. This won't catch global problems, but a local performance test can test if a particular component or function has a performance-worsening bug. Using the profiling tools we discussed in the last chapter, you can find hotspots in your code, areas that take the most time or memory. Local performance tests should be focused on these areas.

Usability Tests

Another vital kind of *nonfunctional testing* is *usability testing*. If your application is simply a batch process, then there is not much need for this kind of test. However, if your application has real end-users, like customers, you should definitely have this. When people are working with NLP-based systems there can sometimes be inflated expectations. For example, let's say we are building a sentiment analysis tool. This tool predicts a sentiment and highlights the terms that led to the prediction. The model may identify words that make sense statistically for the corpus it was trained on, but a human may consider them silly. To find these inflated expectations you should find test users who are as similar as possible to the actual users. If you just use colleagues who are also familiar with software, then they may have a more realistic understanding of what the system can do. If you find that users have these inflated expectations then you should consider how you can modify the user experience to better set expectations.

Since intuitions are not infallible, especially when it comes to language, we need to make sure that we test our assumptions. However, testing stakeholder assumptions is harder. There is another test, of sorts, that the application needs to pass—the demo.

Demoing NLP-Based Applications

Properly demoing an NLP-based application is as much a matter of technical skills as communication skills. When you are showing your work to the product owner and the stakeholders, you will need to be prepared to explain the application from three NLP-perspectives: software, data science, and linguistics. When you are building your demo, you should try and "break" the system by finding data and language edge cases that produce poor-looking results. Sometimes, these results are reasonable, but if someone does not have a technical understanding of such systems, the results look ridiculous. If the client finds an example like this, it can derail the whole demo. If you find one beforehand, you should prepare an explanation about either why this is the correct result given the data or how you will fix it. Sometimes "fixing" a problem like this is more aesthetic than technical. This is why you should be considering the user experience from the beginning of the project.

Because these apparently bad, but statistically justified, examples can be embarrassing, it can be tempting to cherry-pick examples. This not only is unethical but also moves their discovery to production, which would be worse. Even if the problem is not a "real" problem, you should try and be as upfront as possible. The intersection of people who know software engineering, data science, and linguistics is small, so the stakeholder may very well have difficulty understanding the explanation. If the problem is found after it has been fully deployed, your explanation will be met with extra skepticism.

As with any application, the work doesn't end with deployment. You will need to monitor the application.

Checklists

Consider the questions in each of these checklists.

Model Deployment Checklist

- Is this an internal (only used within the organization) or an external application?
- Will the application use sensitive data (e.g., personal health information)?
- Will the model be used in a batch process or real time?
- What are the performance (time) requirements?
- Will this model require specific hardware (e.g., GPUs, more than 8GB of memory)?
- How often do I want to deploy a new model?
- Spark NLP model cache checklist

— Will my application be able to download from the internet if the cache is absent/empty?

- The Spark NLP and TensorFlow integration checklist

  — Can I (or DevOps/IT) install TensorFlow on the production machines?

  — Will I be using GPU or not?

  — Will I need a GPU for serving the model?

Scaling and Performance Checklist

- How long does my application take to run?

- How much memory does my application need when running?

- How much memory does my application need when *not* running?

- How much disk space does my application need?

- How parallelizable is my application?

- If batch, when is the best time to run my application?

- If real-time, how many calls per second, minute, or hour does my application expect?

- If real-time, can I scale out if necessary?

- Profiling tools

  — What tool will be used for monitoring resources when the application is running?

  — Are there pieces of code that require extremely high levels of performance?

Testing Checklist

- Who is deploying my application?

- Do I have deployment tests (integration tests, smoke tests, performance tests, etc.)?

- How do I demo the application?

- How am I monitoring my application?

- Do I need to handle sensitive data?

- How will I review my application's performance?

- Testing NLP-based applications

  — How much coverage do my unit tests have?

  — What systems/components am I integrating with?

— Who will run my smoke/sanity tests?

— Can I do global performance tests?

— Where are my performance hotspots?

— Will my application have actual users?

— Has a potential user tried my product?

- Demoing NLP-based applications

— Who am I demoing my work to? What is their background (technical, domain expert, neither?)

— What are the limitations of the system?

— If there are potentially problematic results, why are the justified? Alternatively, how will I fix them?

Conclusion

In this chapter, we talked about the final steps needed before your NLP application is used. However, this is not the end. You will likely think of ways to improve your processing, your modeling, your testing, and everything else about your NLP application. The ideas talked about in this chapter are starting points for improvement. One of the hardest things in software development is accepting that finding problems and mistakes is ultimately a good thing. If you can't see a problem with a piece of software, that means you will eventually be surprised.

In this book, I have talked about wearing three hats—software engineer, linguist, and data scientist—and have discussed the need to consider all three perspectives when building an NLP application. That may seem difficult, and it often is, but it is also an opportunity to grow. Although there are statistically justifiable errors that can be difficult to explain, when an NLP application does something that makes *intuitive sense* it is incredibly rewarding.

There is always the balance between needing to add or "fix" a thing and wanting to push it out into the world. The great thing about software engineering, sciences like linguistics, and data science is that you are guaranteed to have a mistake in your work. Everyone before you had mistakes, as will everyone after you. What is important is that we fix them and become a little less wrong.

Thank you for reading this book. I am passionate about all three disciplines that inform NLP, as well as NLP. I know I have made mistakes here, and I hope to get better in time.

Good luck!

Glossary

algorithmic complexity

The complexity of an algorithm is generally measured in the time it takes to run or how much space (memory or disk space) is needed to run it.

annotation

In an NLP context, an annotation is a marking on a segment of text or audio with some extra information. Generally, an annotation will require character indices for the start and end of the annotated segment, as well as an annotation type.

annotator

An annotator is a function that takes text and produces annotations. It is not uncommon for some annotators to have a dependency on another type of annotator.

Apache Hadoop

Hadoop is an open source implementation of the MapReduce paper. Initially, Hadoop required that the map, reduce, and any custom format readers be implemented and deployed to the cluster. Eventually, higher level abstractions were developed, like Apache Hive and Apache Pig.

Apache Parquet

Parquet is a data format originally created for Hadoop. It allows for efficient compression of columnar data. It is a popular format in the Spark ecosystem.

Apache Spark

Spark is a distributed computing framework with a high-level interface and in memory processing. Spark was developed in Scala, but there are now APIs for Java, Python, R, and SQL.

application

An application is a program with an end user. Many applications have a graphical user interface (GUI), though this is not necessary. In this book, we also consider programs that do batch data processing as "applications".

array

An array is a data structure where elements are associated with an index. They are implemented differently in different programming languages. Numpy arrays, `ndarrays`, are the most popular kind of arrays used by Python users (especially among data scientists).

autoencoder

An autoencoder is a neural-network–based technique used to convert some input data into vectors, matrices, or tensors. This new representation is generally of a lower dimension than the input data.

Bidirectional Encoder Representations from Transformers (BERT)

BERT from Google is a technique for converting words into a vector representation. Unlike Word2vec, which disregards context, BERT uses the context a word is found in to produce the vector.

classification

In a machine learning context, classification is the task of assigning classes to examples. The simplest form is the binary classification task where each example can have one of two classes. The binary classification task is a special case of the multiclass classification task where each example can have one of a fixed set of classes. There is also the multilabel classification task where each example can have zero or more labels from a fixed set of labels.

clustering

In the machine learning context, clustering is the task of grouping examples into related groups. This is generally an unsupervised task, that is, the algorithm does not use preexisting labels, though there do exist some supervised clustering algorithms.

container

In software there are two common senses of "container." In this book, the term is primarily used to refer to a virtual environment that contains a program or programs. The term "container" is also sometimes used to refer to an abstract data type of data structure that contains a collection of elements.

context

In an NLP, "context" generally refers to the surrounding language data around a segment of text or audio. In linguistics, it can also refer to the "real world" context in which a language act occurs.

CSV

A CSV (Comma Separated Values) file is a common way to store structured data. Elements are separated by commas, and rows are separated by new lines. Another common separator is the tab character. Files that use the tab are called TSVs. It is not uncommon for files that use a separator other than a comma to still be called CSVs.

data scientist

A data scientist is someone who uses scientific techniques to analyze data or build applications that consume data.

DataFrame

A DataFrame is a data structure that is used to manipulate tabular data.

decision tree

In a machine learning context, a decision tree is a data structure that is built for classification or regression tasks. Each node in the tree splits on a particular feature.

deep learning

Deep learning is a collection of neural-network techniques that generally use multiple layers.

dialect

In a linguistics context, a dialect is a particular variety of a language associated with a specific group of people.

differentiate

In a mathematics context, to differentiate is to find the derivative of a function. The derivative function is a function that maps from the domain to the instantaneous rate of change of the original function.

discourse

In a linguistics context, a discourse is a sequence of language acts, especially between two or more people.

distributed computing

Distributed computing is using multiple computers to perform parallelized computation.

distributional semantics

In an NLP context, this refers to techniques that attempt to represent words in a numerical form, almost always a vector, based on the words' distribution in a corpus. This name originally comes from linguistics where it refers to theories that attempt to use the distribution of words in data to understand the words' semantics.

Docker

Docker is software that allows users to create containers (virtual environments) with Docker scripts.

document

In an NLP context, a document is a complete piece of text especially if it contains multiple sentences.

embedding

In an NLP context, an embedding is a technique of representing words (or other language elements) as a vector, especially when such a representation is produced by a neural network.

encoding

In an NLP context, the encoding or character encoding refers to the mapping from characters, e.g. "a", "?", to bytes.

estimator

In a Spark MLlib context, an estimator is a stage of a pipeline that uses data to produce a model that transforms the data.

evaluator

In a Spark MLlib context, an evaluator is a stage of a pipeline that produces metrics from predictions.

feature

In a machine learning context, a feature is an attribute of an input, especially a numerical attribute. For example, if the input is a document, the number of unique tokens in the document is a feature. The words present in a document are also referred to as features.

function

In a programming context, a function is a sequence of instructions. In a mathematics context, a function is a mapping between two sets, the domain and the range, such that each element of the domain is mapped to a single element in the range.

GloVe

GloVe is a distributional semantics technique for representing words as vectors using word-to-word co-occurrences.

graph

In a computer science or mathematics context, a graph is a set of nodes and edges that connect the nodes.

guidelines

In a human labeling context, guidelines are the instructions given to the human labelers.

hidden Markov model

A hidden Markov model is a technique for modeling sequences using a hidden state that only uses the previous part of the sequence.

hyperparameter

In a machine learning context, a hyperparameter is a setting of a learning algorithm. For example, in a neural network, the weights are parameters, but the number and size of the layers are hyperparameters.

index

In an information retrieval context, an index is a mapping from documents to the words contained in the documents.

interlabeler agreement

In a human labeling context, interlabeler agreement is a measure of how much labelers agree (generally unknowingly) when labeling the same example.

inverted index

In an information retrieval context, an index is a mapping from words to the documents that contain the words.

Java

Java is an object-oriented programming language. Java is almost always compiled to run on the Java Virtual Machine (JVM). Scala and a number of other popular languages run on the JVM and so are interoperable with Java.

Java Virtual Machine (JVM)

The JVM is a virtual machine that runs programs that have been compiled into Java bytecode. As the name suggests, Java is the primary language which uses the JVM, but Scala and a number of other programming languages use it as well.

JSON

JavaScript Object Notation (JSON) is a data format.

K-Means

K-Means is a technique for clustering. It works by randomly placing K points, called centroids, and iteratively moving them to minimize the squared distance of elements of a cluster to their centroid.

knowledge base

A knowledge base is a collection of knowledge or facts in a computationally usable format.

labeling

In a machine learning context, labeling is the process of assigning labels to examples, especially when done by humans.

language model

In an NLP context, a language model is a model of the probability distribution of word sequences.

latent Dirichlet allocation (LDA)

LDA is a technique for topic modeling that treats documents as a sequence of words selected from weighted topics (probability distributions over words).

latent semantic indexing (LSI)

LSI is a technique for topic modeling that performs single value decomposition on the term-document matrix.

linear algebra

Linear algebra is the branch of mathematics focused on linear equations. In a programming context, linear algebra generally refers to the mathematics that describe vectors, matrices, and their associated operations.

linear regression

Linear regression is a statistical technique for modeling the relationship between a single variable and one or more other variables. In a machine learning context, linear regression refers to a regression model based on this statistical technique.

linguist

A linguist is a person who studies human languages.

linguistic typology

Linguistic typology is a field of linguistics that groups languages by their traits.

logging

In a software context, logging is information output by an application for use in monitoring and debugging the application.

logistic regression

Logistic regression is a statistical technique for modeling the probability of an event. In a machine learning context, logistic regression refers to a classification model based on this statistical technique.

long short-term memory (LSTM)

LSTM is a neural-network technique that is used for learning sequences. It attempts to learn when to use and update the context.

loss

In a machine learning context, loss refers to a measure of how wrong a supervised model is.

machine learning

Machine learning is a field of computer science and mathematics that focuses on algorithms for building and using models "learned" from data.

MapReduce

MapReduce is a style of programming based on functional programming that was the basis of Hadoop.

matrix

A matrix is a rectangular array of numeric values. The mathematical definition is much more abstract.

metric

In a machine learning context, a metric is a measure of how good or bad a particular model is at its task. In a software context, a metric is a measure defined for an application, program, or function.

model

In a general scientific context, a model is some formal description, especially a mathematical one, of a phenomenon or system. In the machine learning context, a model is a set of hyperparameters, a set of learned parameters, and an evaluation or prediction function, especially one learned from data. In Spark MLlib, a model is what is produced by an Estimator when fitted to data.

model publishing

Once a machine learning model has been learned, it must be published to be used by other applications.

model training

Model training is the process of fitting a model to data.

monitoring

In a software context, monitoring is the process of recording and publishing information about a running application.

morphology

Morphology is a branch of linguistics focused on structure and parts of a word (actually morphemes).

N-gram

An N-gram is a subsequence of words. Sometimes, "N-gram" can refer to a subsequence of characters.

naïve Bayes

Naïve Bayes is a classification technique built on the naïve assumption that the features are all independent of each other.

named-entity recognition (NER)

NER is a task in NLP that focuses on finding particular entities in text.

natural language

Natural language is a language spoken or signed by people, in contrast to a programming language which is used for giving instruction to computers. Natural language also contrasts with artificial or constructed languages, which are designed by a person or group of people.

natural language processing (NLP)

NLP is a field of computer science and linguistics focused on techniques and algorithms for processing data, continuing natural language.

neural network

An artificial neural network is a collection of neurons connected by weights.

notebook

In this book, a notebook refers to a programming and writing environment, for example Jupyter Notebook and Databricks notebooks.

numpy

Numpy is a Python library for performing linear algebra operations and an assortment of other mathematical operations.

object

In an object-oriented programming context, an object is an instance of a class or type.

optical character recognition (OCR)

OCR is the set of techniques used to identify characters in an image.

overfitting

In machine learning, our data has biases as well as useful information for our task. The more exactly our machine learning model fits the data, the more it reflects these biases. This means that the predictions may be based on spurious relationships that incidentally occur in the training data.

pandas

> pandas is a Python library for data analysis and processing that uses DataFrames.

parallelism

> In computer science, parallelism is how much an algorithm is or can be distributed across multiple threads, processes, or machines.

parameter

> In a mathematics context, a parameter is a value in a mathematical model. In a programming context, a parameter is another name for an argument of a function. In a machine learning context, a parameter is value learned in the training process using the training data.

partition

> In Spark, a partition is a subset of the distributed data that is collocated on a machine.

parts of speech (POS)

> POS are word categories. The most well known are nouns and verbs. In an NLP context, the Penn Treebank tags are the most frequently used set of parts of speech.

PDF

> Portable document format (PDF) is a common file format for formatted text. It is a common input to NLP applications.

phonetics

> Phonetics is the branch of linguistics focused on the study of speech sounds.

phrase

> In linguistics, a phrase is a sequence of words that make up a constituency. For example, in the sentence "The red dog wags his tail," "the red dog" is a noun phrase, but "the red" is not.

pickle

> The pickle module is part of the Python standard library used for serializing data.

pipeline

> In data processing, a pipeline is a sequence of processing steps combined into a single object. In Spark MLlib, a pipeline is a sequence of stages. A Pipeline is an estimator containing transformers, estimators, and evaluators. When it is trained, it produces a PipelineModel containing transformers, models, and evaluators.

pragmatics

> Pragmatics is the branch of linguistics focused on understanding meaning in context.

process

> In a computing context, a process is a running program.

product owner

> In software development, the product owner is the person or people who represent the customer in the development process. They also own the requirements and prioritizing development tasks.

production

> Production is the environment an application is deployed into.

profiling

> In an application context, profiling is the process of measuring the resources an application or program requires to run.

program

> A program is a set of instructions given to a computer.

programming language

> A programming language is a formal language for writing high-level (human readable) instructions for a computer.

Python

> Python is a programming language that is popular among NLP developers and data scientists. It is a multi-paradigm language, allowing object-oriented, functional, and imperative programming.

random forest

Random forest is a machine learning technique for training an ensemble of decision trees. The training data for each decision tree is a subset of the rows and features of the total data.

recurrent neural network (RNN)

An RNN is a special kind of neural network used for modeling sequential data.

register

In linguistics, a register is a variation of language that is defined by the context in which it is used. This contrasts with a dialect, which is defined by the group of people who speak it.

regression

In a machine learning context, regression is the task of assigning scalar value to examples.

regular expression

A regular expression is a string that defines a pattern to be matched in text.

repository

In a software context, a repository is a data store that contains the code and or data for a project.

resilient distributed dataset (RDD)

In Spark, an RDD is a distributed collection. In early versions of Spark, they were the fundamental elements of Spark programming.

scale out

In computing, scaling out is when more machines are used to increase the available resources.

scale up

In computing, scaling up is when a machine with more resources is used to increase available resources.

schema

In data engineering, a schema is the structure and some metadata (e.g. column names and types). In Spark, this is the metadata for defining a Spark DataFrame.

script

In programming, a script is a computer program that is generally written on a runnable code file (also called a script).

Scrum

Scrum is a style of agile software development. It is built around the idea of iterative development and short daily meetings (called scrums) where progress or problems are shared.

search

In computing, search is a task in information retrieval concerned with finding documents that are relevant to a query.

semantics

Semantics is a branch of linguistics focused on the meaning communicated by language.

sentence

In linguistics, a sentence is a special kind of phrase, especially a clausal phrase, that is considered complete.

sentiment

In an NLP context, sentiment is the emotion or opinion a human encodes in a language act.

serialization

In computing, serialization is the process of converting objects or other programming elements into a format for storage.

software developer

A software developer is someone who writes software, especially using software engineering.

software development

Software development is the process of making an application (or an update to an application) available in the production environment.

software engineering

Software engineering is the discipline and best practices used in developing software.

software library

A software library is a piece of software that is not necessarily an application. Applications are generally built by combining libraries. Some software libraries also contain applications.

software test

A software test is a program, function, or set of human instructions used to test or verify the behavior of a piece of software.

Spark NLP

Spark NLP is an NLP annotation library that extends Spark MLlib.

stakeholder

In software development, a stakeholder is a person who has a vested interest in the software being developed. For example customers and users are stakeholders.

stop word

In an NLP context, a stop word is a word or token that is considered to have negligible value for the given task.

structured query language (SQL)

SQL is a programming language used to interact with relational data.

syntax

In a linguistics context, syntax is a branch of linguistics focused on the structure of phrases and sentences. It is also used to refer to the rules used by a language for constructing phrases and sentences.

tag

In an NLP context, a tag is a kind of annotation where a subsequence, especially a token, is marked with a label from a fixed set of labels. For example, annotators that identify the POS of tokens are often called POS taggers.

TensorFlow

TensorFlow is a data processing and mathematics library. It was popularized for its implementation of neural networks.

TF.IDF

TF.IDF refers to the technique developed in information retrieval. TF refers to the term frequency of a given term in a given document, and IDF refers to the inverse of the document frequency of the given term. TF.IDF is the product of the term frequency and the inverse document frequency which is supposed to represent the relevance of the given document to the given term.

thread

In computing, a thread is a subsequence of instructions in a program that may be executed in parallel.

token

In an NLP context, a token is a unit of text, generally—but not necessarily—a word.

topic

In an NLP context, a topic is a kind of cluster of meaning (or a quantified representation).

Transformer

In a Spark MLlib context, a Transformer is a stage of a pipeline that does not need to be fit or trained on data.

Unicode

Unicode is a standard for encoding characters.

vector

In a mathematics context, a vector is an element of a Cartesian space with more than one dimension.

virtual machine

A virtual machine is a software representation of a computer.

word

In linguistics, a word is loosely defined as an unbound morpheme, that is, a unit of language that can be used alone and still have meaning.

word vector

In distributional semantics, a word is represented as a vector. The mapping from word to vector is learned from data.

Word2vec

Word2vec is a distributional semantics technique that learns word representations by building a neural network.

XML

Extensible Markup Language is a markup language used to encode data.

Index

A

abjads, 30
Addin, Saif, xii
alphabets, 29
Anaconda, 5
analytic languages, 23, 305
annotation libraries, 63
annotation, in document-annotation model, 63
annotators
    defined, 12
    in document-annotation model, 64
    Lemmatizer, 70
    POS tagger, 71
    SentenceDetector, 68
    Spark NLP library, 67-71
    Tokenizer, 69
ANNs (artificial neural networks), 79
Apache Hadoop, 43
Apache Hive, 44
Apache Pig, 44
Apache Spark (basics), 44
    architecture, 44-51
    getting familiar with, 7-11
    loading/viewing data with, 8-11
    logical architecture, 46-51
    natural language processing, 39-77
    physical architecture, 45
    resources, 77
    setting up/starting, 6
    SparkSQL and Spark MLlib, 51-62
        (see also MLlib)
    starting with Spark NLP, 8
App, Spark jobs and, 48
Arabic writing system, 30

architecture, Apache Spark, 44-51
    logical architecture, 46-51
    physical architecture, 45
Argument Reasoning Comprehension Task, 229
artificial neural networks (ANNs), 79
ASCII (American Standard Code for Information Interchange), 33
ASCII tokenizer, 35
assertion status detection, 189-191
attention modeling, 227

B

backpropagation, 85-96
backpropagation through time (BPTT), 97
bag (multiset), 113
bag of words, 113-115
    in classification/regression, 142
    CountVectorizer, 114-115
BasicPipeLine, 72
Baum–Welch algorithm, 162
Bidirectional Encoder Representations from Transformers (BERT), 228
Binarizer, 55
boosts, 270
bound content morphemes, 23
bound functional morphemes, 23
BPTT (backpropagation through time), 97
Branzan, Claudiu, xii

C

cache, 318
categories, in wikis, 257
CBOW (continuous bag-of-word)

E

edge, defined, 253

8-bit Unicode Transformation Format (UTF)-8, 34

Elasticsearch, 267

elementwise multiplication, 89

Elman networks, 98

Elman, Jeffrey, 98

embeddings from language models (ELMo), 228

    (see also word embeddings)

emotion detection (see sentiment analysis and emotion detection)

encoding systems

    ASCII, 33

    Unicode, 33

    UTF-8, 34

encodings, 33-34

English alphabet, 29

English language

    paralinguistic features, 21

    tokenizing, 35

environment, setting up, 6

Estimators, 57-60

    CrossValidator, 61

    MinMaxScaler, 57

    Pipelines, 61

    StringIndexer, 58-60

Evaluators, 60-62

executors, 46

expert system, 251

Explain Document ML pipeline, 72

exploding (vanishing) gradients, 98

F

f-score, 246

Facebook, 227

fastText, 227

feature selection, for classification/regression, 145-148

federated search, 268

filters, CNN and, 96

Finisher, 16, 74-75

Finisher Transformer, 16

Firth, John R., 197

formality, sociolinguistics and, 26

Fukushima, Kunihiko, 96

Function, 47

functional morphemes, 23

functionality libraries, 63

fusional languages, 24, 305

G

gain (index metric), 275

Ganglia, 322

gaps parameter, 35

Garbe, Wolf, 110

Geez (Amharic) writing system, 31, 36

generative models, 169

generic NER, 180

Gensim topic modeling library, 65

GloVe (Global Vectors), 226

golden sets, 313

GPUs (graphics processing units), 319

gradient descent, 84

graphical models, 155

Greek alphabet, 30, 35

H

Hadamard product, 89

Hadoop, 43

Hadoop Distributed File System (HDFS), 44

Han Chinese writing system, 32

handwritten text conversion, 292

Hangul alphabet, 30

hashing trick, 137

HashingTF, 137

head-word (lemma), 108

Hebrew writing system, 31

hedged speech, 190

hidden Markov models (HMMs), 156-163

Hiragana writing system, 32

Hochreiter, Sepp, 98

home signs, 20

homonymy, 227

HTCondor, 43

Hubel, David H., 96

human labeling, 309-315

    academic paper classification, 310

    checklist for, 315

    classification, 314

    guidelines, 310-311

    inter-labeler agreement, 312

    iterative labeling, 313

    labeling text, 314

    tagging, 314

    where to find labelers, 312

human language, origins of, 20

I

IDF (inverse document frequency), 134-137
idiolect, 25
implied negation, 190
indefiniteness, 180
indexing
    inverted indexes, 124-130
    latent semantic indexing, 202-205
IndexToString Transformer, 59
inference engines, 251
inflectional affixes, 23
information extraction, 179-196
    assertion status detection, 189-191
    coreference resolution, 187
    exercises, 196
    named-entity recognition, 179-187
    relationship extraction, 191-195
information retrieval, 123-138
    (see also search engines)
    exercises, 137
    inverted indexes, 124-130
    resources, 138
    stop word removal, 133
    vector space model, 130-137
input data, 322
integration tests, 323
intents, 277
inter-labeler agreement, 312
International Phonetic Alphabet (IPA), 22
inverse document frequency (IDF), 134-137
inverted indexes, 124-130
Iris Data Set, 52
isolating languages, 23
iteration cycle, classification/regression, 150-152
iterative labeling, 313

J

Jakobson model of pragmatics, 27
Jakobson, Roman, 27
Java Microbenchmark Harness (JMH), 322
Java Virtual Machine (JVM), 40
Jupyter Notebook, 5

K

K-Means clustering, 198-201
Keras (see sequence modeling with Keras)
kernel, 8

knowledge bases
    building, 251-264
    business metrics, 262
    defined, 251
    designing the solution, 253
    implementing the solution, 255-262
    infrastructure metrics, 263
    model-centric metrics, 262
    planning the project, 253
    problem statement and constraints, 252
    process metrics, 263
    review process, 264
    testing/measuring the solution, 262-264

L

labeler fatigue, 314
labeling, human (see human labeling)
language models, 169
language topology, 303
language, human
    origins of, 20
    spoken versus written, 21
languages, supporting multiple, 303-308
    checklist for, 308
    compound words, 304
    language topology, 303
    morphological complexity, 305
    searching across languages, 307
    text processing in different languages, 304-306
    transfer learning and multilingual deep learning, 306
latent Dirichlet allocation (LDA), 209-210
latent semantic indexing (LSI), 202-205
LeCun, Yann, 96
lemma (head-word), 108
lemmatization, 108-110
Lemmatizer, 70
letterbox, 28
lexical morphemes, 23
libraries (see specific libraries)
linear models, 149
linear separability, 80
linguistics, 22-25
    morphology, 23
    phonetics and phonology, 22
    syntax, 24
local mode, 45
locking, 41

About the Author

Alex Thomas is a principal data scientist at Wisecube. He has used natural language processing (NLP) and machine learning with clinical data, identity data, employer and jobseeker data, and now biochemical data. He has worked with Apache Spark since version 0.9, and with NLP libraries and frameworks including UIMA and OpenNLP.

Colophon

The animal on the cover of *Natural Language Processing with Spark NLP* is a chimango caracara (*Milvago chimango*), a bird of prey belonging to the Falconidae family.

The chimango lives in South American shrubland, at the edge of water and near towns and fields. They live in large flocks and are aggressive and territorial. They often chase larger raptors.

Both the male and female chimangos build and defend nests, and incubate and feed the young. These birds eat insects, vertebrates, and carrion, and they can catch fish on the surface of the water.

The chimango is considered common in its habitat. Many of the animals on O'Reilly covers are endangered; all of them are important to the world.

The cover illustration is by Karen Montgomery, based on a black and white engraving from *Encyclopédie d'Histoire Naturelle*. The cover fonts are Gilroy Semibold and Guardian Sans. The text font is Adobe Minion Pro; the heading font is Adobe Myriad Condensed; and the code font is Dalton Maag's Ubuntu Mono.

O'REILLY®

There's much more where this came from.

Experience books, videos, live online training courses, and more from O'Reilly and our 200+ partners—all in one place.

Learn more at oreilly.com/online-learning

9 781492 047766